Life of the Blessed JOSEPH OF COPERTINO

An early Biography (1753) written by

Paolo Antonio Agelli

Translated from Italian by

Christopher David Costanzo

Copyright © 2014 Christopher David Costanzo
All rights reserved
ISBN: 1502377527
ISBN 13: 9781502377524
Library of Congress Control Number: 2014917229
CreateSpace Independent Publishing Platform
North Charleston, South Carolina

TRANSLATOR'S PREFACE

This biography was written by Paolo Antonio Agelli, an 18th century Franciscan Brother and Inquisitor. It was published in 1753, shortly after the beatification of Joseph of Copertino but several years before his canonization as a saint in 1767. It is a typical hagiography of the period, replete with formulaic phrasing which can at times be tiresome to modern readers. I have tried to preserve the flavor of the original, but have taken some liberties to improve its flow and readability.

The biography describes Joseph of Copertino with vivid frankness, including his childhood, his relationship with his mother, and his humiliations at the hands of family and acquaintances. It is clear that Joseph came across to many people as a simpleton, slow of wit and clumsy in manner, given to fits and seizures for which he endured contempt and ridicule through much of his life from those who found his mental and physical shortcomings exasperating. The narrative also catalogs the miracles and prodigies attributed to him (including his alleged ability to fly) and also, in somewhat uncomfortable detail, his asceticism and self-mortification.

The story of Joseph of Copertino should be of interest to psychologists with respect to Joseph's domineering mother and his manifest shortcomings as a youth among his peers. Physiologists might be interested in the metabolism of those who fast a great deal, as he did, and the resulting ketosis that sometimes produces acetone to which the so-called "odor of sanctity" is often attributed. Neurologists might be interested in the release of opiates in the brain of people under extreme physical duress, as is hypothesized regarding many ascetics who mortify their bodies and thereby seem to experience indescribable episodes of intense joy. Medical diagnosticians might be interested in the symptoms of the many illnesses that Joseph is said to have cured, and also in his own illnesses and his autopsy.

Despite the cold, scientific possibilities regarding the bodily and mental state of Joseph of Copertino, his character and personality shine forth through the many pages of hagiographic language of this book. He was clearly a man of deep faith, bereft of malice, with a self-deprecating and playful sense of humor, and was suffused with an intense and infectious happiness that drew people from near and far. His charisma and lovability jumps out from the pages of this biography. He seems to have had that great gift of making others happy.

When I first read this biography of Joseph of Copertino, I got the definite impression of being in touch with an exceptional personality. I have translated this early account of his life to describe a remarkable mystic who I think is worth knowing, and to elucidate the impact of his spirituality on others.

Effigies Beati Patris Josephi
a Cupertino Ord. Min. Conv.
S. Francisci.

THE LIFE
OF THE BLESSED

JOSEPH
OF COPERTINO

*Of the Order of Minor Conventuals
of St. Francis*

DEDICATED

TO THE MOST SERENE HIGHNESS

OF JOSEPH
ARCHDUKE OF AUSTRIA

IN VENICE
At Giambattista Recurti

MDCCLIII
Under License and Privilege from Higher Authority

MOST SERENE HIGHNESS:

I hope that the great daring with which I've undertaken to consecrate to Your Highness the Life of the BLESSED JOSEPH of Copertino, a member of my Order, will find in your Spirit a favorable reception, for it was written for many reasons of which I will remain silent but are of just and weighty import, and presented in an abridged form, since it was only a few days ago that the reigning Supreme Pontiff, Benedict XIV, placed him among the blessed.

Given that this great Servant of the Lord, with his heroic virtues, surprising ecstasies, continuing prophecies, and his great miracles, gained the love and veneration of the whole Catholic World, your most August House was more than any other highly partial and devoted to him, and could not restrain itself in repeated instances from procuring from the Apostolic See his recognition at the Altars of public worship.

Emperor Leopold I, a Monarch of firm piety and religion as everyone knows, along with His most August Consort Eleanor, expressed their great interest in Joseph to the Venerable Innocent XII. Wilhemine Amalia, as the August Consort of that Glorious Emperor whose name you carry, MOST SERENE PRINCE, also shared the victories that this Blessed person wrought on the good soul of her great Father John Frederick, Duke of Brunswick, and she caused her religious petitions to reach Clement XI. Likewise, the most august Charles VI and his most August Consort Elizabeth, for whose glory it is sufficient merely to name them, who were the happy Parents of Your Immortal MOTHER so luminous for the rare virtues which adorn her, and for the splendor of the three Diadems which the Royal Augusti gird the temples, employed their much respected offices to intercede with Benedict XIII and Clement XII.

You know therefore, MOST SERENE LORD, that while in the act of placing obsequiously before your eyes the Holy memories of my Blessed one, I do nothing more than justify the holy concerns of Your great Grandparents who, guided always and always by the spirit of religion and piety, were moved and excited by a special light from Heaven which clearly proved to them the facts and the evidence. You also know that since it not possible to render to my Order the adornment of the humble thanks that is due to them, it is appropriate to address them to You who are the Heir of their lofty prerogatives. You are the one in whom the glory, the good sense, the valor, and the mercy of the most illustrious Houses of Europe are united as a beautiful scion - you, who in your countenance, and in your actions, are fully inspired by the Majesty and the Clemency of Your Most August Father, which makes the peace of the Empire and the good fortune of these your most happy States - you, in short, who do not cease to be the Hope of those far away, in the manner of a fresh Sun which, upon first rising, gilds the peaks of the high mountains to the great wonder of those around it.

For that reason, it is to YOUR MOST SERENE HIGHNESS that I render this reverent tribute of my most profound respect, dedicating to you a small Volume as a testimony of my great and eternal duty, enjoying it for myself as well the beneficial influence which from the far off Imperial Throne diffuses itself on these most happy States.

Receive it kindly, I beg you, MOST MERCIFUL PRINCE, because in creating the portrait of a Blessed person and evincing the amazement of people near and far, one then understands all the more how admirable is the Lord in his Saints.

You will also have in him a new Protector in Heaven who will gaze at you with a partial eye for sharing the same name with him, and he will oversee with untiring concern your greatest exaltation, for you will merit it greatly. Deign, then, to bestow on me, despite my unworthiness, a ray of Your Most Clement Patronage, permitting me to kneel forever to kiss the Royal Mantle with the most humble obsequiousness.

Your Serene Highness'
Most Humble, Devoted, Grateful, and Attentive Servant
B(rother) Paolo Antonio Agelli, Inquisitor

Florence 1 March 1753

THE PRINTER
TO THE READER

With my printing there comes into public light the compendium of the life of BLESSED JOSEPH *of Copertino, corrected and amended, and so seen emerging from the devoted pen of the writer. It deals with the full life of this most clear beacon of sanctity, as the very celebrated Bernino has said in his Roman edition of 1722 and in other editions reproduced by me, and purports to having been composed on the basis of the inquiries made by the Apostolic authority in Nardo, Assisi and Osimo where this great Servant of the Lord lived and performed stupendous marvels. Anyone who might wonder whether the summarizer labored with good results in examining these works may easily clarify the matter. He has taken the greatest care not to deviate one single word from those of the depositions of the sworn witnesses which form the substance of the biography. The last chapter of Part Two contains twenty-two incidents of grace and miracles which, being more recent, Bernino was unable to use to adorn his history of Joseph. All of them, however, were unearthed with great fidelity from authentic evidence worthy of faith. Live in Happiness.*

INDEX

OF THE CHAPTERS

IN THE

FIRST PART.

CHAPTER I. *His Birth, and education up to his entrance into Religious life.* Page 1.

II. *He takes the Habit of the Capuchins as a Lay Brother. He returns to the Secular World. He is received into the Order of the Minor Conventuals of Saint Francis, and is ordained a Priest.* Page 5.

III. *Having been made a Priest, his stay at the Monastery of Grottella, and the Virtues he practiced there.* Page 13

IV. *Supernatural gifts from God shared by the Blessed Joseph in the Monastery of the Grottella, and his miracles.* Page 20.

V. *At the orders of his Provincial Superior he travels around to the Monasteries of his Province of Bari, and then returns to the Monastery of the Grottella.* Page 29

VI. *His summons to the Holy Office of Naples, his stay in that City, and his assignment to his Father-General in Rome.* Page 35.

VII. *His trip from Naples to Rome. His stay in that City, and his departure for Assisi.* Page 43.

VIII. *The arrival of the Blessed Joseph at the Sacred Monastery of Assisi, and his internal and outward distress.* Page 48

IX. *The stay of the Blessed Joseph in the holy Monastery of Assisi, and the marvels of his life that happened there.* Page 56.

X. *The Gift of Wisdom, by which the Blessed one was enriched by God in Assisi.* Page 71.

XI. *The flocking of qualified people from every country to the Blessed Joseph in Assisi. Prophecies, Conversion of Heretics, and miracles carried out by him.* Page 75.

XII. *Taking of the Blessed Joseph from the holy Monastery of Assisi to the Monastery of the Capuchins of Pietra Rubea (Pietrarubbia), and his stay there of about three months.* Page 89.

XIII. *The new taking of the Blessed Joseph by order of the Holy Inquisition to the Monastery of the Capuchin Fathers of Fossombrone, and his stay there of around three years.* Page 98.

XIV. *By order of Alexander VII, the Blessed Joseph is restored to his Minor Monastic Order of Osimo. His trip from Fossombrone to the aforementioned city.* Page 106

XV. *The stay of the Blessed Joseph among his coreligionists of the Minor Monastic Order of Osimo, until his death.* Page 111.

XVI. *Illness and death of the Blessed Joseph of Copertino.* Page 119.

XVII. *His Burial; the flocking of the public, and the miracles at his Sepulcher.* Page 127.

INDEX

OF THE CHAPTERS

IN THE

SECOND PART.

CHAPTER I. *Of his great love towards God.* Page 133.

II. *Of the continuous praying of the Blessed Joseph.* Page 140

III. *Of the ecstasies, and the wondrous raptures of the Blessed Joseph.* Page 145

IV. *Of the tender love of the Blessed Joseph towards the Mother of God.* Page 153.

V. *Of the gift of penetrating the thoughts and secrets of others, bestowed by God on the Blessed One.* Page 159.

VI. *Of the continued and admirable gift of Prophesy of the Blessed Joseph.* Page 167.

VII. *Of his great charity towards his neighbor.* Page 176.

VIII. *Of the unsullied purity of the Blessed Joseph.* . Page 185.

IX. *Of his most deep Humility.* Page 191.

X. *Of the heroic Poverty and blind Obedience of this markedly Blessed person.* Page 198.

XI. *Miracles wrought by the Blessed Joseph.* Page 203.

XII. *Other miracles of God wrought through the intercession of the Blessed Joseph.* Page 216

THE LIFE OF THE B. JOSEPH OF COPERTINO

FIRST PART

one

His Birth, and education up to his entrance into religious life

The Blessed Joseph was born in Copertino, an illustrious and populated town in the Kingdom of Naples, in the year of our salvation 1603, on the seventeenth day of June. His parents were Felice Desa and Francesca Panara, common families albeit honest and honorable. The mother was a woman of singular piety towards God, of such austerity and diligence in the religious education of her son that his behavior was never marked by the usual defects of boyhood. For this reason he used to say that *he never had need for his novitiate in his religious life, having gone through it effectively under her maternal will.*

God wanted Joseph to be a seraphim of love, and for his body to be almost always suspended in air, ever engrossed with his soul and ever carried away by it. He had Joseph born in a stable like his seraphic patriarch St. Francis, for Joseph's poor mother had taken refuge there from the frightening abuse of the authorities who were stripping her home to gather security for the debts of her husband.

Reborn at the holy baptismal font, Joseph in the course of time was duly confirmed after learning the basic tenets of our holy faith and acquiring the first rudiments of literacy. Even more, he learned to be so enamored of God and of knowledge of the saints that as a lad of only five years he gave obvious signs of a heroic holiness. From this came Joseph's frankness and simplicity of heart, as manifested in his speech, his wisdom, his astuteness in his work, and his great humility in his dealings, all of which brought forth love and wonderment from everyone.

Churches were Joseph's delight, and he decorated them with flowers and visited them frequently, praying in them with the greatest fervor. He did so in his paternal home as well, where despite his poverty he erected a small altar and genuflected before it for the greater part of the day and night while consumed by his recitation of the rosary, the litanies, and other devotional prayers.

These first gleams of grace which molded his innocent soul were from the Lord who wanted to keep him separate from others, imbuing him with the blessed destiny of the saints, whose ecstatic purpose was infused in his soul. Even when he barely understood his destiny, it was so luminous that it carried him away from worldly things to the contemplation of the heavenly. And it happened not just a few times. Often when his schoolmaster was teaching the more advanced students, little Joseph's book would fall from his hand, and he would remain immobile, with his eyes fixed heavenward and his mouth half open, as if he were listening to the singing and the sound of the angels up there.

Joseph had not yet completed his seventh year when he fell from spiritual consolations to bodily anguish. At that tender age he was assailed by an internal abscess in his flesh which developed into a large growth and then into a horrible cancer. It was followed by very bad sores on his head which required knife and fire but without results. The pain lasted four years, ravaging his tender little body.

But more than the pain, what really cut into his heart was the severity of his mother for whom Joseph's heroic suffering was not sufficient, for she demanded in him the strength of Job. She did love him, but wanted him to be holy. Although she knew how to hide her compassion, she couldn't hide her tears. When her son asked her for the reason for the tears, she explained by saying to her son, *I weep for the passion of Jesus Christ.*

The savage disease became more and more cruel until Joseph was unable to move, and he was living in agony. But it never induced him to forego Holy Mass. With prayers and tears he forced the his good mother to bring him to Mass every morning. When the fourth year had passed, that heavenly hand, which strikes and heals, was filled with pity for such a long martyrdom, and Joseph was healed with a bit of unction made for him by a hermit from the oil of the lamp of the Madonna of Galatone where his devoted mother had brought him. A fact equally worthy of remembrance and of marvel is that from the place where he had gone the day before while still cancerous, on horseback and lying across a sack in front of his mother, he was able on the following day to return to his own home over nine miles of road, healthy and on foot, which he did with no help or support other than a walking stick.

Freed from so harsh an illness and with due thanks tendered to God, Joseph thought to give back to Him that life which he had received anew. Though already poor in his patrimony, he thought more about mortifying his body to keep it subjected to the spirit rather than about how to sustain life. Thus he arrived at the most austere penances in order to elevate his mind, and God did favor him. Joseph dressed himself in sackcloth with prickly hairs, and did not feed himself with anything except bread, fruit, cooked vegetables, and herbs all of which he flavored with dry and very bitter wormwood powder. His fasts were continuous, and he would go very frequently for two or three days without food. To those who reproved him he would answer that he had forgotten to eat.

Most amazing were his prayers, especially as a youngster untutored in learning. Since he read in some book about he purpose of meditation and that its mysteries were elevated and sublime, he identified with those mysteries with such alacrity of spirit that everything changed in him. While he persevered in this, the Lord worked to make his soul worthy of things that were surprising and wonderful. And so, ascending with great strides the mountain of Christian perfection, Joseph happily gained its highest peaks, as we will go on to see.

two

He takes the Habit of the Capuchins as a Lay Brother. He returns to the Secular World. He is received into the Orders of the Minor Conventuals of Saint Francis, and is ordained a Priest.

Joseph at the age of seventeen years old and in the flower of his youth lived an austere and innocent life like a lily among thorns, despite the corrupting depravity of those times. For that reason he did not feel secure, so he was impelled by divine grace to seek admission to the safe harbor of a religious Order and thereby consecrate himself to the majesty of the Lord. He selected the Order he loved most, and to which he sensed God was calling him, and that was the Franciscans.

He had been born, it was said, with a resemblance to Saint Francis, so his mother put him under the protection of that great saint. During the horrible torments of Joseph's infirmity he had been entrusted to Saint Francis. It was to that glorious patriarch that he always directed his prayers and, he wanted ardently to live and die in his Order. Joseph fixed his mind on the Minor Conventual Order that had always been the repository and faithful custodian of the sacred remains of its angelic founder in Assisi, and he also thought of the miraculous Saint Anthony in Padua - two sanctuaries that are the wonder and consolation of the whole Catholic World.

Joseph's paternal Uncle, Father Franceschino Desa, was in the Franciscan Order, as well as his maternal Uncle, Father Giovanni Donato, Master of Theology, who enjoyed a high reputation among his co-religionists. Through them, Joseph's application seemed assured. Instead it was precisely because of them that his application was turned down and he was excluded. His uncles knew that Joseph possessed low literacy, and that without literacy he couldn't rise to the priesthood. For that reason alone they firmly rejected his admission.

Joseph bowed his head but didn't lose hope. Like a deer who runs the crags of a hill in search of water, he was greatly aroused in his yearning to serve the Lord under the banner of S. Francis. Seeing the first door closed to him, he knocked on a second door by presenting himself to the Provincial Head of the Capuchins, and asked for the habit of a Lay Brother, which he received speedily.

He was given the name of Brother Stephan. And there, in the town and Monastery of Martina, which otherwise could not boast of any saints in their poor cloisters, he lived a saintly life for nine months. But, oh, the greatness of divine judgment! It seemed that his very saintliness rendered Joseph incapable of serving in that holy establishment. Those ecstasies which he had from early youth as a privilege from God increased within him and became more pronounced while he was there. He went about not only in the enclosure of the church but throughout the monastery in a state of rapture, almost bereft of feeling and conscious only of God.

And it so happened that when he was assigned to serve in the refectory, the dishes frequently fell from his hands for which he was punished by having to carry cooking pots tied around his neck. When he placed bread on the table he was unable to distinguish between white and black bread, and was reprimanded for not paying sufficient attention to his superiors. When ordered to put wood on the fire, he knocked over the hanging water pots instead, frightening and burning the monks.

Wherever God surprised him with rapture, there he fell to his knees. By lowering himself so often in uncomfortable places, he contracted a painful tumor on one knee. He cut it off with a knife, leaving the agony to himself and the healing to God, who cured him immediately. But the emaciation of his appearance from the cut that he had endured, together with his life spent in continuing contemplation, rendered him less and less capable to serve in a religious establishment, for such service requires a strong spirit and perfect health to endure its toil.

Upon being told that he was not fit either for a monastery or for a spiritual life, he understood that *it was important for a spiritual being to be the first to arrive at a church and the last to leave, and to pray constantly and so forth,* so he gave himself to the choral enclosure and to prayer. Such was his stay, and he busied himself with it night and day. Inasmuch as manual labor was tedious to him as one who was in continuous touch with the spirit of God, he either skipped his work in part, or totally neglected it.

Such was his way of life, but the monks didn't understand it, for God kept hidden from them His marvelous plan for Joseph. First they suspected, and then they believed that Joseph was dull of wit, unhealthy of body, intolerant of spirit, and lacking the capacity for the manual labor of the monastery. So they dismissed him.

It was inexpressible - the pain and the mental confusion that the young Saint experienced regarding his inability and ineptitude which he understood were the reasons for his dismissal. He later said, when he was more experienced, that *when he felt his tunic being removed, it was as if his skin was being peeled off and his flesh separated from his bones.* Also in him was bitterness and confusion when he had to dress himself again in secular clothing. He was unable to find either his hat or his shoes or his socks, so he had to depart half naked. He didn't have the courage to head for Copertino, knowing full well that his mother would have stabbed him with reproach, and his acquaintances with sneering derision.

He headed towards Vetrara where his paternal uncle was preaching Lent. Who can tell of the tests to which God put his servant during his trip! When it grew dark and night fell, Joseph had still not eaten. He was about to be devoured by dogs who rushed out madly from a nearby establishment. He escaped the dogs, but shortly afterwards some shepherds thought he was a spy for bandits and almost finished him off. But Joseph was rescued by one of them who recognized him and gave him a piece of bread.

Upon going on his way he heard a terrible voice shouting, *stop spy, stop spy,* and saw a bold-looking man on horseback coming at him. The man held a naked sword at Joseph's breast and accused him of being a spy for the government. Assisted and protected by divine clemency, Joseph was not frightened at all. So, although he was told to walk and not look back under pain of death, he had full faith in God and after a few steps looked back anyway. He saw neither the horse nor the rider on the plain, and said to himself, t*his was Malatasca* (as S. Catherine of Siena called the Devil) *who wanted me to be afraid and to make me despair.*

Victories of such import did not put an end to Joseph's battles. When he arrived at Vetrara, he quarreled with his Uncle who looked at him unfavorably, threw him out, and accused him for being inept, a vagabond, having the same defects as his father. His uncle confronted him with his father's debts which, since his father was dead, Joseph would have to pay or else suffer perpetual incarceration. Nevertherless, Joseph stayed there until Easter, when his uncle brought him secretly to Copertino to save him from the law.

But in Copertino he had to endure the tighter grip of his mother who, with her usual rigidity, displayed her inexorable judgment of him in her expression and in her words, even if in her heart and by her actions she was his untiring protector. To guard her son from imminent danger, she offered incessant prayers to God. Nor did she hold herself back from the monks attached to the Grottella. She said so much, and worked so hard that she prevailed, softening the hardness of Father-Superior Giovanni Donato, who finally gave in. He installed

Joseph as a tertiary Oblate in the rule of the Monastery and assigned him to watch over the monastery's mule.

Having been admitted among the monks to this lowest and most base grade and condition, Joseph's poor afflicted heart relaxed and he exulted greatly, seeing himself now as a companion of the above mentioned Father-Superior. This person was a monk of great good sense and of esteemed kindness who, when he had found himself in Vienna at the court of Emperor Ferdinand II, was so worthy that the image of the Mother of God appeared to him and commanded him to go to the Church of the Minor Conventual Order of Grottella, a mile and a half from Copertino, to serve Her there.

In that monastery, safe from the annoyances of the secular world, Joseph showed evidence of every kind of virtue, which at the outset attracted the eyes and then the heart of everyone. He used to go about barefoot to get the bread for the monastery, and while at the monastery, before the Lord who was born poor, Joseph's humble and patient activity, his frankness and the sincerity of his words, and his exemplary modesty inspired his devout benefactors to flee from vice and to love the Christian life.

On top of the nakedness of his feet, and the coarseness of his hair shirt, Joseph added a rough iron chain which he always kept tight around his side. His fasts were rigorous and continuous. His bed was very hard, made up of only three boards. A threadbare bearskin served as a mattress and a coarse bag of straw was his pillow. So, his rest was painful and brief, and weariness embraced his eyes, but it gave him time for prayer and for the study of the rudiments of Latin. Amidst such austerities he always appeared merry and spoke simply but emphatically, but with such total obedience and readiness to carry out the most laborious and menial tasks of the monastery that he seemed tireless.

So much was the virtue infused into his heart by God's kindness, which is so consoling to a suffering spirit in its travails, that Joseph was deemed worthy to be accepted into the Order of the Minor Conventuals of Saint Francis as a seminarian. He was now received as a son of the Monastery of the Madonna of Grottella where he became a novice.

In his novitiate Joseph was a paragon of sanctity, withdrawn from any congress with others, as if God was about to call him at any moment. He talked and lived all the time with God. He used to say humbly that he was dressed as he was solely because of the kindness of the monks. He was so tolerant that he endured any correction howsoever harsh, even for things that weren't his fault. He was so obedient that he never transgressed the arduous requirements placed upon him by his superiors to test the resignation of his spirit.

He understood that the condition in which he found himself required him to acquire a knowledge of letters, so he applied himself to it with every effort. But God wanted him to be miraculous even in this matter, so Joseph found that despite all his efforts he was incapable of learning. He recognized his own inability and whenever he was reproved by his teacher or saw by his teacher's face and his trembling voice that he was annoyed, Joseph would shrug his shoulders and say with his own unvarying patience, *be patient and in that way you will gain more merit.*

And in this manner his novitiate ended. Because of the good evidence of sanctity that came from him, he was admitted to solemn vows and regular religious practice, at which he wept with great tenderness upon thinking how different are the ways of men from the ways of the Lord that led Joseph to be ordained by Him. Furthermore Joseph was not distrustful as to his difficulty and near incapacity when it came to letters. Inspired by bigger things, he abandoned himself wholly to God, and devotedly turned to the Mother of Wisdom so that from her most divine Son, he obtained the capacity needed for the degree of Priest, knowing that through ordinary paths it would have been impossible to acquire it.

In fact Joseph was never able to explain the Gospels adequately except for the passage that begins, b*eatus venter qui te portavit* (blessed the womb that bore you). And this was the very passage that guided him to the Deaconship after he had received, without examination by virtue of his good reputation, the Minor Orders on January 3, 1627, and the Sub-Deaconship on February 27 of the same year. The Bishop of Nardo, Monsignor Giovanni Franchi, in accordance with the Sacred Canons, wanted to examine Joseph formally for the Deaconship itself, so Joseph, full of God and in full faith of the patronage of the Virgin Mother, presented himself promptly for the examination. The Bishop opened the book of the Gospels and, guided by an angelic hand, the passage that presented itself was *Beatus venter qui te portavit*, which the Bishop put to Joseph to explain. Joseph then rejoiced in his heart, and engrossed in God and in his great Mother, he read it and explained it with such happiness and frankness that he ended up passing. He was then ordained a Deacon on March 20 of the above-mentioned year 1627.

There remained the priesthood, the examination for which had to be conducted by the Bishop of Castro, Monsignor Giovanni Battista Deti, a rigorous prelate, who was very zealous in ascertaining the abilities of those to be ordained. The Blessed One went to him, along with the young students of the Monastery of Lecce who were his co-religionists, all of whom were well endowed with learning and of ready spirit, although all were uncertain as to whether they would be able to do honor to themselves or to their Order at such a feared trial. The first ones answered the questions wonderfully, and so did the next ones. The Bishop reasoned that the abilities of the few applied to all, so he went on to approve all of them without further ado. Thus Joseph was miraculously approved, becoming on March 4, 1628, nothing less than a priest of God. Later on, still without the arsenal of literacy, God made Joseph a teacher of correct doctrine to heretics, a teacher of higher learning to theologians, a teacher among Cardinals and sovereigns, and even admired by Supreme Pontiffs.

Full of the Grace of the Sacred Unction, Joseph returned to his monastery in Copertino, and prostrated himself before the statue of the Virgin Mary, proffering to her his humble thanks for what had been a supernatural event. Here he later celebrated his first Mass on March 28 of the same year, after having seen the world that exists beyond that mere empty aspect that is seen by those who love it insanely. He resolved to lead a supernatural and heavenly life. In this he was so fired up in his devotion to the Mother of God *that he could not go for a single hour without seeing that sacred image, which enraptured his body and soul,* as he himself told Monsignor Bonaventura Cleverio, of the same Order of the Minor Conventuals, who was attached to the Bishopric of Potenza.

three

Having been made a Priest, his stay at the Monastery of Grottella, and the Virtues he practiced there.

Having overcome so many obstacles, our Blessed Joseph decided to die within himself in order to live for God, whose goodness deserves the respect of everyone's heart. In order to achieve it in a place that is full of temptation and of enemies, one has to do battle and subdue them. But Joseph so shunned the world with all its beckoning that he seemed, in fact, outside of it. Mean, dark and narrow was his cell but it still did not seem to him sufficiently remote from the eyes and ears of the curious, so he left it frequently. His most frequent abodes were either in a little room over the vault of the church or in a small chapel dedicated to Saint Barbara that had been built in an olive grove inside the same monastery compound. There he passed whole days in intense contemplation, with continuous ecstasies and in harsh penitence.

During an astonishing rapture, which we will discuss at the appropriate place, he gave up into the hands of his superior everything he had for his personal use, even the garment that was needed for celebrating Mass. He offered all this in imitation of his Seraphic Patriarch who renounced to his indignant father everything that he had gotten from him. In the same manner Joseph also gave back everything, including his shirt, to his severe but devout Mother who because of her devotion did not appear to approve the heroic act of her son. But she accepted them as a dutiful obligation towards his religious state. And after his departure she covered with a thousand tender kisses the blessed objects he had left behind, rendering infinite thanks to the Most High for what He had bestowed abundantly on her Joseph.

So, left only with a tunic, he cast it at the foot of the crucifix saying, h*ere I am, Lord, entirely poor and without anything, for inasmuch as you are my only good, I regard anything else as hurtful, dangerous and ruinous to my soul.* But such courageous resolve did cost him dearly! He proved in fact that anyone who practices to serve God must expose his soul to temptation, for he did not yet understand that poverty does not consist in not having external things but rather in not having a craving for anything. He was overcome inside by a fierce melancholy, by prolonged distrust, and a deep affliction of spirit *that the Lord with all his charity would not relieve,* and as Joseph himself later confessed to the Archbishop of Avignon, Monsignor Libelli, *he doubted that he could endure it.*

These doubts came after he saw himself almost devoid of his tunic since over time it had become worn out and torn, and he did not know where to get another. He himself admitted, *God perhaps permitted that the Order not provide everyone with necessary food and clothing so as to cleanse me in that way.* For he well knew that at the center of his heart was the Lord who from time to time exhorted him to have patience.

He confessed that this struggle between himself and divine goodness lasted two whole years. After those two years had passed, while he was in full spiritual dread, he reached a state of extreme need. Almost disconsolate, he entered his poor cell and threw himself on his poor little cot, renewing his lamentations to God, saying finally, *Lord why have you abandoned me?*

After invoking God with great fervor and with his breath hotter than usual, he gave forth a most bitter cry accompanied by deep gasps, which lasted a long time. As he was sobbing, a monk beat on his door which Joseph did not open. Since it was not locked, the monk entered and drew near the bed, asking Joseph the reason for his cry. After Joseph begged the monk to go away and leave him buried in misery, the monk answered, *no, I want you to stop weeping, to take heart, and since I think you need a tunic I've brought you one.* The monk laid it on the bed and went away.

Then Joseph rose full of wonder, donned the new tunic, and recognized within himself that it was a prodigy of divine kindness, infallible in its promise to liberate from anguish anyone who confides in that kindness, and to render him glorious. Immediately his gloom dispersed and his heart filled with the sweetest joy. He detested his past distrust, and from then on he served the Lord with a calmness so great that even an empire of a thousand worlds couldn't degrade the honor that he rendered to God. He was never able to find out who the monk was *but*, he said, *if he was not an angel sent from heaven, he certainly carried out the office of a consoling angel.*

And there he was, with every weight of the world unloaded from him, content in his extreme poverty, seeking neither nourishment nor clothing, and ready to fly directly to heaven. He used to go forth wherever obedience sent him, without stockings on his legs, with only slippers on his feet, and covered only by a single mean tunic. He frequently returned to the monastery with half of the tunic torn away by the veneration of the public, which snatched away even his waist-cord without his even noticing it since he was so engrossed with God.

But God, who dresses and paints the meadows in beautiful green and feeds and nourishes the smallest flying things, did not neglect his faithful servant, so on one occasion among many, Joseph was provided with a tunic, waist-cord, shoes, stockings, and a hat by a far off citizen of Lecce.

Now that Joseph had with his voluntary poverty defeated the world along with its vain pomp, he set about to fight with the Devil. And with divine aid he achieved victory. In that battle, obedience was his shield and humility was his spear with which he defeated the obstinate and arrogant enemy. On many occasions he did not wait for a command to fight but anticipated it. To bring an end to his raptures and to bring him back from them, the simple call of the monastery's superior was enough, although no obedience to anybody else could induce him to leave the monastery or eat meat. He used to say *that the virtue of humility is the most efficacious spell to triumph over the Devil.*

After gaining the priesthood, Joseph plunged deeply into true Christian humility since he saw himself unworthy of that divine priestly role. In exercising the function of priest, Joseph desired that something other than his fingers touch the Most Sacred Body of Jesus Christ. He used to tell himself that he was a sinner and a reprobate, and that he was the only reason for every evil thing in the world. He wanted everyone to call him a sinner, even youngsters, but even with them he couldn't fulfill his wish.

He taught a three-year old, who still could barely speak, to say, *Brother Joseph is a great sinner and when he dies he will go to Hell.* But instead he heard the child say twice in a loud and clear voice, *Brother Joseph is a great Saint and after he dies will go Heaven.* Before the child could say it a third time, Joseph playfully pulled his hair and ears and frightened him with his voice to make the child repeat the words as he had taught him instead. But the child, who spoke with the voice of God, did not know how to deny the truth. So he said again with even more spirit, *Brother Joseph is a great Saint and after he dies will go to Heaven.*

Bystanders were astounded by the novelty of what had happened, but it did not go to the Blessed One's head. Instead he plunged yet deeper into humility. He set his hands to the most vile tasks of the cloister, and subjected his shoulders to the greatest weights during the construction of the Church which was then in progress. It was work that for decency's sake he was later prohibited from doing because of his status as a priest. Although Joseph did not violate his prohibition, he compensated for his daily repose by undertaking other hard trials at night.

In discussion with others he would say, in imitation of the Royal Prophet (King David) who talked about himself with God, *uti jumentum factus sum apud te* (although I am made into a beast, I am with you). Joseph actually called himself a beast. *Let us go and wash and clean this beast,* he used to say whenever his superior ordered him to shave his beard. With patched clothing, and on bare feet, he would go about the land in all seasons in search of bread in support of the monastery. He appeared as a priest only when he was before the altar, but he was more of a layman in the debasement and burdens he placed on his person.

It did not seem to Joseph that his efforts were enough to overcome the call of the flesh, so he began to fight it with such vehemence that it was a wonder that he didn't die in achieving his victories. Twice a week he beat himself with such fury that thirty years later one could see marks of blood encrusted on the walls where he used to go in retreat. Nor was he content with this, but he begged others to beat him in order to keep the pain alive. If ever he was assailed by an impure image, or a vanity, or a distraction, he seized the whips to skin himself. His first instruments of severity were small cords with twisted needles. These were followed by little steel pins with hard points which ripped him in such a way that when he swooned at the end, there were streams of gushing blood.

The prudence of Joseph's superior moderated Joseph's excess of severe penitence, with which it was feared that he would end up losing his life. His superior limited it to only once a month, and to the use of some braids of brass only. But for Joseph these were materials for even cruder torment because they bruised him without lacerating the flesh, and he had to submit to the hand of the surgeon to open and squeeze out the contusions. His coarse hair-shirt served as a bandage for his many wounds, and a horrible chain squeezed his loins and his sores against the hair-shirt, and pushed the hair-shirt itself against the chain in such a way that his body had the aspect of a torn cadaver rather than a living man. Joseph went even further in torturing himself because over the knotted chain, he placed an iron plate so that when the knots were pressed down strongly they penetrated deeply almost to his bones.

But this cruel and ingenious martyrdom lasted only a little while. One day Joseph found himself with Don Girlolamo di Domenico, an outside priest, who loved the Monastery of Grottella. This priest saw Joseph returning to his cell barely alive as if about to expire at every step, and he brought the matter to the attention of the superior, exhorting him to look into the matter personally. They went together to visit Joseph who in obedience was forced to take off his habit and even his little tunic, which was actually his usual bristly and prickly hair shirt. Instead of flesh they saw with horror the sores, chains, and the iron plate, which for obedience's sake Joseph was also made to remove. They discovered a man whose body was a whole single sore, wearing only underpants, and barely alive with only a slight breath of life left in him. It was here that he was prohibited by the superior from wearing such horrible clothing any more. The chain and iron plate remained at that time in the possession of the priest as a worshipful memento of harsh penitence.

It is not known whether this major incident brought about confusion in Joseph or just obedience. It is well known that the devil was full of rage, and at night wanted to repay Joseph's merit by beating him so ruthlessly that in the monastery one could hear not only the laments of innocent Joseph but also voices of screaming demons who had become the targets of Joseph's living faith and who gave themselves in shame to hasty flight.

Joseph rounded off such severity with a continuing fast. After having been made a priest, for seven years he didn't eat bread, and for ten years never drank wine. His diet consisted of herbs or dried fruits or cooked beans, seasoned only with a very bitter powder. A person who on one occasion took some of that powder and tasted it thinking it to be pepper called it a death powder (as David did). What's more, Joseph didn't eat anything on Fridays except some herbs that were so bitter and disgusting that just to lick them with the tip of the tongue would leave one's stomach nauseous for days. During Blessed Lent, as it is called in the Franciscan Order, Joseph took some food only once a week. Likewise during other religious fasts he fed only on bitter herbs, or fruits, or beans, and did so only on Sundays and Thursdays. During the other five days he lived only on the diet of the Eucharist. Others observed that before celebrating Holy Mass, Joseph was so languid and listless that he seemed to be expiring. But afterwards he was agile in movement, with color and serenity in his face, which well showed that his best nourishment was the bread of the Angels.

As for eating meat, that was out of the question. Once when his superior ordered him to eat it, Joseph obeyed with usual promptness but he was immediately overcome by a stomach irritation and regurgitated it. It was the same with fish. For the sake of obedience, he once ate some fish with certain citizens of Lecce who had arrived deliberately well provided, but once the dinner was over he took leave from his table companions, locked himself in his cell, and those who were outside without his knowledge heard him vomit all the food because of the weakness of his stomach. He then grabbed an iron chain and, beating himself horribly fifty times, said with the words of his Seraphic Father, *Now brother ass you are well.*

Joseph's frugality with food was matched by the brevity of his rest. He did not sleep more than two or three hours at night on that bed which, as we already said, served more to bring out bitter sighs than sweet repose. Such a tormented and penitential life that he practiced, to the extent that it submitted the baser aspects of life to the higher ones, did not continue with the same aforementioned rigor, either for obedience to his superiors or because of his changes of residence or because of his different vocations, which we will describe. But finally, having seen what our Blessed One did for God, we will see in the following chapter what God for him.

four

Supernatural gifts from God shared by the Blessed Joseph in the Monastery of the Grottella, and his miracles.

God was pleased to privilege his servant with the gift of ecstasy in Joseph's most tender years and again after he became a priest, which made Joseph not only a wonder to the public but also to the most sublime and elevated minds.

Father M. Lorenzo Brancati of his Order, who was later Cardinal di Lauria, said of Joseph, *as soon as he began to meditate he found himself outside of himself, thereby entering into contemplation through the grace of God.* And once entered into contemplation, with such an elevation of the mind and alienation from his senses, it was well understood that his prayer was a complete communication with God, who in his delight in finding him, filled Joseph's soul with much of Himself, and united it so much to Him.

In that state Joseph could produce neither feeling nor movement in his body. He was frequently seen lying immobile, either with his arms outstretched, his eyes turned upward, his body almost stilled, or his feet in the act of walking, and there was no skill nor force that could move him from such a position. Neither pull nor blow or even flame, but only the voice of his superior, and Joseph's obedience to it, could make him come back from such his blessed raptures. When they were over, his countenance was tinged with a holy glow and his eyes were full of tears. He would then turn to bystanders and, in order to cover up the divine activity, would ask them to pardon what he called his daze and his imperfections.

All it took was for him to hear singing or music in a church, or discourses about God, or any indication of the mysteries of our faith, and he would immediately burst out in a cry and remain immobile for a remarkable time so alienated from his senses that he could not hear or see. On the eve of holy Christmas, a good number of shepherds who were invited to play music in the Church of the Grottella were met joyfully by Joseph at the door, and when they had barely touched their bagpipes and flutes, he began dancing in the nave in the center of the Church, like David before the ark. Then, taking a breath and giving a very loud cry, he flew *like a bird through the air to the great altar more than ten meters away, and he embraced the tabernacle with both his arms.*

The greatness of the spectacle filled those devout shepherds with holy fear. Added to it was a further marvel. For Giuseppe, having finished his flight, came to rest on the altar, full of lighted candles, without causing any of the candlesticks fall. He stayed kneeling on the altar in that embrace for a quarter of an hour, and then came down without causing a single upset.

Upon drawing away from the shepherds Joseph said, his eyes and face covered by tears, *no more, brothers, no more, be ye blessed in your praises of God.* It was a great miracle, this, and it continued within himself; for when the Mass was over, he ran hastily to his cell, and barely upon reaching it he uttered his usual cry, fell to his knees and remained there for a long time ecstatic, all engrossed in what God was showing him.

Lord Cardinal Lauria asked Joseph in the third person, *what might those in ecstasy see during their Ecstasy?* And Joseph answered also in the third person, *they find themselves as if in the middle of a great gallery of beautiful things and they see in one glance in a very shiny mirror hanging there, every type of arcane and longed-for mystery that it pleases God to reveal to them in that great vision.* And certainly afterwards Joseph saw astounding things as well. For the quality of the visions remained impressed upon on him, so that, following their fruition and enjoyment, he was drawn from one ecstasy and raised to another.

Joseph was an ecstatic from the time he acquired the priesthood, and it didn't end until his death. For that reason, for thirty-five years his superiors would not admit him to the chorus area of the church, nor to processions, nor to the refectory, since his raptures and ecstasies would have disrupted the events there. This is not the place to list all the ecstasies. It is enough to say that while he was staying for sixteen years in the Monastery of Grottella in Copertino, he was seen, upon approaching the altar wearing the cope, to leap high onto the highest step of the pulpit; and on Holy Thursday to throw himself from the ground into the air as far as the Sepulcher of Jesus Christ; and on Saint Francis' feast day to betake himself in flight onto the altar of Saint Francis; and, on the feast of the Madonna del Carmine, to raise himself from the ground and fly onto the altar of the Blessed Virgin upon the intoning of *Holy Mary.*

Similarly he was seen rising up high in his cell with lighted embers in hand without being hurt, also in the Refectory rising in the air from his seat with a sea urchin in his hands, and in the countryside flying onto an olive tree; and on another occasion onto a high cross that he had with miraculous strength brought to its spot. Joseph added to his raptures and his ecstasies continuous prophecies and a continuous penetration of the most hidden secrets of other people, even smelling out and discovering enchantments and witchcraft from afar.

But I have said enough here of such high and sublime gifts, and will refrain from talking about them more specifically until later chapters. We will now pass on to say a few things about his miracles.

For those many miracles that he performed in those sixteen years in Copertino Joseph acquired such fame in that land of his, and in the whole province as well, that he was held to be not only a great saint but a miracle of sanctity. With the sign of the cross, or with the blessing of Saint Francis written in his own hand, or with the oil of his lamp, he would cure any kind of infirmity saying, *my children, trust in God.* With these abilities that were given to him by God, he was liberal not only with local people but even with outsiders who came from afar to see him.

When he was visiting the sick, a mother showed him one of her daughters who had become so withdrawn and crippled by smallpox that she could not get on her feet. Joseph sat down somewhat away from her and drawing out a crucifix from his breast said, *come here, hold this crucifix, kiss it, and then bring it to your Father and Mother to kiss.* The command was a miracle. The girl went and kissed the crucifix, brought it with unhesitant step to her father and mother to kiss, and was perfectly cured in an instant.

With only one touch, this servant of God cured another person of a deep wound between his index finger and thumb. He did the same by touching the eyes of Joseph Turi, who had lost almost all his sight, inspiring him to trust in the great Mother of God and causing his sight to come back so markedly that he was able to betake himself right away to the Church of Grottella to render thanks to his distinguished benefactress.

The same thing happened to Pomponio Imbeni. The wretch was glued to his bed with stinking, disgusting sores, but with a simple touch from the hands of Joseph they immediately dried up, the crusts fell off, and he became completely whole.

Onofrio Rizzo, had bites on his mouth that was clenched shut by convulsions, and it couldn't be opened even by force with a piece of iron, but it opened with a simple touch from the fingers of the Blessed One, and he was cured entirely, being commanded by Joseph to say *the Blessed Virgin had cured him.*

When summoned to visit Pietro Paolo Schifeio who was reduced to agony, Joseph went, declared him cured, and so he was. And the following morning, in fulfillment of a vow to prepare a feast for the monks of Grottella, Joseph took part and miraculously multiplied the food they were eating up.

Also in agony was Pompeo Morelli, but being told by the Servant of God, *go, for you are well*, he recovered his life which had been doomed. With a bundle of plants of Saint Nicholas, Joseph freed Joseph Maria Gallo from a fatal fever, and with his touch he cured Father Giovanni Maria Volente of atrocious pains.

These were the fruits of his living faith in God. If we wanted to add the many other deeds brought about by him in Copertino this narrative would never end.

Windstorms and even whirlwinds obeyed Joseph. One of these that was very frightening, rose up one day, shook his Monastery of Grottella, and threatened the final destruction of everything around it. Joseph kneeled before the altar of the Madonna, and with a scream said, *eh, faith, faith*, and turning to the stormy airs shouted *ah, dragon, ah dragon*, then ran out of the church, dispersed the storm, and left the sky clear where he passed by.

The clouds obeyed him in the same way, as when he dissolved them during a heavy rainfall after a procession that he had organized for the Most Holy Madonna of the Grottella. And, that monastery of Joseph's did not know any shortages as long as Joseph was there, whether he went about in search of food, or multiplied it with omnipotent hand when there was need. Thus he multiplied honey, leaving a basin of it full to the brim for the Monastery of the House of the Ziuli as a reward for their charity to his own monastery. He also multiplied some stored wine for ten citizens of Nardo' who arrived at night at the monastery and asked for some wine to relieve their weariness. When they were politely denied because there wasn't enough there even for the monks, Joseph felt sorry and produced as much as they wanted to drink, and there was enough left in abundance for the brothers that evening and for subsequent days.

Francesca, his mother, reduced to poverty and without bread, would come to her Joseph, reminding him that she was his mother, and he would answer her, *the Madonna is my mother. I have nothing because I'm poor. Entrust yourself to the Madonna, for she will provide.* As soon as she would return home with a living faith in Mary, she always found as much bread as she needed that day.

In this way, Joseph's faith performed so many acts that were even more wonderful than those we have mentioned. Joseph's prayers, and the evident infallible promises of Jesus Christ, rendered even dumb animals obedient to his commands. When a certain ram was bitten by rabid dogs in the hamlet of Mollone near Copertino, it was locked up in the fenced enclosure of a small garden to protect the people and the herds from the rabies it had contracted. The Blessed One went there by chance and was warned not to get close in order not to suffer the animal's fury. But he, with his usual trust in God, called the ram to come to him and said, *mad, mad as you are, what are you doing here? Go back now to your sheep, and see to it that we don't hear more about your complaints or your affairs.* The ram obeyed the voice and immediately returned to care for his flock, docile and cured.

In the Convent of Saint Clare of Copertino, a wonderful white lamb was known which the Servant of the Lord had given to the abbess. That simple animal, as if sent there to the nuns as an example of correct observance, was always ready at the sound of the bell to be the first to run to the refectory and then to the chorus enclosure. There it would go to each nun begging for food and then rested quietly until time to leave. But within the chorus it behaved zealously with respect to the divine service, and would go around and shake any nun who was dozing off. If it saw anyone wearing an item of vain attire, it would go and rip it away with its feet or its teeth. It lived and died among them, pleasing all of them, and respected for the uniqueness and mystery of its manner.

Joseph also promised to send a small bird to that convent as an incitement and stimulus to good singing. And so it was. For five straight years when the nuns first assembled, whether to sing matins or vespers, a single gentle sparrow would fly in from the window of the chorus and, with its own sweet and unusual melody, would anticipate the singing of the nuns, inspiring all of them to praise the Lord.

There was one occasion when two novices were arguing after the service and seemed about to come to blows. The solitary sparrow first became excited and shrieked at them with a hoarse and unharmonious sound, then tried to separate them by beating its wings and scratching with its nails, but it was driven away by one of them with insults and threats. It left in sorrow and did not come back. After four days in which it did not show itself, the other nuns, grieving, let the Blessed One know of its absence to which he replied, *serves you right; why did you insult and threaten it? It doesn't want to go back anymore.* But, won over by their entreaties, Joseph sent it back. And, more gentle than ever, the sparrow reestablished its place among those holy virgins, becoming so tame that it let itself be caressed, and even allowed one of them to tie a tiny bell to its little leg.

This went on for two months, and since the sparrow was always the first one in the chorus, the nuns were summoned by her bell. But then when Holy Thursday came, the solitary sparrow disappeared, and did not show herself the next day or the morning of the following Saturday. Again the nuns went to Joseph who answered immediately, *I sent it to sing and you wanted to make it play music by attaching the little bell to its foot; it hasn't come because these recent days I've been watching the Sepulcher, but now I'll have it come back.* And in fact it did come back, and continued with the nuns as long as the Blessed One stayed in Copertino, who upon leaving then took his miracles elsewhere.

No less obedience was reported regarding two hares, whom Joseph saved wonderfully from the danger of hunters and the greed of some dogs. Upon seeing the hares in the olive grove of the Grottella, he said to them, *don't leave the proximity of the church of the Madonna, because many hunters are going after you.* The timid little animals obeyed him. But one of them, while grazing, would have become prey of the swift hounds if it hadn't, when fleeing, gone around and found the door of the Church and upon entering it thrown itself into the arms of the Blessed One. He took it, caressed it, and said to it, *didn't I tell you not to stray from the church, because the dogs will tear your skin?* At this point the hunters caught up and boldly asked for the hare. But Joseph, with serious words and countenance, answered, *this hare is under the protection of the Madonna; have patience, for it is not your turn, so bear it some regard.* Confused, they put aside their boldness and left quietly, and the Servant of the Lord blessed the hare and commanded it to return safely to its grazing. Then his companion arrived, also chased by the dogs in that little meadow that lies between the Church of Grottella and the Little Chapel of. S. Barbara, and it ran under the tunic of the Blessed One, who was passing by there. The hunter, D. Cosimo Pinelli, Marquess and Lord of Copertino, who was following the hare, met up with the Blessed Joseph, who when asked if he had seen the hare answered him, *this hare is mine, Lord Marquess, don't bother it, and don't come to hunt any longer, so as not to frighten it.* Turning then to the hare, and placing him on the ground, Joseph said to it, *go and escape into that bush, and don't move.* The tiny animal obeyed. The Marquess and his hunters were amazed, and they marveled greatly when they saw the dogs fix their eyes on the hare and then tremble with fright without moving a step.

We have portrayed Joseph's dominion over the birds of the sky and the beasts of the field that God had granted to innocent Adam. But that which follows is more resounding, and raises us up to admire even more a vestige of God's omnipotence that he communicated to his servant. An enormous and furious hailstorm from the sky killed almost all the sheep on a large farm known as *li Quarti* near Copertino. Smitten by the pain of such a slaughter, the poor shepherds ran to the Church of Grottella to seek comfort and relief from the Blessed Joseph. He saw their tears, understood the harm, consoled the shepherds as much as possible, and betook himself to the place of the killing. Upon arriving he lifted the heads of the sheep one at a time, and said to each one, *get up in the name of God,* and each one got up alive. When he raised the last one and said the same words it got up, but immediately fell down again dead. Then Joseph, as if in growing anger, lifted it again with great force, and in a loud tone of voice said, *get up, I tell you, in the name of God,* and the little sheep got up and didn't fall down again. Then Joseph departed leaving the shepherds - I don't know who they were - either very astonished or very comforted by the novelty of such an unheard of marvel.

After the miracle of the little resurrected sheep, there came other instances that renew with increasing force our astonishment and wonder. Every Saturday it was the custom of our Blessed One to recite the litanies in a small Chapel near the Church of the Grottella in the company of shepherds and farmers from the nearby countryside. On a certain Saturday none of them appeared, since all were distracted and busy with the harvest. Joseph's regret was great. His eyes turned here and there, but seeing only some flocks of sheep without shepherds he uttered with holy enthusiasm, *you there, come here, sheep of God, to honor the Mother of your God and of my God.* And oh, what a prodigy!! To these words, that were uttered at such a distance so that not even the most acute hear could hear it, all the sheep of those flocks overcame barriers and obstacles and ran towards the little chapel without heeding the stalks in the fields or fearing the rod of authority. Having arrived leaping at the chapel, the Blessed One, all joyful, intoned the blessed litany, and they all answered from refrain to refrain. Joseph would say *Holy Mary* and the sheep would answer with devout bleats, *beee.* He would go on. *Holy Mother of God,* and the little sheep responded *beee.* So, at the end of every word of praise for Mary as sung by her devoted servant, the little sheep would answer, *beee.* When the holy praises were over, and after receiving the blessing from the Blessed One, they returned joyfully to their pastures, and he, satisfied with having had those innocent little animals praise the Virgin, turned his steps back to his Monastery.

five

At the orders of his Provincial Superior he travels around to the Monasteries of his Province of Bari, and then returns to the Monastery of the Grottella.

Upon witnessing a life that was so religious and so perfect, and seeing the many marvelous things that God caused to happen in his subject Joseph, the Provincial Minister of the Province of Bari ordered Joseph to go around to all the monasteries in his jurisdiction and stay three or four days in each one. He thought that upon showing the Blessed One to the public it would suggest to the monks under his authority the idea of proper religious observance. For every one of them would be able to see with his own eyes how a true son of the Patriarch S. Francis of Assisi ought to be.

Our Joseph knew his orders but didn't know their reason, nor did he try to figure it out. His only concern was the value of obedience in which he traveled as in a *carriage to paradise*, as he used to say. But the fathers in the Monastery of the Grottella did not react to Joseph's departure that way, nor did the inhabitants of Copertino who had become accustomed to Joseph's miracles, and who thought that by losing him they would lose all the goodness they enjoyed in the world. For that reason they brought their concern to the Provincial Minister, but he was fixed on the will of God and wanted it to be carried out with obedience.

So Joseph departed, dressed in his poverty with a rod in his hand, with only his lay companion Brother Lodovico, and without knowing where he was going or which road to take. God knew Joseph well, and wanted his servant to be accompanied through that province by an array of miracles in a triumph of holiness. But He wanted to test him first. So Joseph, who was not known by sight even though he was known through fame, was allowed at the beginning of that trip to find himself now derided as a wretch, now taken as a tramp, and now as some slovenly beggar. He endured hunger, thirst, discomfort, and disgust, but always with joyfulness and with his only consolation in knowing that he was being obedient.

But in walking through the land, Father Joseph of Copertino, whose fame had already made him an apostle of the kingdom, soon become known to the people, and great throngs flocked around him. In order to flee their acclamations and adulation, it became more convenient for him to lose himself in the countryside, or to travel at night. or else during the hottest time of the day, or when the sky was discharging lightning, hail, or heavy rain.

That's why on many occasions, feeble either from perspiration or lack of water, Joseph would be forced to rest in some broken down hut in a meadow. Even though his spirit was happy, his distress was felt by his body which, as a result of his penances, was reduced almost to a cadaver and could have barely sustained the rigor of his trip had he not from time to time gained from heaven the strength and vigor with which to sustain himself and to support his good companion Brother Lodovico. The latter become seriously ill with fever, unable to go further, and he threw himself in agony onto the road. The servant of God comforted him, being himself also in need of comfort. Taking Lodovico's hand, he raised him from the ground saying, *be of good heart, brother, and have faith in the great Mother of God, for she will free you of this evil so that we can complete our mission.* Indeed that's what followed. With some effort Joseph led Lodovico to the nearby city of Andria. There, with a bit of oil from the lamp that was in front of the Image of Virgin Mary, drew the sign of the cross on his forehead.

Instantly the fever left him and he became healthy - in the most perfect health.

When they got near to Conversano, Joseph noticed that some youngsters ran into the city when they saw him. Being, as he was, averse to human praise, he feared an encounter with the public. So with hurried step Joseph skirted outside the walls and directed himself to Cartellona which was Brother Ludovico's home town, expecting that nobody would know him there except his co-religionists. But it was specifically there that God made him known to others by a rare miracle.

It was late at night when they reached the monastery and the doors were shut and locked. Three times Brother Ludovico knocked loudly but nobody heard the sound, even though certain workers of the monastery were sleeping nearby. So they went to Brother Ludovico's home, but their knocking was in vain there as well because nobody answered, even though from outside they could hear the voices of those whom they had awakened. The Blessed One said, *let's go back then to our monastery, because God will find a good way to make them open the door.* They went back and at Joseph's single knock the doors opened wide to the wonderment of some peasants who were sleeping nearby, and to the even greater amazement of the monks and of the guard who had the keys.

In the Monastery of Monopoli the chorus enclosure served as Joseph's cell. In the Monastery of Nardo he was often seen in ecstasy, and even publicly in the Church of Saint Francis there, in view of the whole populace which was left surprised and stunned. Joseph was also seen in ecstasy in the home of the vicar of the above-mentioned city. There, upon hearing the song of a town girl, he gave his usual cry and raised himself above the level of a small table.

Finally, in the same city, D. Antonio Nestorio, vicar of the bishop, was stricken by a fierce headache whose sharp stabbing made him yell and shout with spasms while in bed. Brother Joseph visited him and upon placing his hand on the place where D. Antonio felt the pain said, *does it hurt here?* When the sick man answered, *yes sir*, the Servant of God answered, *does it still hurt?* And the sick one said, n*o sir*. To confirm his answer, he immediately got up from the bed now free of his unendurable pain. While the bystanders were standing amazed at such a prodigious recovery, yet another even more stupendous event revealed itself. The Blessed One, upon uttering the last aforementioned words, saw a painting representing the *Ecce Homo*, which was hanging over the head of the bed of the sick man. Breaking out in a very sharp scream, Joseph lost his senses, went into ecstasy and stayed that way like a statue until the Father- Guardian drew close to his ear and told him to come to back to senses. Joseph did come back but was confused. He acted as if he had been asleep, rubbing his eyes and covering his face with his hands so as not to be seen.

Upon passing through Lecce, Joseph visited the head of that city who was ill, and immediately cured him, at the same time predicting great things, all of which came true.

That's how our Blessed One toured his province. His trip left an imprint of a continuous path of holiness, miracles, ecstasies, and proof of contrition wherever he passed. Rich and happy in his holy poverty, he refused to receive the offerings from all sorts of people, howsoever generous, spontaneous and continuous, either for his own use of for the monasteries, poor as they were. Then he returned to his Copertino after having benefited the image and reputation of his Order in all those places where he had gone.

The joy displayed by his town, which recognized all the good that was in him, was indescribable. Also indescribable was how much they enjoyed knowing that they themselves were part of his desire. Nevertheless, being accustomed to his penitence, retreats, contemplations, and to the presence of his beloved Image of the Madonna of the Grottella, he was too afraid to wander about where he would always be tempted by plaudits, even though he was reassured by virtue and obedience not to be seduced by them. So, arriving at his cell, he once again carried out those usual marvels which God is always pleased to work in this his humble and most simple servant.

At his little window there hung a poorly-made little cage with a marvelously beautiful finch. Within its confinement, it would go towards Joseph beating its wings whenever Joseph entered his cell, and it would often say these words which Joseph had taught it, *Jesus Mary, Jesus Mary.* And when the time came for Joseph to say his office, the finch would move here and there, jumping around in its cage and admonishing him in a clear voice, *Brother Joseph, Brother Joseph, recite your office.* One time when the Blessed One was praying in the oratorio next to his cell, this gentle little bird was spied by a hawk which threw itself on the cage and killed it with its talons. Joseph heard the noise, saw the sad event, and also saw the killer fly next to the cage wanting to take his prey. *Ah, you scoundrel,* he yelled at it, *you've killed my little finch? You deserve to have me kill you.* Frightened, the hawk went and placed himself on top of the cage as if waiting in penance for the Servant of God to punish it for its crime. Then, Joseph struck him lightly with his hand and said, *go away because I forgive you, but don't do such things again.* The evildoer departed, more saddened for his crime I would say than happy for the pardon he received.

Nevertheless, the most renowned of Joseph's miracles was his life itself, which was a complex of his most noble virtues and drew to him the eyes and wonderment of everyone. Among these virtues, humility, of which Jesus Christ approved so much, was foremost in anything Joseph did and especially in his miracle works. For that reason, knowing that these miracles came from omnipotent virtue, Joseph was full of saintly horror when he heard a blind man whose sight he restored ask him how he did it, and answered, *go away, go away, because with my own sins I couldn't by myself do other than make you even blinder.* On other occasions, in a loud voice during the very act of a miracle, Joseph said with great simplicity and truth, *God did the miracle.* And so, in disapproval of praise and of approbation given to him, he would never accept any of it for himself. *Non nobis Domine,* he used to say, *sed nomini tuo da gloriam* (not to give glory to us, Lord, but to your name).

On the other hand, when dealing with his own humiliation, oh here yes, his humble spirit rejoiced without restraint! A monk of his monastery who was unable to move because of infirmity had by necessity to betake himself frequently to Copertino. Joseph built a portable chair to help him, and with one of the laymen carried the invalid back and forth with ropes on their shoulders with such liveliness in his face and loveliness of words that he himself seemed to be the beneficiary.

When undertaking such menial activities, or on other occasions when walking, if Joseph found some young person bearing a stain of dishonesty, he would draw close to him and say in his ear, *go clean your face since you are covered with ink*. To another person guilty of some sin he would say, *fix your crossbow*, by which it was understood that he was referring to his conscience. To another who was thoughtful and sad, Joseph would reveal the secret reason for his sadness, or he would console him with compassion, or reprove him charitably.

Joseph wanted to remind those who betook themselves from Copertino to the Grottella of the passion of Christ by raising in certain eminent spots some large crosses, and he wanted the crosses blessed by the hand of the bishop. The Vicar General of Nardo, who was enduring the excessive heat of the season declined, but Joseph, full of faith, said to him, *the Most Holy Madonna won't let you get hot*. With that promise, the Blessed One prevailed. And he was so right because in the ceremony, which lasted from nine o'clock to midnight, the Vicar, although dressed in his cope, admitted that he hadn't felt a hint of heat, while his attendants and everyone else were soaked in sweat.

six

His summons to the Holy Office of Naples, his stay in that City, and his assignment to his Father- General in Rome.

Although God did not openly reveal this coming distress to his servant, he did give him some indications of it so that he would recognize it when it came. At the blessings of the crosses mentioned earlier, Joseph prostrated himself before one of them after the ceremony and he felt a twinge in his heart and heard a voice in his ear that said to him, l*eave the dead crosses and take up the living ones.* And not much before the coming of this great trial, while in extreme contemplation, Jesus was shown to Joseph as a tender and unclothed child with a large cross on his shoulders, who allowed himself to be watched for a certain length of time without saying anything, and then disappeared.

Much the same happened three years earlier, when it was thought that he might be called to Naples to that Holy Tribunal, and was sought out by some Monks to see if he would willingly go to see that city. Joseph replied straightforwardly *that he would go but under orders from the Holy Office.* When he was further asked *why* and *when*, he could only shrug his shoulders and say, *I don't know anything else.*

The reason for Joseph's summons was an accusation against him to the Ministers of the Holy office lodged by the vicar of a bishop whose name is not given. It was set forth in a letter in these terms: *A man of about thirty-three years of age goes about these provinces inducing the public to think he is another Messiah, using prodigies every step of the way, which is believed by the masses who will always believe anything, and who can never distinguish appearance from reality. One, therefore, provides knowledge of this to the Superiors so that either a remedy might prevent a bad outcome, or that a bad outcome not become fixed and incapable of remedy.*

One does not know or need to know about the zeal with which the accuser acted by mixing truth and falsehood. It can only be said that the iniquity was a lie in itself, and that the vicar was touched by overwhelming pangs of conscience. He fell into profound sadness. Little by little he went mad, and he left life in a wretched state.

When the accusation reached Naples, the Holy Office sent to the alleged guilty party an immediate order, addressed to the Guardian of the Grottella, to send Joseph from there to the Inquisition. A monk of the same Order brought it to Copertino. Joseph was coming back from a visit to his crosses when the monk suddenly arrived with the dispatch. Joseph saw him, and was in no way in doubt and had a premonition that some unexpected command was coming from the superiors of his Order. Joseph asked him courteously *if some order from them was either for him or against him.* The monk was cautious not to reply and kept it secret, pretending not to know what it was about, and he consigned the letter to the Father-Guardian, and departed.

The Father-Guardian, surprised by this unexpected summons, kept its contents to himself more than he should have. Since summer was underway, which is very hot in those parts and made it uncomfortable to travel at that time, the Father-Guardian hid his great regret about the forthcoming departure of our Blessed One, and did not tell him anything. But Joseph heard a voice in his heart that presaged something about his great forthcoming distress, and he with spirit fully composed went to the Guardian several times and said that *he was uncertain if there might be an order for him to depart.* The Guardian, won over by Joseph's importuning, gave into Joseph's hand the letter and the summons. Joseph kissed one reverently and the other adoringly, making up for delay in his being notified with a dauntless resolve to hasten his departure. He judged useless and vain the clamoring that people make in similar instances by those who love others, and was intent only on following the command of God.

Joseph asked for and was lent a beast of burden through the kindness of a fellow priest, and in the company of his Brother Lodovico, departed from his beloved Grottella with a serene expression and a tranquil heart. He was never to return. All of Copertino was immediately in tears, its inhabitants saying to each other, *oh what a loss, oh what a loss!.*

Joseph's journey was like the one he had already made within his province, replete with virtue, ecstasies, and sufferings. His utterances to Brother Lodovico were these: *that he was not worthy to be dressed in that sacred vestment of an Order whose fame is now so prejudged by his evil habits, that God was punishing him strongly with the current contempt that he was enduring, and he added promptly that he would pay for the time he wasted earlier in his life in the past.* And so, upon thinking of his supposed sins, Joseph turned from time to time to beseech divine compassion and then would become ecstatic and rise up from the ground. The fact was that in heaven, where the truth about Joseph was known, his defense was being prepared to dispel the slanders about him.

In his passage through Monopoli, the fathers of his Order wanted to show Joseph a well-made statue of Saint Anthony of Padua that had just been placed in their Church. No sooner did Joseph see it that he gave a shout and flew towards it over a distance of fifteen handbreadths. In a very short time he came back by the same path to where he started because, upon turning his eyes, he had noticed the altar of the Immaculate Consolation nearby. He flew again from the ground to the top of that altar, and then returned by the same route to where he had been.

With this string of marvels behind him, Joseph arrived in Naples and found the monks of his Monastery of Saint Lorenzo more regretful about his call to the Holy Office than gladdened by the fame of his holiness. How much, then, was his spirit afflicted as evident that night when he remained awake throughout, weeping and saddened, doing nothing but, Joseph maintained, placating the anger of God whom he had provoked with his sins.

But it never occurred to God to punish Joseph angrily, but to console him instead with a stupendous miracle. For upon leaving the monastery the following morning in the company of Brother Lodovico to go to the pious seat of the Holy Office, Joseph was joined by a young monk of graceful and devout appearance, who first greeted him, then went along with him, and by means of his conversation calmed the turmoil in Joseph's heart. Joseph looked at him fixedly, rejoiced in seeing him, and discerned a certain sweetness in the young monk's soul that soothed the tempest within him and restored his usual calm. *Remain joyful Brother Joseph*, the young monk told him, *because God will help you, and the Mother of God will help you, and our Father St. Francis as well.* The facts bore out the promises, and in entrusting himself to God, Joseph found comfort in that certain aid was assured.

With this good companion, the Servant of God would have walked as far as the Indies, but upon entering the Palace of the Inquisition, that companion disappeared. Joseph asked Brother Lodivico *where might they have lost the young monk or left him behind,* and Brother Lodovico answered *not to have seen anyone accompanying them,* whereupon Joseph told himself that he must have been St. Anthony of Padua, who came in flight to him just as he himself had flown towards him in Monopoli.

Full of holy faith, Joseph therefore entered that holy tribunal of the faith, which is unbiased towards everyone and always renders correct judgment, either when absolving the innocent or punishing the guilty. Three times Joseph was examined, and once he was asked about the source of his knowledge. Such exams are buried in secrecy, but when they probed his abilities, Joseph answered with a miracle which was a prophecy that was later verified in the passage of time. It was as follows.

The Holy Minister presented him with an open Breviary and Joseph was required to read and explain it. Fortuitously to men, although caused mysteriously by God, there fell before Joseph's eyes the lesson of St. Catherine of Siena, who was his great advocate. It read *Catharina Virgo Senensis ex Benincasis piis orta parentibus* (Catherine, a maiden of Siena, from Benincasa, born of pious parents). But Joseph read, *Catharina Virgo Senensis piis orta parentibus*, (Catherine a maiden of Siena born of pious parents) leaving out the words *ex Benincasis* (from Benincasa). When the tribunal admonished him to repeat the reading, Joseph did so right away, again leaving out those words. And so again a third time. Upon being told to look again at the lesson in which he had neither read nor uttered *ex Benincasis*, Joseph constantly affirmed *that he did not see those other words that the tribunal articulated just before.* By this, God wanted Joseph to predict that the words *ex Benincasis* had to be removed from the Roman Breviary, which the Holy Congregation for Rites did for just reasons.

After some weeks in the palace of the Holy Inquisition, the goodness of Joseph's spirit became most truthfully evident as well as the truth of his miracles. So Joseph was honorably dismissed and sent with some dispatches to his Father- General in Rome with further permission to first rest for a month or so in his Monastery of San Lorenzo in Naples. But his repose was his usual penitent life, humble, contemplative, and full of miracles. The public and the nobility gathered to see him in wonderment, and his fellow monks regarded him as the victor over his past tribulation, as if gold had been gleaned from a great crucible. They rejoiced yet more because of his proven innocence and that he was not made to suffer for a supposed crime. Joseph alone did not applaud the approbation that he got, *calling himself a sinner, unworthy to live among his devoted brothers, and only worthy to return to the horses of the stable.* It was in those terms that he spoke of himself to the nuns of S. Ligorio in Naples on the occasion of a great event that follows.

The Superintendent of the holy Tribunal imposed an order on Joseph requiring his obedience to celebrate Holy Mass in the Church of San Gregorio of Armenia, where the nuns of S. Ligorio are enclosed in a noble convent. The Blessed One went there and celebrated Mass in the secret chapel, and while kneeling to recite one of the of chants of the Church, he was immediately raised into high contemplation, wherein he was brought to heaven. He first gave a loud shout, rose in flight and placed himself standing straight on his feet on top of the altar with his arms extended in a cross, and he bent at the waist among the flowers and the candles which were burning there in great numbers. The nuns, seeing him first in the air and then on the flames screamed loudly, *he is burning himself, he is burning himself.* But Brother Lodovico, Joseph's companion who was accustomed to such marvels, answered them calmly, *have no fear nuns, for he is not going to burn himself,* and in fact neither Joseph nor his habit burned. Then upon giving a new shout, Joseph returned in flight to the middle of the church, jumping with his knees, turning around very fast, full of inner joy and outward exultation, and he danced, singing, *oh Blessed Virgin, oh Blessed Virgin,* and then, having removed all sensation and his person being immobile, again went into ecstasy.

Upon being shaken by Brother Lodovico, and coming back to his senses, Joseph provided some pious teachings to those holy nuns, some of whom wanted him to make the sign of the cross over them, while others surreptitiously cut off various parts of his tunic, being as they were full of astonishment and wanting his relics. Once back in his cell, the Blessed One, saw the cuts on his tunic and burst into tears. Brother Lodovico found him in that state and asked him *why he was crying.* Joseph answered, *because I'm poor and the nuns have cut up my whole tunic.* Brother Lodovico then told him not to cry because those good servants of the Lord would make him another one. But Joseph wanted the remnants of this one. *What do those nuns want from me, a great sinner,* he asked weeping once again, *I would rather wear this tunic, cut up as it is, than their new one.* And in fact that's the way it was.

Being informed about the above-mentioned rapture, and of others that will be described shortly, a trusting fellow countryman, who at that time was a fellow monk but later became Cardinal Lorenzo di Lauria, sought Joseph out and asked him, *what does certain dancing and singing in a low voice on one's knees mean in some Servants of God?* The Blessed One answered, *those kinds of raptures, which are jubilant raptures, are those that God grants to some of his Servants.*

Now, returning to the prodigies of our Blessed One, even though he wept for his cut-up tunic he did laugh with modesty because of the following event. A Neapolitan knight came brazenly into his cell and began to revile him. *You wicked hypocrite,* he said, *I have no respect for your person, which I hold in no regard, but I revere and have faith in the habit you wear. Make the sign of the cross over this wound and cure me* (and he then uncovered his wound). Joseph calmly looked him in the face and then from head to foot, and began to laugh with pleasure, and then answered humbly between his laughs, *you tell the truth; come here.* And, making the sign of the cross over the wound, Joseph healed it, and the knight attributed the miracle that Joseph worked on his person to the saint's abilities.

By this act of heroic docility, God glorified his servant not only among those who were present at the miracle, but also before the people who gathered together in a large and universal flock of noblemen and also the immense population of Naples. Joseph, not being able to endure it, decided to leave for Rome. But his departure turned into a flight since the Count of Monte Rey, Viceroy of Naples, at that time, along with his consort, let Joseph know that they wanted to attend his Mass with all the ranking people of the kingdom in the chapel in the Royal Palace, with the pomp of holy music and full display. Regarding this, the Blessed one did not know how to restrain the force of his own humility, and in order to turn away from such human esteem he secretly set out on the road to Rome.

The fathers of the Monastery of S. Lorenzo found out, and were worried that the royal authority would be disappointed and slighted, and would resent the change of plans. So they immediately sent off two monks to make Joseph come back, having convince themselves that it would certainly be the Holy Office's intent to recall him so as not to disobey the command. Joseph doubted that such would be the intent, but he judged it better to obey, so he came back. Nevertheless it pleased the Lord to endorse the humility of his servant. So, for a different reason the holy function was deferred, and Joseph took advantage of the time and the opportunity offered by the delay and took the road to Rome again.

seven

His trip from Naples to Rome. His stay in that City, and his departure for Assisi.

That journey of his was more of a continuous meditation than a tiring trek. Joseph traveled the road from Naples to Rome with his feet on the ground and his mind on heaven, uplifted by high contemplation of the sight of so many beautiful things that adorn heaven and earth that never cease to give praise to the creator. But even more, he contemplated that blessed and happy place to which he was betaking himself: the resting place of the remains of the Prince of the Apostles, bathed in the blood of innumerable martyrs, the head and the center of the Christian religion.

From this high perception there came into his soul a horror of entering the city unless he entered it humbly, devout and poor just as his great Father and Patriarch S. Francis entered it four centuries before. Discovering near the walls of the beloved metropolis that his companion, Brother Lodovico, had in his possession a small silver coin which had been advanced to them for a few provisions during the trip, Joseph made him leave it on a stone for the benefit of whoever might find it, saying that *upon entering the holy City it was fitting to enter totally abject and poor.* And so he entered, and so he was received into the Monastery of the Holy Apostles.

At that time the whole Order of the Minor Conventuals of S. Francis was governed by Father-Master Giovanni Battista Berardicelli of Larina, a personage well recognized for his good judgment and knowledge of doctrine. To him Joseph consigned the orders from the Tribunal of the Holy Office to send him to some remote monastery so that he could lead his life in solitude far from any intercourse with others. The governor was startled upon reading it. Not only did he little appreciated this new and not well-known guest, but he debased him emphatically, confining him to a small room in that monastery until he could eventually make arrangements for him.

On that occasion the humanity of the Blessed One was subjected to the bold attacks of pride, but God kept his eyes on him to cleanse him, as if separating gold from its impurities. Joseph saw himself in a religious Order that he much desired, to which providence brought him by force of miracles, yet within that Order he saw himself tried by the Holy Office, badly viewed by his superiors, an object of disdain and of reproof. He blamed his own unworthiness, but he was could not avoid the pain of knowing that albeit in some innocent way he had dishonored his fellow monks. So he stayed in his cell, retired and alone, entrusting himself vigorously to God, resolved to let himself go along that apparently rough but secure and sweet road of holy obedience *like a blind man guided by a dog*, as he was wont to say.

God, who rejoices in putting down his servants in order to more highly elevate them, humiliated Joseph even here so as to pull him from a sea of contradictions to the comfort of internal spiritual peace. So just as he freed Joseph with great glory from the confinement of the Holy Office, so he freed him from his cell and made him appear wonderful not only in the eyes of Rome but even in the eyes of the Supreme Pontiff. Outside of Rome his fame truly spread *that Father Joseph worked many miracles in that city, so that he was held by everyone as a saint*. It certainly had to be like that. If God had left him without the splendor of those marvels with which he frequently glorifies even on this earth the heroic life of his beloved servants, most memories would thus die after which there would none left, such as the memories of the flocking to Joseph of the most conspicuous personages of that noble metropolis.

Here we record things that remain beyond doubt. Giuseppe Mozzicchi, whose fatal illness was the despair of physicians, prayed to the Blessed One as recommended by his relatives, and was instantly cured. Marcello, Cardinal Lanti, Dean of the Sacred College, Protector of the Franciscan Order, a man of great wisdom and recognized merit, was moved by the fame of our Blessed One and could not contain himself from going to visit him in his poor cell in the Holy Apostles. The Cardinal remained with him for a long time in devout conversation and it satisfied him so much than it seemed that he didn't know how to detach himself. He offered Joseph aid and protection, which Joseph unhesitatingly declined, but promised that in exchange for such kind solicitude he would never forget to pray to God for him, that he might enjoy a long life and a healthy mind, as indeed happened, and then, as one would hope, enjoy the glory of paradise.

The general of his Order was now no longer censorious but an admirer of Joseph's saintly virtue and the rare gifts with which heaven had splendidly adorned this monk, his subject. He took Joseph to kiss the feet of Urban VIII, in order that the wise Pontiff might know face-to-face the man who had been portrayed to him by such great public fame. The humble Servant of the Lord went to him, and his fame was vindicated in the Pope's presence. Joseph entered the chamber where the Pope was holding audiences that morning, and saw him fill the place with the divine glow of the Prince of the Apostles, with the great authority of the Vicar of Jesus Christ. When Joseph lowered himself to kiss the holy feet, he took leave of his senses and rose up in a rapture. It lasted until the general called him back to himself, concerned as he was for the Supreme Pontiff. The latter turned to the general and said that if Brother Joseph were to die during his pontificate, he would testify as to what had happened. He ordered that Joseph be placed in some monastery that observed a strict rule.

Also during his stay in Rome, there is a story about Joseph that is so prodigious that one reads about it regarding only a very few Saints. It is about finding himself in several places at the same time. One day, Ottavio Piccino of Copertino, an old decrepit man, had betaken himself with much hardship to the Grottella, wanting them for charity's sake to commend his soul to God at the time of his death which he saw as already imminent. He was called by the nickname "father," either for his advanced age or for the sake of respect. In answer to his loving request, the Blessed One agreed, and answered him, *yes, I'll come to commend your soul, even if I should find myself in Rome.* Now it might seem that this is an exaggeration, but it was true; for the year had not yet passed when the good old man got sick, and Joseph at that time was in Rome. Joseph recalled his promise and hurried to the old man in his agony. It astounded a devout tertiary named Teresa Fatali who was on the road outside when the Blessed One knocked on the dying man's home. She said, *Father Joseph how is it that you find yourself here?* He answered, *to commend the "father's" soul.* When she recounted the incident she added, *that same morning, when I heard that the old "father" was dead, many said that they had seen Brother go into the house of the old man Ottavio Piccino, who, as I said, died.*

But Joseph, either for being averse to receiving visits, which were being made by the principal personages of Rome, or desirous of a retreat more fitting for his soul, showed an inclination to hide himself in some remote monastery in accordance with the command of the Holy Office. But God would settle him otherwise in a far different manner, and instead had him placed in the holy Monastery of Assisi.

Ever since he was a youngster, Joseph had conceived a deep veneration for those sacred places, having heard his devout mother tell about them, along with her brother who was a Monk in the Grottella whom we have mentioned elsewhere. In listening to those discourses, little Joseph much enjoyed the story of the sacred tomb of the Seraphic Father S. Francis and of the description as to how his body was placed, and of the flocking of people to it. And he felt the birth in his heart of a certain warmth of devotion, which would later flare up into a fire.

And in fact it did flare up, but the great distance of those places and Joseph's responsibilities to his Order rendered it difficult to visit those sanctuaries, so it made him give up the hope of going there.

But a strong desire to go there was nourished within him. To fulfill it, he used to imagine with sweet deception that whenever he went from the Madonna of the Grottella to the Church of S. Francis in Copertino, that he was really making a trip to the Madonna of the Angels at S. Francis of Assisi, and when on the road wrapped in such heavenly contemplation, his spirit was sweetly pacified. Such was the state of affairs when he was called from Copertino to Naples, and from there to Rome. There he felt that the gentleness and fragrance of the Sanctuary of Assisi was closer, and he prayed secretly to the Lord to make him worthy of access to it.

But obedience prevented him from even breathing of it, knowing full well that with his orders from the Holy Office, the Father-General was meanwhile thinking of sending him to the Monastery of Monte Rotondo near Rome, a delightful but solitary place. But a new thought now diverted the Father-General. Thinking of monastery after monastery, he couldn't decide where to place Joseph, for God does silence and govern the heart of a superior in accordance with its ability. Finally, with the aid of a higher light, the Father-General recalled that the Pope had ordered him to place Joseph in a monastery with a strict rule. He decided on that of Assisi, in order that the holiness of the place would gain greater luster by Joseph's observance of its rule. So on the last day of April 1639 he sent Joseph to Assisi, along with his companion Brother Lodovico. We will see next how much Joseph endured and wrought there.

eight

The arrival of the Blessed Joseph at the Sacred Monastery of Assisi, and his internal and outward distress.

It was with great happiness that Joseph arrived in Assisi, showing his desire to follow Christ in that sanctuary and to walk in the footsteps of that great Father who, with his poverty and his wounds, was a true image of Jesus Crucified.

Joseph got from S. Francis an appreciable and sure confirmation of his own wishes. For no sooner had Joseph set foot in that holy monastery than he prostrated himself with full tenderness and devotion before S. Francis' altar in the Church, and, overcome by a sudden impulse that burst forth within him, said, *Holy Father, in life you so loved poverty, and you are now among silver and brocades and so many rich adornments!* And his Holy Father, by means of a brilliant internal illumination, made Joseph understand that those ornaments weren't for him but for the most Holy Sacrament that resided in that altar, while his own remains were beneath ground in the dark, in no splendor at all. Joseph understood from this that since his Seraphic Father was abject, poor, and humble, he who was his son in his house should be that way too.

Joseph was kindly received by the monks, and especially by the Father Master Gabbrielle di Caravaggio, a man of great kindness and esteem, and by Father Eutimio da Campo, master of novices, all to whom the Father General had commended Joseph. But God, who was the director of that good soul, wanted to test Joseph's firmness in the midst of spiritual storms. Three times his room was changed, now for one reason, now for another. Finally he was placed in a room near the novitiate where he stayed a long time, near a small oratory where he found his delight, where he celebrated Holy Mass, and where he rose from the ground to heaven in loving raptures. In that tour where he was moved to different cells, he obeyed as if he were a dead weight, allowing himself to be moved about without complaint.

Then there was the Custodian of the sacred Monastery of Assisi. He was the same Father-Master Antonio di S. Mauro who previously as the Provincial head had sent Joseph around the Province of Bari. Taken by God as an instrument to hone the patience of his servant, the Cusodian began to treat Joseph at first with haughtiness then with contempt and finally with threats and penitential punishment. In this case Joseph did not resort to quick expediency or caution, but followed his saintly custom of humiliating himself more and more as he was pushed down, attributing to his own deficiencies his superior's rigidity.

God added most to these afflictions, namely with a lack of spiritual feeling, a great trial to which God often subjects those souls he loves most. Little by little the waters of divine consolation dried up. The ecstasies and the raptures disappeared, as did all that gentle sweetness which in great abundance had raised his spirit, and which had brought comfort to every affliction. Joseph's Masses seemed uninspired, and when he celebrated them he seemed not to enact the sacrifice but to be making himself nothing but a victim of spiritual sterility and of his previous mental backwardness.

He sought out the fervor of his religious Order by reading its chronicles, but he couldn't discern it there. He would resort to exclamations to his God, but he called in vain; for even though He heard him well, He pretended not to hear so that He would call again. A gloomy sadness came into his heart, which passed its poisonous mood into his very eyes, rendering him incapable of lifting them.

To add to his sadness, a satanic angel came who pierced him day and night with visible and dishonest portrayals that were most hateful to Joseph's pure spirit, forcing him to endure them at the angel's pleasure. And thus poor Joseph, from the sublime heights of his wonderful contemplations, was cast down deep by these attacks, by his sadness, by spiritual sterility and by temptations. He wept copiously seeing that all the protection of his combative spirit had been beaten down.

Despite this, it seemed to him that he was still left with his will intact, capable of hidden resistance and secret strength, even though he didn't know whose strength it was. It was God's. Joseph turned to the crucifix throughout his distress, but he seemed to see the crucifix of an unknown God, for such was the trouble, fog, and darkness in which his spirit was wrapped. From the bottom of his heart he prayed and begged, but as is usual in similar situations, to his great sorrow he couldn't discern the effect of his prayers or his entreaties.

The Blessed One remained for a long time in that great struggle where the outcome illustrates the difference between bodily and spiritual battles. In the former, the more one strives the more one tires. But in the latter, the more one exerts himself the more he is invigorated and strengthened, with the grace of God always growing inside him along with the energy of the Saints.

Meanwhile, the opposition of the Father-Custodian went on, as ordained by God in order to crown Joseph's victories. Since Joseph was more fixed on the God of consolation than the consolation of God, he responded to the words *hypocrite and disobedient* with humble words and true innocence. So it happened that because of his reaction to his vexations and because of his increasing virtue, heaven loved him all the more, and undertook more to protect and comfort him.

Father-Master Bonaventura of Copertino, who at that time was President of the holy Monastery of Assisi, was named, by order of the Father-General, to be Joseph's superior. The Blessed one, who steadily recognized God throughout, benefited greatly from this divine will which worked to his advantage.

But meanwhile, the internal distress didn't cease, nor the internal temptations, so that Joseph continuously raised his voice from the bottom of his heart up to the Most High, waiting for the only remedy for his woes to come from Him. But God, when it comes to testing his servants, does not always grant a diminishment of discomfort, but rather an increase of His grace so that his servants can more courageously fight the arrival of new travails. And that's what he did with Joseph.

In the two years that the described afflictions lasted, the infernal enemy saw that he couldn't defeat him with impure images. Changing then from hateful to pleasing weapons, he frequently depicted in Joseph's mind the sweet life that he had enjoyed back in the Monastery of the Grottella where he had always been absorbed in ecstasy, always elevated in rapture, and always favored by God. In all this, the Angel of Darkness transformed himself into the Angel of Light, and engendered in him a fiery devotion towards the image of the Madonna of the Grottella, and made every effort to make Joseph understand that, without seeing it, it would be impossible to resurface from the abyss of spiritual sterility in which he was lying almost lost.

These thoughts took such possession of the imagination of the innocent and simple Joseph, and he gave so much credence to them, that now he no longer yearned for the holy places of Assisi, a yearning which he judged to have satisfied, and instead he said silently to himself and out loud to others, *I would like to go back to the Madonna of the Grottella, because that one is my mother, and the other one of this world nourished and nursed me there.* With that utterance, as an affectionate son, he would call for Maria for whose memory he pined. And in his desire to see Her again he prayed for his return to that Church.

His burning desire received another impulse from the intense effort that his fellow countrymen made for his return. Not satisfied with the incessant petitions that they sent to the Father-General to get back this fellow-citizen saint of theirs, they dispatched representatives to the Father-General. But since they were going against the divine will, they all suffered a bad journey. Some were surprised by fever, others robbed by thieves, and the Auditor of the Treasury, who was committed more than the others, was struck by a sudden accident and sadly lost his life on the trip.

Throughout these troubling trials it was never possible for the Blessed One to open his mouth to the superiors for an end of his yearning. It was only with God that he remonstrated, and only to Him did he manifest his desire. For that reason, God had compassion for his servant and began to prick his heart with these voices: *What do you want? What do you seek? Am I not the same here as there?* Joseph pondered their significance, and being familiar with the voice of his beloved, was left consoled. Falling into the same thoughts as before, he returned to his earlier wish and undertook a noble battle between God's grace and himself, which having both been removed from humanity were rather in harmony and friendly with each other rather than discordant and combative.

Meanwhile it pleased the Lord to relieve the anguish of his servant by creating an opportunity for the previously-mentioned Father-General Berardicelli to call Joseph to Rome and have him observe all of Lent there in 1644. Joseph went, and on the journey was impelled by Brother Lodovico to think once again of going back to his town of Copertino, and he came close to deciding to request it of his superior. But this wasn't the design of divine providence, and for that reason when they were near Rome a strong ray of light flashed in Joseph's mind that stopped him unexpectedly in his very tracks. There he was seized by God and he recognized the deceit and the vanity in which he had put his trust. He turned to his companion and said, *companion of mine, we will later return to Assisi.* Upon arriving in Rome, he placed himself fully in the hands of the Father-General, without any discussion either of his native town or the Grottella.

Bonaventura Calverio, Bishop of Potenza, mentioned elsewhere, at that time was in the Monastery of the Holy Apostles and was in charge of Joseph. He remembered exactly Joseph's summons to that city, and said, *Casimir, who later was King of Poland, was a novice of the Company of Jesus at San Andrea di Monte Cavallo, under the discipline and direction of Father Alessandro Pellegrini of the same Company. The Young Prince, having heard of the fame of Father Joseph begged Father-General Berardicelli to summon him from Assisi.* Joseph came to Rome and knew Casimir's heart and his secret, and said to him *that he should put off his holy ordination, that God would soon show him his will. And, in fact, after a short while the King, his Brother, was moved by the Pope, as was all of Poland, to prevent Casimir's ordination. In due course as it happened, Casimir was crowned King.* It was that, therefore, which was the reason for Joseph's trip to Rome. The esteemed bishop went on to say that so great was the reverence and obedience with which this Royal Prince dealt with our Blessed One in that short period, that he always had his name on his lips and continuously entrusted himself to him.

In the company of the above-mentioned prelate, Joseph went to visit the seven churches, and each time upon entering and leaving them Joseph was taken in ecstasy so that it was necessary for the bishop to command him, by virtue of his holy obedience, to come back to his senses. Upon entering the Church of Saint Peter, which was the first one Joseph visited, he walked with his eyes not only lowered but almost closed so that he could barely see the pavement. Upon being exhorted to gaze at the altars, the chapels, and at the magnificence of that temple, Joseph never raised his eyes but said, *I believe, I believe and I want nothing else but the holy faith.*

He was also taken by the mitred one to visit Cardinal Lanti, the Protector of the Order, and Cardinal Mont' Alto, and it is said also to Cardinal Borghese. In each one of these visits, which all took place the same morning, as soon as they sat down and the bishop began to explain some point about the passion of Jesus Christ, Joseph immediately gave a great shout and with a bursting heart was taken up in ecstasy, leaping in an instant from the kneeling bench onto the ground with his arms extended and his eyes towards heaven, open, immobile and unconscious. He would not have left his state of ecstasy if the bishop hadn't commanded it by holy obedience. Great therefore was the joy of the purpled ones who having themselves been uplifted by him, recommended him to others.

The Lord Cardinal of Lugo gave him his own rosary, and having then written to the Blessed One regarding an incident that had distressed him a great deal, and having received Joseph's answer, said, *I'm satisfied and happy, Father Joseph is a great Servant of God.*

Even the Venerable Father Bonaventura di Martina of the Order of the Minimi, living in his Monastery of S. Andrea delle Fratte in Rome, who later died in the odor of sanctity and was distinguished for his many miracles, became devoted to Joseph after having learned of him. He wrote Joseph frequently, and preserved his replies like relics. In one of them, alluding to Virginal purity, our Blessed one wrote, *Lucia Virgo, quid a me petis, quod ipsa non poteris praestare* (Lucy, virgin, what do you want from me that you cannot do yourself), meaning that even though at a distance, Father Bonaventura's bodily and mental well-being was sufficient. Such was the declaration of the named Bishop of Potenza, who entrusted himself to Joseph, and concluded by talking about himself saying, *truly I admit to inner spiritual aid for which I begged through his intercession.*

The Blessed One regretted his stay in Rome, wearied by the flocking of the great to him, each of whom wanted to have him for himself. But with heroic virtue he suppressed every other wish including his burning desire to return to behold once again the image of the Madonna of the Grottella in Copertino, and he returned instead to Assisi. But since he couldn't go to Copertino, the Image of the Virgin Mary came to him, and with so much grace that after she appeared, every affliction in his heart dissolved and Joseph was restored to what he was before. Once again taking the trip to Assisi, upon seeing the Church of Saint Francis in the distance, he was taken up in ecstasy, a quick forerunner of that grace which flooded his spirit.

Father-Master Michel Angelo Catalani, at that time Assistant and then Father-General of the Order, and eventually Bishop of Isernia, passed through the holy monastery a few days after Joseph's arrival. Knowing well not only Joseph's afflictions but also his great desire to see the Madonna of the Grottella, he had a copy made and brought it with him as a gift to Joseph. Upon finding himself together with Joseph in a cell of the monastery discussing the usual religious matters, Catalani said, *Father Joseph do you want me to show you a beautiful thing?* And while speaking began to unwrap the painting on one side. First there appeared that sacred Virginal Countenance, not completely revealed, but Joseph recognized it. *Ah my mother,* he exclaimed, and placing himself face-to-face with her was taken in a swoon of loving ecstasy in which he would have expired if he had not been invigorated by such a pleasing and unexpected image, and he found himself free and loosened from every inner turmoil. He ran immediately from his cell to the church, prostrated himself before his Seraphic Father and begged him to forgive his thought of leaving that sanctuary where one lives happily, and where one is more blessed when one dies.

nine

The stay of the Blessed Joseph in the holy Monastery of Assisi, and the marvels of his life that happened there.

Joseph's renewed appearance in Assisi was like a solemn triumph accompanied by the gladdest acclamations from every class of society of that renowned city, the glorious mother of that Seraphic Order and of its son Saint Francis who is worthy of endless praise.

The city was greatly rewarded for having reacquired such a precious treasure in whom it could continuously see with wonderment a living portrait of its Seraphic Patriarch with his heavenly virtues. The nobility gathered in council with demonstrations of joy, and immediately gave Joseph the most meaningful evidence of its joy with a voice vote making him a citizen of Assisi, and sending a special delegation to him with the written declaration to that effect:

Confalonerius, & Priores Illustrissimae & Seraphica Civitatis Assisi admodum R. Patri Josepho de Copertino Ordinis Minorum Conv. S, Francisci de Familia sacri Conventus Assisiatis salutem, ac prosperos ad pia opera succesus.

Amor insignis, quem erga Civitatem hanc, quam singulari divinae miserationis beneficio communem cum glorioso Patriarcha pauperum D. Francisco Patriam, licet immeriti nacti sumus, praetulisti & preces, qua pro animarum salute, & pro spiritualibus, temporalibusque bonis publicarum, privatarumque rerum, semper dignatus es, & dignaris salubriter in Domino ad Dominum efficaciter effundere, praesertim dum veram charitatem restaurando, divisos Civium animos reconciliare conaris, aegros etiam afflictos solaris, & omnes denique bonis consiliis adjuvare solitus es, & signanter auxilium, quod nobis per finitimarum regionum bella inter sacrilegas hostium invasiones, verbo, & opere superioribus mensibus praesentissimum exhibuisti, eo nos adduxerunt, ut Assisiensium Civium corda rapueris, tibique Assisiensis omnes immortalis obligationis vinculo devinctissimos reddideris. Et cum pariaparibus referre nulla ex parte valeamus, ad effugiendum ingratitudinis vitium, in signum grati animi Te praedictum Admodum R. P Josephum a Copertino in publicis generalibus Consiliis inter nos Civem aggregavimus, viva omnium voce, & aggregamus per praesentes cum omnibus Praerogativis, & Privilegiis Assisiensibus Civibus in ipsa Assisinate Civitate, Oriundis, competentibus, & competituris. In quorum fidem, & testimonium has Litteras fieri, & nostri sigilli impressione muniri, ac per nostrum Cancellarium subscrbi jussimus. Dattum Assisi ex Palatio nostro Priorali hac die 4. Mensis Augusti Anni MDCXLIV.

Loco Sigilli.

Grandilius Lucidus Canc. mandato, &c.

Those who had the privilege of bearing Joseph the glad news had the good fortune of seeing heaven in his countenance. For he answered the delegation with words of pleasure *for being made a fellow countryman of his great Father Saint Francis, Standard-Bearer of Christ stigmatized.* The thought of it brought Joseph to sweet ecstasy. He took leave of his senses, and was taken up in the air in rapture to the ceiling of his cell. It seemed as if he was going to bear the news to Saint Frances in Heaven, or else that the Patriarch was bringing Joseph up to him to receive his thanks. When Joseph then returned to his senses they heard him say in a low voice these words, *sicut cor tuum, sicut cor tuum* (so your heart, so your heart), and turning to the others said, *have the grace to forgive me, for these are defects of nature.*

To the public demonstration by the City, there was a corresponding and equally fine demonstration by the monks. They declared

Joseph a Father of the Holy Monastery of Assisi, which almost brought tears to Joseph's eyes as he saw himself admitted as a son into that great house whose father is a Seraphim.

The Blessed One's return to the holy monastery become famous thanks to one of his typical but still stupendous marvels which should be mentioned. Through a small door he entered the church where the monks and primary nobility had convened. A few steps after he entered, he raised his eyes and saw an image of the Most Holy Virgin painted on the vault above the adornment of the Altar of the Immaculate Conception. This holy Image of the Madonna with the Baby Jesus in her arms was very similar to that of the Madonna of the Grottella, and upon seeing it, Joseph at once gave a scream and went in flight eighteen paces through the air towards her, He then embraced her and said, *ah my mother, you have stayed with me.* One couldn't tell which of these acts came first.

Now settled in the monastery with the aforementioned honors, Joseph never let up in the main rigor of his life. Vegetables and herbs without any condiments were his food. For obedience's sake he took a little wine mixed with water to warm the stomach, but the concoction rendered him almost without any strength, and it made him suffer pain and bleed from the mouth. Out of pity, the priest Don Giovanni Martelli brought Joseph a bib padded with goose feathers to protect and aid him. Joseph took the bib, but on the following day he gave it back saying, *Saint Francis rolled in the thorns and in the snow and I should be among softness and delight? Take back your gift, since it doesn't suit me.* If it happened that, obliged out of obedience, he had to partake of fatty dishes, he would vomit them immediately, hurt as he was not just by their flavor but by their smell.

As we've said before, Joseph's sleep was very short and uncomfortable, and he weakened his body with whips and chains and hair shirts. A direct illumination from on high made him understand that in order to bring himself to God, the mortification of his internal passions was of greater value than his physical body inasmuch as the soul, more than the body, is disposed to know God. In this way Joseph's mind was, like a ship in a port, less exposed to passing storms. Once again he wandered through the ample paths of heaven, which shared with him their secrets and inexpressible sweetness.

On the morning of July 29, 1644, after celebrating Holy Mass, Joseph ran hurriedly to the room of the Father-General who happened to have stopped in Assisi on a journey, and in his presence told Father Master Roberto Nuti, *I have to confide something to you, but I fear you will repeat it in which case I don't want to tell you.* Nuti promised him secrecy, so Joseph added, *know that the Pope is dead, and I know it because this morning when I said Mass, during the recollection of the living I couldn't find the Pope there, but I found him immediately in that of the dead, and on Sunday the news will be known throughout the city.* And so it was. Urban VIII died in Rome on Friday, July 29, 1644, and on the following Sunday Marino Nati, Secretary to Cardinal Antonio Barberini, brought the news to Assisi.

Francesco Angelo, Cardinal Rapaccioli, vexed by temptations and scruples, expounded on his tribulations in a very long letter to his close friend Joseph, begging him for advice and help. But in giving the sealed letter to his secretary to be consigned to the mail, the Cardinal was at the same time given the letters that had just arrived, among which was a letter from the Blessed One. In it Joseph answered point by point the very letter that Cardinal Rapacciolo had just written to Joseph but was not yet sent. The purpled one was left beside himself, and in an instant found himself totally free of his internal distress.

Certainly it was a great thing for Joseph to penetrate the secrets of the heart and to see things from afar, but even greater was that he knew the saints of heaven face to face even though he had never seen them during his life. Joseph was very devoted to Saint Philip Neri who seemed a living example of the innocence of life in the simplicity of his habits as well as the greatness of his miracles. Now it happened that upon coming to the Holy Year 1650, Graziano Benigni, Confaloniere of Assisi, was summoned by Father Giuliano Giustiniani, a Priest of Saint Philip of the Oratorio of Rome who told him that he had learned that in the holy Monastery of Saint Francis of Assisi there was a Father Joseph of Copertino, a monk who led a holy life. Father Giuliano begged the Confaloniere to bring Joseph, as a gift in his name, a portrait of Saint Philip which was thought traditionally to be very similar to the original, and to give it to Father Joseph, the Servant of God, so that Joseph would pray for him. The Confaloniere accepted the task and upon his return to Assisi, he saw the Blessed One but before he spoke to him, he heard Joseph say, *that is indeed the true portrait of Saint Philip Neri*, and brought it into his cell. Joseph then showed the Confaloniere his own portrait of Philip, and added, *this is not similar to it.* Thus Joseph made it understood that he not only foresaw the messenger and the gift, but that Saint Philip had also appeared to Joseph visibly and that he knew him by appearance, which is why Joseph had elected him as his specific advocate.

From such foreknowledge of his, Joseph's good mother also gathered a beautiful fruit. She died in Copertino while he was sojourning in Assisi. Upon dying while, being attended by some monks of the Minor Conventual Order, she exclaimed, *oh Brother Joseph, son of mine, I'll never see you again!* Immediately a great light appeared which illuminated the whole room, and once again you could hear the dying woman exclaim, *oh Brother Joseph, my son!* It is a certain that Joseph had become aware that his mother was in her extreme hour, for at that same moment in Assisi he said to one of his confidants, *now that poor little mother of mine is dead, and the next letter that is to arrive in Assisi will bring that very painful news.* The letter came to the Custodian, who asked Father Caravaggio, the Confessor of the Servant of God, to give Joseph the news. When he found him Joseph said, *you are perplexed about giving me the news of my mother's death. It has been fifteen days since God has taken her. One has to be content with what He does, and conform oneself to His holy will.* Nevertheless, Joseph wept over the death of his mother, and his tears provided a fair natural tribute, along with his ready example of resignation to the divine will.

But enough about his predictions and his penetration of the conscience of others, for he predicted and revealed much, and spoke and said much to others. We will pass, therefore, to a list of some of his miracles that he worked in Assisi.

He used to visit the sick, and merely by embracing them they were healed in an instant. His companion, Brother Lodovico, had such wonderful luck himself, for he was reduced to agony but upon being embraced by Joseph who said, *don't abandon me dear companion*, he was fully healed.

Brother Giovanni Battista Cruciani of the Third Order of Saint Francis was afflicted for three years by a fierce headache accompanied by deep hypochondria, so that he seemed more like a corpse than a man. The Blessed One went to him, and immediately cured him by putting his hand on his head and reciting the benediction of Saint Francis.

Aleide de Fabiani received the same grace. And with a single touch Joseph healed Ottavio Arometario of an abnormal pain in his legs, and also healed Doctor Paolo Santinelli of spasms that tormented his body.

Even the touch of things that had been used by Joseph had similar benefit. Thus, Olimpia Benigni, who was undergoing a very dangerous childbirth, miraculously lived with the touch of the Blessed One's belt, and so Portia Pontani was able to live thanks to a touch of his cap. The son of a peasant recovered the ability to swallow when confronted by the benediction of Saint Francis that Joseph had written. With a touch of a handkerchief stained with Joseph's blood, Chiara Leonelli was cured of a growth that had devoured almost her whole face. With the same touch, Apollonio Bianchi who had thrown himself in a fury from a window into a fountain, was cured of fever. Even the water in which Joseph's tunic had been washed, which had been saved because of the sweet odor that it gave off, restored the health of many people who were desperately ill.

There are innumerable witnesses as to the power of Joseph's prayers. At Mass, Joseph prayed for the above mentioned Ottavio Aromatario and also for Girolamo Ferri, whose physicians were desperate regarding a deadly fever, and they were cured at that instant. He prayed for the settlement of a bloody brawl between soldiers of Assisi and those of Bastia, and those two inimical factions became reconciled without any other mediation. Upon seeing Joseph once (and I don't know what greeting passed between them) a gardener ceased his dishonest behavior and took up an exemplary life, having been persuaded solely by Joseph to undergo such an advantageous change.

The prayers of Joseph gave indications as to future events. There was a war going on between the Pontiff Urban VIII and the Florentines. On the night of the Holy Stigmata of Saint Francis, they slipped down to the plain of Assisi where fires could be seen blazing here and there in the surrounding area. The night-time fighting and the fires suddenly alarmed the whole population of Assisi. Those not adept at arms were frightened and took refuge in the Churches of the Franciscans as secure asylums. Bishop Baglioni and the Governor Valeotti went straight to Joseph's room and found him amidst the frightening clamor peacefully engaged as usual in prayer. Upon seeing them so highly agitated, the Servant of God told them without moving from his place, *ah souls with little faith, go away and trust in God, for I promise you that the Father Saint Francis, who is your fellow countryman, will never permit any harm to this city.* No sooner had he said this that all the fires went out without doing any damage, and the land remained ever after immune from any military injury even though Todi, Perugia, and Citta di Castello, suffered much in that war.

Fourteen other miracles wrought by Joseph when he was alive can be read in the pages of his beatification file, but these are enough to give an understanding of his marvels.

Of equal efficiency were his prayers on behalf of the holy monastery. On one occasion it found itself with such a lack of grain that the custodian, Father-Master Saurino di Sutri, despaired of government help and wanted to abandon the monastery so the monks wouldn't die of hunger. After trying everything, he turned to the Blessed One explaining to him the great need for food. The Blessed One replied, *trust in God for he will provide; iacta cogitatum tuum in Dominum et ipse te enutrie* (place your understanding in the Lord and he will nourish you). Then, kneeling with the custodian, they recited together the litanies of the Mother of God. They had just finished when a group of monks rushed to Joseph's cell where the Custodian was, and reported that Cardinal Rapaccioli had sent a donation of four large measures of grain. Joseph wept with joy along with the Custodian, and turning to him said, *didn't I tell you that God would provide? Modicae fidei quare dubitasti?* (How could you doubt, you with such little faith?) *Don't you know that the Father Saint Francis said that if you can find a loaf of bread in the world, half of it will be for his Order? So now if he provides for all his brothers in every place, how could he fail in this place where his body rests by the will of God for all eternity! Oh this God is good. So we serve him and he provides for our needs.* Then the monks kneeled in the cell and sang the *Te Deum*, but Joseph at the third or fourth verse went into an ecstasy.

Similarly, on another occasion, Father-Master Roberto Nuti was the Custodian and was in distress about not knowing how to pay the debts of the Holy Monastery because of the scarcity of donations during the first two days of the Festival of Forgiveness in August. Joseph boldly took his head in his hands and said to him, *don't doubt; are you afraid? Providing for this monastery occupies the thoughts of Saint Francis more than yours.* Then they recited the litany of the Most Blessed Virgin and there were even greater donations in the days that followed than those made three or four years before.

As much as he offered relief to others, Joseph offered even more in defense against abuses by the infernal enemy. By command of his Father-Custodian he betook himself to Cascia to attend to an offense and clear it away. This trip of his was a path of the just, scattered with light so that at each step there sprouted a fullness of miracles. Having entered into a rural Church that was much neglected and without lamps, Joseph said to his companion, S. Bernardino Benaducci, *do you think that the Most Holy Sacrament is here?* His companion said *who knows?* But Joseph's heart knew it right away, whereupon breaking out in a loud scream he flew through the air to the tabernacle, embraced it, and there he adored God who was un-perceived by the others but whose fragrance Joseph could discern even at a distance.

Upon continuing their voyage, a man of bad reputation with a firearm came up to him and said into his ear *that he was going to kill an enemy of his, but having seen Joseph he repented his sin and now willingly condoned every offense that had been done to him.*

Upon arriving at a river, one could see that Joseph and his horse were unexpectedly carried off by the current. Brother Ludovico threw himself into the water up to his chest, grabbed Joseph by the arms, and pulled him out to the river bank. Then looking at Joseph closely, he found that he and his clothes were as dry as if he had come from a dewy meadow, with only a light sprinkling on his shoes and on the edge of his tunic. Later, recounting this incident to a confidant, Joseph said that at that moment of great danger, the Devil urged him towards despair with the words, *die here you big hypocrite, abandoned by God and left derelict,* and that Joseph answered to the contrary, *I always hope in God. God always helps and I will not fail to trust in his compassion.*

They finally arrived at Cascia, and when the Devil saw him, and adding insult to injury said, *didn't I do you in while on the road?* And Joseph, all simple and humble, answered *nothing happened to me because I was obedient.* It has been said that the words of the Blessed One were a very powerful exorcism to drive away the Devil, and here too Joseph drove him away.

The Devil was furious with Joseph and waited for his return to Assisi to avenge himself by means of frightening attacks and horrible blows. He tried at first to frighten Joseph during the night while he was reciting the office in the chorus enclosure of the church, appearing to him in the image of a large black butterfly. The Devil blew out Joseph's lamp with a great breath, and at other times made him hear an explosion nearby like a firearm that had been fired, making a great sound and causing the ground to tremble under his knees. But since none of this worked, there was one last attempt that was driven by the Devil's infernal rage. During the night when the good servant of the Lord was praying in church, he heard the door open loudly and a man entered who seemed to be wearing iron clogs. Joseph watched him, and as he came closer he saw the lamps around the Altar of Saint Francis go out. When the last one was extinguished, Joseph was left in front of the altar with the man shod in iron. Entrusting himself to the Holy Father, Joseph received deliverance at the very moment of the assault. The Devil threw himself upon him with such force that Joseph was knocked to the ground, and with a hand on his throat tried to strangle him. Joseph was about to die under the weight of such a pitiless enemy, but then he invoked his Seraphic Father, and saw him come out of his tomb which was under the dais of the main altar, and with a small lighted candle relight the lamps, while the enemy fled in terror at the light. Thereafter Joseph called Saint Francis by the name *Candlelighter of the Church*.

The Devil renewed the struggle on another occasion. It was at night when the Blessed One was praying in a confessional. He saw the same man come forward with a horrible face and with iron on his feet, and kneel next to him. Nevertheless, he appeared more than usually worshipful, mouthing prayers, and conveying that he was a good servant of God. So Joseph said to him devoutly, *brother, pray to God for me*. The traitor then rose, threw himself upon Joseph and grabbed him so fiercely that Joseph, thinking himself dying and not knowing him to be the Devil, resolved immediately to grab him in his arms as well as he could and to win the fight. The Devil then howled at the Blessed One, shouting, *ah you wretched hypocrite, to what end do you want to stay in this Monastery?* Thus he made himself known for what he was, and without waiting for an answer he betook himself to flight.

For these victories Joseph rendered thanks to God and attributed his triumphs to Him, even inviting dumb animals to speak in behalf of God's glory. He used to tell a finch which he kept in a cage, *praise God,* and the little bird's voice would dissolve in song and he wouldn't cease until the Blessed One bade him silence. A goldfinch was once given to him, and when gazing at it with pleasure Joseph considered that the divine omnipotence by which such beautiful creatures were made to delight men, so he put him at liberty saying, *go and enjoy it, for God gave it to you. I don't want anything else from you other than you come back when I call you to praise together your God and mine.* The little bird obeyed and never left that neighborhood, sometimes hopping about, sometimes beating its wings at the window of the Blessed One, sometimes sitting in the small trees of the nearby garden. And whenever he was summoned, he went to Joseph to sing the divine praises of God with him.

But who wouldn't have joined with Joseph to praise the Lord when the Angels themselves, who never cease to praise God, felt it worthy for them to be with him! On the day that Joseph entered Assisi, a great Servant of God, a woman, saw him accompanied in his entrance by two angels. And to another venerable woman, a Servant of the Lord, Sister Cecilia dei Nobili of Nocera, a Lay Sister whose holy life is now being examined, had it revealed by her Guardian Angel that Joseph's own guardian was an angel from the supreme Chorus of Angels. That's why it is attested that Joseph never entered his cell before first venerating his Guardian Angel and inviting him with distinct deference to go in first. On two other occasions, the above-mentioned Sister saw the spirit of our Blessed One in the ribs of Jesus Christ. On another occasion, she saw Joseph being caressed with extreme joy by the Mother of God. And finally when the Sister was conducted in spirit to the top of a mountain, which was said to be the mountain of perfection, she saw Joseph among some of the souls in that holy height.

One cannot be silent about a certain declaration as to the holiness of the Servant of the Lord made by a Demon by command of God. Father Santinelli deposed as follows, *finding myself in the year 1651 at the Borgo San Sepolcro where Lucia Migliorati was possessed by a Demon, I took a belt that had been blessed by Father Joseph and I went into church to put it on her. But when she saw me she got up and said with great fury, friar, don't come near. If you only knew how much you are burning me. What is that thing you want to give to this woman? This wretched woman will never take that which you bring her.* And as I drew the belt from my pocket I said these words, *I command you from God to take this belt.* And she replied, *this she will never do, nor will I take it. Finally as I repeated my words she took it and quieted down for the short period that it would take to recite the creed three or four times. Then that Spirit started up again and said,* if you knew the virtue of that friar, and how much his soul is pleasing to God, you would be astonished. Yet it's necessary for me to say it because God is forcing me. That friar subjects himself to discipline and to continuous meditations which are all acceptable to God, particularly those of the morning. God and the Blessed Virgin speak to him. But I want to punish you and Father Joseph, although there are other Demons stronger than I who punish him. *In the meantime she tried to remove that belt that was on him, but when it was put back on her he ceased molesting the woman.* He added that the odor, of the Blessed One that could be smelled in the room came from his virginal chastity and, referring to a Statue of Saint Anthony of Padua, he said that there was no difference at all between it and Joseph, except that the former was already sanctified, and the latter probably would be also. He finished by saying that he was willed by God to say these things which he would not have wanted to say, since that friar was the worst enemy that the Demons had.

Hell hated Joseph as much as he was loved and favored by Heaven. Having overcome those two years of spiritual dryness of which we spoke, there came to Joseph the culmination of heavenly grace. Every day he celebrated the Holy Mass in the private oratory next to his cell where he was always brought by the mind of God into the deepest ecstasy, and many times raised from the ground in the most sublime raptures, so that as we said elsewhere, for 35 years his superiors did not admit him to public ceremonies because his great union with God would carry even his body away from people and up towards Heaven.

Upon being asked what he saw in those raptures, Joseph answered, *on some occasions I can see the Attributes of God, all admirably together, mentally indistinct and in confusion, so that one couldn't be distinguished from the other. On other occasions I could see each one itself, always new and precious, as if one were opening his eyes in a large gallery in which human intelligence is astonished by seeing everything together, as well as every separate part.* On another occasion, prodded by similar questions, he answered with his usual simplicity, *what do you want me to see? I am united with God.*

One day while watching fixedly the portrait of Saint Francis hanging on the wall of his cell he went into ecstasy, and when ordered to come back to his senses he said to those present, *forgive me that I was overtaken by sleep.* Then on the following day he confided to a monk who was his friend, *yesterday when you came with your countrymen and sleep overcame me I saw beautiful Father Saint Francis, of which one can't say more, and I was curious to see how he was attired. I also understood that all these countrymen* (and these were the Knight Barocci and three others from Modena) *had not come out of curiosity but for devoutness.*

Joseph was for the greater part of the day and night swamped by a torrent of these heavenly delights, so much so that rather than being an inhabitant of earth he seemed to inhabit that great house where God, with indescribable abundance, fills the hearts of his friends with joy and sweetness.

From his great union with God it emerged that not only was he frequently carried into the air, but as a new and unusual wonder he would, when carried upward, also carry others with him to bring them to God. As part of the festival of the Immaculate Conception in 1642, the novices of the Holy Monastery solemnly sang the Vespers in their private Chapel. When it was over, the Father-Custodian arrived, who at that time was Father-Master Raffaello Palma, later Bishop of Oria in the Kingdom of Naples. This man, upon seeing Joseph next to the altar, said to him in confidence, *what are you doing here, my fellow countryman?* The Blessed One, who had had many ecstasies in the course of the Vespers and was filled with the beautiful glory of the Mother of God, turned to the Custodian and indicating the Image of the Immaculate Conception said, *Father-Custodian, Beautiful Mary. Beautiful Mary!* And, after fixing his gaze on her for a while, Joseph, merry and festive, repeated, *Father-Custodian say beautiful Mary, say beautiful Mary, beautiful Mary*. The Custodian said it in a restrained and low voice, but Joseph not wishing such restraint when exalting her added, *say it louder, Father-Custodian, beautiful Mary, beautiful Mary*, and with his fervor growing stronger in his heart, drew close to the Custodian, embraced him tightly on both sides, exclaimed *beautiful Mary, beautiful Mary!* Being taken by surprise by a sudden rapture, Joseph was transported high off the ground carrying the Custodian with him. When the rapture was over, and when they both returned to the ground, the Custodian left right away, not only as an admirer but now a participant in divine greatness. And the Blessed One turned to the novices who had gazed at the prodigy and said, *little lambs have patience. I have slept a little bit*. Then with his hood pulled over his face he returned to the secret delights of his cell.

Similar to the rapture already described was one that followed, this one more marvelous than the first one in which he had taken up in the air with him a very devout monk, but in this second one it was a furious madman: the Knight Baldassarre Rossi, who had fallen into such a fury that he treated and abused everyone crazily. Many times his people referred him to Joseph and finally with great effort they brought him forward tied up on a chair, moving Joseph to pity for his great illness. His bonds were untied and with great force he was made to kneel. Getting up from his seat, the Blessed One placed his hand on the knight's head and said, *Knight Baldassarre, don't doubt yourself. Entrust yourself to God and to his Most Holy Mother*. In saying this he took his hand which was on the sick man's head and tightened it around his hair. Breaking out with his usual cry, *oh,* he went up in rapture high from the ground, bringing the madman up with him. Both stayed in the air for the eighth part of an hour, and then returning to earth Joseph said, *be joyful knight*. The knight regained his mind, and returned to his home praising God and his blessed liberator.

It was not in Assisi that God bestowed this superior gift on Joseph for the first time but in Copertino, and we will mention it here not so much as part of a chronology of events but for the evenness of the subject, so that the similarity of the miracles will render him who worked them even more illustrious. Joseph was attending the installation of some novices in the Monastery of Saint Clare in the aforementioned town, and was praying on his knees in a corner of the church. Upon hearing the musicians intone, *Veni Sponsa Christi* (Come, Betrothed of Christ), he gave his usual scream and ran towards a Reformed Father, a native of Secli, who was participating in that function, and when the nuns made their confession, Joseph squeezed his hands and grabbed the Reformed Father with supernatural strength in a joyful rapture and took him in a violent dance through the open space of the church. While turning and turning like David before the Ark, both of them were raised into the air, he being carried by Joseph, and Joseph carried by God in an extremely marvelous ecstasy following the divine immaculate lamb, which pulls to itself those of pure and virginal heart in order to fill them with its inexpressible heavenly sweetness.

ten

The Gift of Wisdom, by which the Blessed one was enriched by God in Assisi.

As was said from the beginning, Joseph was born into a poor family, not at all educated in the sciences or letters. It was not by favor but by a miracle that the clergy elevated him to Holy Orders and then promoted him to the priesthood. From then on he began to show an abundance of divine compassion, feeling himself brought to the highest level of contemplation, and through it to an intimate communication with God. In the school of such a lofty teacher, he acquired such a knowledge of superhuman things which, after he explained them, filled the most trained and educated theologians with wonderment.

Those who knew him would admit *that he was a most simple person and could barely read, that he wasn't a theologian, nor had he studied any science, and he himself was of low capacity, that he was an idiot, that he could barely read or write.* Cardinal di Lauria, among others, says *Father Joseph was ignorant, had never studied, nor did he understand other than basic Latin.*

Observe the Blessed One after his arrival in Assisi, and you will see to what heights of knowledge he climbed, for it is more than true that our God is the God of knowledge, who in one instant can fill his beloved servants with the light of his doctrines. The much-praised Cardinal di Lauria attests, *Father Joseph, upon being questioned by some of us scholars regarding some difficult mystery, answered firmly with deep and clear doctrines, thereby resolving any difficulties for us.* Regarding the subject of "grace freely given" he says, *Pater Josephus a Cupertinus onimo ignorans, legere tantum sciens, in spiritu fervore mira de altissimis, & de agibilibus me praesente, saepissime eructabat* (Father Joseph of Copertino, ignorant of everything, hardly knowing how to read, very often in my presence with fervor and spirit held forth on the most amazing and sublime matters.)

As Father Anonio Martinelli has deposed, Joseph *spoke with such frankness about things pertaining to God and about Holy Scripture that it was a thing to marvel at.* He adds that on one occasion Joseph explained to Monsignor Claverio, Bishop of Potenza, a former monk of the Minor Conventual Order, the mystery of grace which is such a difficult subject in Sacred Theology, and that the said prelate, who was very learned, couldn't have his fill in praising him. One finishes with the testimony about Joseph by Father-Master Pietro di Correto, Regent of the College of Saint Bonaventura in Rome, a highly lettered man, that when he was Regent of the Holy Monastery of Saint Francis of Assisi, he had heard Father Joseph speak more profoundly about theology than could the foremost Theologians of the world.

There were many more witnesses as well. Among them was Father Michael of Monte Albotto, a Capuchin, who deposed as follows, *Father Joseph was endowed with a lamp that was superior to the natural intelligence acquired in the schools, because he used to answer most adequately certain doubts about Sacred Theology that were put to him, but with answers spoken in common speech, even with some low examples, so that I was left extremely astonished, and that marvel has always stayed in my mind. The subjects were about predestination, the Most Holy Trinity, the efficiency of grace, free will, and the like.*

The Bishop of Potenza, Monsignor Claverio, before he was appointed to that office a short while ago, said that *every night Joseph would go to the Church to say the Office, and that he himself noticed that Joseph understood all the meanings of the Psalms, which could not have been so if not through supernatural illumination, since he was, after all, an idiot.*

With permission from this prelate, Father Giovanni Battista Cruciani di Spello, a priest of the Third Order of Saint Francis, deposed as follows, *on one occasion Monsignor Claverio, Bishop of Potenza, a greatly lettered man, recounted to him that during a month's stay in Assisi, he learned more about moral Theology in his conversations with Father Joseph than he had in the course of his studies with books on theory.*

And also very elevated is the testimony of Father-Master Jacob Roncagli, a member the Order of Minor Conventuals, a just and quiet contemplator of the spirit of our Blessed One, of whom he speaks as follows, *he had even the gift of wisdom, because he explained things about God, and passages of scripture, and spoke always in symbols, even though, after all, he never studied and frankly could barely read. At many times I tried to tell him certain things that demonstrated the properties of the Father, the properties of the Son, and the properties of the Holy Spirit. And when he gave me his blessing for which I always begged him* (even if I was obliged to bless him first), *he would say while making the sign over me,* may the power of the father, the knowledge of the Son, and the virtue of the Holy Spirit protect you from all evil. Amen. *On one occasion among others, when I questioned him, I went on to ask what Christ's worst pain was during his passion. Some of those present said it was his encounter with his mother on Calvary. Others said it was the beatings. Others said the thorns. Ah* Joseph said, *but Jesus had another concern, for his thoughts were higher; his greatest pain was the loss of Judas. Joseph then fell silent, speaking more by his silence and his wonderment than with words.*

Another distinguished teacher of the Order, also of the Minor Conventuals, renders this outstanding testimony about Joseph: *Father Joseph always used to talk about the Mysteries of our Holy Faith in ways that were more than ordinary, putting forth in his speech an understanding that exceeded his little training, so that standing out from his words were the gifts of the Holy Spirit, of wisdom, of intellect, and of knowledge which his discourse showed that he possessed, even though it was known that he had not acquired them through study. He used to discourse on the mysteries of the Most Holy Trinity, the Incarnation, and the Redemption, and I especially remember that in explaining the Mystery of the Most Holy Trinity, he suggested that it was similar to fire, referring to the saying of Saint Paul:* Deus noster ignis consumens est (Our God is a consuming fire). And he said that *since fire is a single thing which always produces light and heat, so the divine nature of the Father produces the light of wisdom which is the Son, and together they produce the heat which is the Holy Spirit.* He then adds the same about Joseph, *that even though he was not lettered, he dissolved theological doubts so that you could see that God's knowledge, high and deep was instilled in him. So, Monsignor Bonaventura Claverio, Bishop of Potenza, used to say that Father Joseph had marvelously dissolved his major doubts regarding theology,* especially in matters of justification, grace, sin, and the actions of men, *adding that Joseph had calmed his mind of all the difficulties he had regarding these subjects.*

This most educated prelate, who had studied theology for fifteen full years in our College of Bonaventura in Rome, confirms his depositions made by word of mouth through others, affirming *that Father Joseph through his innate supernatural wisdom discoursed so learnedly regarding divine attributes that he was left astonished and in wonderment, and said now I am learning a new and good theology.*

And finally, others testify that Father Joseph discoursed on very difficult points of theology like a great theologian, and without preparation he superbly answered any doubts put to him regarding Holy Scripture in a way that showed clearly that his knowledge was supernatural and innate, so that the most learned Father-Master and Regent Antonio di Ponte della Trave, admiring such a depth of understanding, frequently said, *he knows more than I.*

eleven

The flocking of qualified people from every country to the Blessed Joseph in Assisi. Prophecies, Conversion of Heretics, and miracles carried out by him.

The city of Assisi was too narrow to confine Joseph's heroic sanctity. Even if it fairly judged his sublime merits and called him its Saintly Brother, still his clear virtue required a greater theater for his splendid miracles. So, the fame of his great goodness went out, and spread not only throughout Italy, but passed into Germany, France, Spain, and Poland, in fact almost all of Europe. For that reason many princes and great lords went to see him in the holy Monastery of Saint Francis, some going for devotion's sake, some under the advice of others, some to venerate the divine magnificence within him. The wonderful thing about these visits was that whoever talked with Joseph was left with unbridled affection for him.

Father Ottavio Lalli of the Third Order of Saint Francis offers the following facts: *Father Joseph of Copertino was revered and esteemed not only by the fathers of our Order and by the men of Assisi, but by princes, lords, and by the most eminent Cardinals Faccinetti, Lodovisio, Caraffa, Ropaccioli, Donghi, King Casimir of Poland, the Infanta Maria of Savoy, and others, and also by the Polish Prince Zomoski, and particularly Prince Alexander Lubomiski and his wife. When they came to Italy for the Holy Year, they went to see Father Joseph and entrusted themselves to his prayers that they might have children since for twelve straight years they had had none. Father Joseph told them to* trust in God and in Father Saint Francis that they might have heirs after they returned to their country. All of this was told to me by these princes in Warsaw when I saw their little prince. These lords told me that they had this son through the prayers of Father Joseph. In addition to the Cardinals mentioned by Father Lalli, are Cardinals Palotta, Verospi, Paluzzi and Odescalchi, in fact as many as are on the list of the Sacred College.

Regarding the cardinals, the ones mentioned above either visited him in Assisi or else had a close correspondence with him through letters. Whenever any of them appeared in his presence, he appeared to them in scenes worthy of tenderness and humble hesitation. Cardinal Francis Rapaccioli, participating in Joseph's Mass, saw him raised more than four palm-widths from the ground, and in reporting it to the custodian he wept with tenderness. When Cardinal Cesare Facchinetti found himself together with the previously mentioned cardinal, both saw Joseph rise from the ground and fly up to the vault of his cell, a rapture that won the heart of Luigi Ficieni who was Fachinetti's Gentleman of the Chamber, who was so touched and humbled by such a prodigious spectacle that he abandoned the world and retired to the Oratorian Fathers of Fano.

A spectator at a similar rapture was Cardinal Niccolo Ludovisio to whom Joseph, in 1644, foretold of his elevation to the purple, *as indicated elsewhere*, and to whom he also revealed his most hidden internal secrets. And Cardinal Giuseppe Spinola, at that time Governor of Perugia, also saw Joseph with his whole body in the air before the Image of the Mother of God.

To Cardinal di Lauria he foretold the purple, saying to him in a familiar way, *my fellow countryman, go to Rome and find yourself a beretta* (the cap worn by Cardinals). He spoke even more clearly but with a different intention to an intimate of Cardinal Facchinetti, at that time Bishop of Sinigallia. This purpled person sent Joseph a letter with the above messenger, and upon seeing it the Blessed One said to the messenger, *aren't you ashamed that you go around with such a dirty and filthy face while you serve a cardinal who is so good*. Upon such reproof, the fortunate bearer of the letter, who had a guilty conscience, went to confess himself right away. Upon his return Joseph said, *oh this is how those who serve such a good Cardinal should be, with beautiful faces.*

He spoke likewise in the spirit of foresight to Cardinal Benedetto Odescalchi, who was later Innocent XI, who visited Joseph in Assisi on his the way from Rome as Legate to Ferrara. This man twice lamented the famine which afflicted the city, and both times heard Joseph answer, *go joyfully because there are certain boats on the sea.* At that time Odescalchi did not grasp the meaning of those words, but later upon arriving at Loreto and going up the steps of the palace, he received letters from Monsignor Sanfelice, Vice-Legate of that city, which comforted him on his journey because they said that two Ships loaded with grain had arrived. The cardinal, admiring Divine Providence and extolling up to the stars the prediction of his faithful servant said, *here are the Ships of Father Joseph.*

On many occasions, the Bishop of Potenza, mentioned earlier, an admirer of the Blessed One's gift of knowledge, also experienced Joseph's gift of bestowing advice. The Bishop, before betaking himself to his pastoral duties, *asked Joseph if he should go to church every day. Joseph answered no, because his life was active and contemplative, and he was also required to govern others. Joseph also gave him a general rule for going to church for preaching and for spiritual exercises. Joseph advised him to do those things that he would be able to continue doing for ever.* To the question as to what to do to reform the clergy and whether he should be strict with delinquents, Joseph answered that he should see to it that his clergy recite the Divine Office with care and celebrate Holy Mass with devotion, because these two holy exercises would reform everything else. With delinquents, he should follow the advice of the Father Saint Francis: that is, not be troubled or become angry over their transgressions and their sins.

Monsignor Cherme, a Polish Bishop, also enjoyed Joseph's counsel. Upon going to Rome on ecclesiastical matters regarding that Royal Domain, he purposely passed through Assisi so that he could participate in the Blessed One's Mass. He had a long and thoughtful conversation with Joseph and upon departing, as a sign of his gratitude, he put in Joseph's hands a folder full of Hungarian money telling him that with it he might satisfy the needs of his monks. Joseph exclaimed *Jesus! Jesus!* and hurled the folder away from himself saying, *I don't need money*. When the Bishop said that it might serve the needs of the monastery, Joseph replied *take it to the superior, not to me, since I don't know about these needs and requirements*.

The influx of princes and secular potentates was not less, and they congregated in Assisi to see this miracle of sanctity. I have already spoken regarding the testimony of Father Lalli, of Prince Alexander Lubomiski and the Princess, his consort, who came on purpose to the Holy Monastery of Assisi in 1650, and also of Prince Zamorski who benefitted from seeing Joseph and talking to him, and returned to Poland with a huge load of holy papers. The Duke of Bouillon came from France for the same reason.

A young Polish knight also betook himself to Assisi and with persistent, almost violent insistence forced himself on the Blessed One to ask *if it would be better for him to take a wife, or else take the cloth as an ecclesiastic. Joseph answered saying neither one or the other*. And that's the way it was, because when the knight returned to his country he died a few months later, neither married nor a priest.

Prince Leopold of Tuscany, who later became a cardinal, went to Assisi for the sole purpose of seeing Joseph, and saw a lot that he couldn't explain. The minute the Father-Custodian opened his own mouth in praise of the Blessed Virgin, the Prince saw Joseph in ecstasy, having fallen down with his mouth closed just as Saint Frances was portrayed in the act of receiving the Holy Stigmata, and his eyes turned to the image of the Mother of God.

Finally, Isabella of Austria, Duchess of Mantua, betook herself to Assisi to confer thoughtfully with Joseph on matters regarding her soul. In the evening in the sacristy, where he first joined her and on the following morning in church where she heard his Mass, that Most

Serene Princess had the good fortune to admire with extraordinary amazement not only Joseph's sanctity and doctrines, but on both occasions his ecstasy and rapture. When she returned to Mantua she brought with her as a valuable relic one of the Blessed One's tunics which she had requested and obtained from the Father-Custodian of the Monastery.

Celebrated and admirable among all laypeople was the visit made by the Admiral of Castile and his consort. This Ambassador of the King of Spain, moved by the fame of such a great servant of God, wanted to pass through Assisi on his way to Rome, and there he met with Joseph in a cell of the holy monastery. Later he told his wife, who was waiting for him in Church, *I have seen and spoken to another Saint Francis*. The Admiral's wife was also desirous of speaking with Joseph, and requested permission from the custodian who, knowing Joseph's aversion to talking with women, ordered him to come down into the church to speak with the Lady and other women of her party. The Blessed One smiled and said *I'll do it out of obedience, but I don't know if I'll be able to speak to her*. In fact, that's the way it was. For having come into Church through a small door opposite the Altar of the Immaculate Conception, he saw the statue of the Virgin Mary, screamed, threw himself into flight with his whole body in the air for a distance of twelve paces over the heads of the Admiral and the women, and brought himself to embrace the feet of the Queen of Heaven. He was there for a brief while, immobile in adoration, then he erupted in another scream, returning by the same route through the air to the spot where he had first taken flight. Having thus made reverence to the sacred image and having kissed the ground with bowed head, he betook himself straight away to his cell with his hood lowered. The Admiral's wife and the other ladies swooned at the unexpected prodigy. The Admiral did not swoon, but with his eyelids lowered and his arms spread wide in astonishment, he lost all feeling and seemed between life and death.

A priest, Doctor Giovanni Martelli of Spoleti, who was present at this rapture, went to Joseph's cell a few days later to talk to him of spiritual matters, and raised the subject of Joseph's aversion to speaking with women, asking him what he would have done if the Admiral of Castile, the lady his Consort, and the other ladies had come to him to speak. Joseph replied, *I went to the Church with the greatest aversion, because it behooved me to do it for obedience's sake. But the Blessed Virgin bestowed grace on me so that they neither spoke to me nor I to them.*

Even Casimir, who was later King of Poland, visited him, as mentioned in Chapter VIII. When this Prince let Joseph know of his resolve to enter a religious Order, Joseph said, d*on't enter any Order except the Jesuits because in time it will behoove you to leave the Order which you won't be able to do from any of the others.* Joseph also told him that he should delay becoming ordained because God in his good time would expressly manifest his will. And so it happened, because after six years of religious life in the Company of Jesus, Casimir was promoted to Cardinal by Innocent X, and when Casimir's brother King Wladyslaw died, the Polish Diet called Casimir to succeed to the throne. Upon thus returning to his kingdom, this monarch passed through Assisi to see his venerated Joseph, who upon seeing Casimir wearing a secular collar and with a sword at his side, smiled and said, *I told you that you'd never be a Jesuit nor a Priest. Go, for you will do more good things for Christianity than as a member of an Order.* Nor was the prediction an empty one, for when this sovereign took up his kingdom, he secured the Catholic religion there in notable battles against the Turks where he was always the victor. The King, going on to Poland, so remembered the affection and holiness of the Servant of the Lord that he never stopped writing to him, and in whose answers Joseph several times interpreted events for the King in Poland.

But the conversion that follows is a complete prodigy of grace. After several trips to the main courts of Europe, Frederick, Prince of Brunswick, a young man of 25 years of age at that time, arrived in Assisi from Rome in the year 1650 to see with his own eyes him who had been described in Germany as being of such great holiness. He brought with him a letter of credence from Cardinal Rapaccioli to secure his lodgings, and by order of Innocent X there was another letter from Rome sent secretly to the Custodian of the Holy Monastery enjoining him to let him speak with Joseph so that the prayers and persuasiveness of the Servant of God might lead to a conversion of this Lutheran Prince which, if it were to occur, would be very advantageous regarding matters of religion in those parts. The Father-Custodian immediately betook himself to the public inn, took the Prince and two Counts in his entourage, one of whom was Catholic and the other heretic, and conducted them to the Apartment of the Holy Monastery, called the Apartment of the Pope. The Prince himself asked to see the Blessed One, declaring that he wanted to leave afterwards. The following morning which was Sunday, he and the two Counts were brought in secret through the old door of the novitiate where Joseph usually celebrated Holy Mass, so that nobody would be aware of their arrival, least of all Joseph himself who knew nothing of it. But soon he could tell who was present at the divine service, for Joseph found the host unusually hard and had to try several times with force to divide it, which was evidence to him that some hardened heart was present at the divine sacrifice. Whereupon, upon breaking the consecrated host, Joseph gave a tearful wail and with a great scream flew through the air five paces while kneeling, and upon returning to the altar remained ecstatic for some while,

The Prince took notice of the wail, observed the ecstasy and asked for the reason. The Custodian interposed his authority since he was dealing with such a great personage and asked Joseph. In accordance with obedience, Joseph answered, *those whom you sent to Mass this morning have a hard heart because they don't believe that which the Holy Mother Church believes, and for that reason the Lamb became hard in my hands this morning, which is why I couldn't break it.* The Prince was quiet and full of thought upon hearing the answer, and was no longer prompt in his departure, neither resolving to depart nor to close his ear to any secret, but overtaken by a strong impulse to embrace the Catholic Religion.

Meanwhile Joseph, having been informed of the intentions of the Pontiff, was stimulated even more by his own great kindness to recover that soul and having already discussed the matter with God, knew that this was granted as seen from that which followed. After dinner, John

Frederick wanted to meet with the Blessed One, and stayed with him alone in his cell until Compline. What the discussions were only God knows, but all we know is that the Prince emerged thoughtful from the cell and betook himself straight to the church where in front of the Altar of Saint Francis he kneeled and then removed himself, perhaps to surrender to that heavenly light, knowing that it was going to triumph over him soon. God, who followed him with his grace, led him to the chorus of the church where he participated in the whole Compline and then descended to the procession in which he showed more curiosity than compunction. But with God one can't dissemble, since his arrow is so penetrating and his grace so victorious. On Monday morning Frederick wanted to participate in Joseph's Mass at which he was struck by another miracle. It was when Joseph raised the consecrated Blessed Host and there appeared on it, visible to all, a cross colored in black and Joseph, with his body one-hand's distance in the air over the dais of the altar, continued to raise the host, thinking but of God. This unexpected prodigy stunned one of the two Counts, the heretic, who disdaining even the miracles that God was working for his benefit, shouted insolently, *damn our coming to these towns. I was in my own town, quiet of spirit, but now here the furies and scruples of conscience shake me.* Not so the Prince who still had not resolved these matters, but the Blessed One could say to one of his confidants, *we are joyful that the stag is wounded, and we can well hope for his conversion.*

After Mass, the Prince returned to private discussions with Joseph until the dinner hour. He returned after dining, during which time Joseph, at the suggestion of the Custodian, was ready to dress him with the Girdle of Saint Francis, of whose miraculous effects the new penitent had been informed. Then the Prince entered into the room of the Servant of God, who upon seeing him ran towards him and dressed him in his own girdle, and in doing so said to him several times, *I tie you up for Paradise.* And so the Blessed One was taken up in ecstasy, but was called back by virtue of obedience. The poor monk then turned to the Prince of Brunswick of the great house of Saxony, lord of great states, and said with great force, *go and adore Saint Francis, participate in the Compline, go devoutly to the procession, and do everything that the monks do.* Frederick obeyed like some humble and devout novice, and followed the instructions imposed on him. Later, having gone in the company of Cardinals Facchinetti and Rapaccioli to the Altar of the Holy Sacrament, prostrate there with his face down, said with firm and clear voice, *here one adores the King of the World, and here I confess myself to believe that which the Holy Catholic Church believes.*

That evening, up until the fifth hour, he confided to Joseph the secrets of his conscience, and in order to carry out a public abjuration of the Lutheran Heresy by his own hand he confirmed that he would return to Assisi the following year, which indeed happened, but wanting first to arrange prudently the public affairs of his states in the interests of the Catholic Religion, and the private matters of his conscience later in the face of the world. Of this noble acquisition, Cardinal Facchinetti deposed as follows, *the conversion of the Duke of Brunswick was granted by God through the prayers of Father Joseph, and when he and the Duke came together, the Duke surrendered to Brother Joseph's prayers which triumphed over his soul because God gave him strength and wisdom.*

Even the Most Serene Princess of Brunswick attests that when Duke John Frederick, her husband, was living at court, *all he could do was to speak of the Servant of God, Father Joseph of Copertino, for whom the Duke maintained a most tender devotion, and kept portraits of him. Regarding all this, the Duke wanted to receive monks in his states and chose the Franciscan Capuchin Fathers, among whom was his confessor, and he kept them there as long as he lived.* One of these fathers was the famous preacher, Father Joseph Bono of Diso, who on Tuesday of Easter 1679, at the end of his preaching in the Cathedral of Hanover, made a long and worthy commemoration of the heroic life of our Blessed One with a tenderness that brought tears to the listeners. The first among them was the most sovereign listener himself who joined in giving witness to the praise.

A conquest of such consequence cost Joseph a lot, for it unchained Hell against him much to his detriment. The first move against him was a speech by a heretical servant of the prince, who threatened Joseph with wounds and death if his master were to change his religion. But the Blessed One calmly answered, *what's the matter with you? Go and kill God if you can, for only He is the author of such good works. I admire his creation and all I want is His glory,*

By these words he countered the agitation of the Prince's servant, but not that of the Devil. On the same day that the Prince had his last encounter with Joseph and was converted, the Servant of God entered his adjoining oratorio to give thanks to the Most High. The Devil appeared to him visibly, threw him onto the ground, and beat him with blows that were so resounding that Brother Ludovico, Joseph's companion, heard them in the next room. Frightened, he ran to the Custodian and gave him a confused account of what was happening. The Custodian was in the chorus enclosure in the company of two principal monks and of the Prince himself who was participating in the divine praises. They betook themselves to the oratorio where they found the Blessed One, who had already won the struggle, giving continuous thanks to God.

Questioned by the Custodian and ordered to give the reason for the din, Joseph replied *Malatasca* (that was his name for the Devil, as he is also called elsewhere) *came to bully me, and he threw me to the ground with great fury, and I was a bit hurt in the neck.* In fact one could see a great bruise on his neck as if someone had tried to strangle him. Upon being asked why the Devil had later departed, Joseph replied, *because I grabbed the stole that was on the altar of my oratory and beat him with it and asked what do you require of me? The Devil then stopped beating me and he asked, shouting, how do you dare dress with the girdle of Saint Francis someone who is not yours, nor of your Order, but mine? I answered, I did it out of obedience to the command of my superior,* and he replied fiercely, *I'll fix you and your Superior.* And so he vanished.

But the seducer is not lacking in deceptions and falsehoods, so he entered Joseph's cell again in the form of a pilgrim. By the fire, he set about to reason with him calmly and displayed powerful arguments as to the evil Joseph wrought by undertaking the conversion of that Prince without orders from the Pope. Joseph shielded himself by saying *that he was ignorant, that there were many things he didn't know, and everything he did was in obedience to his Father- General and the superior of the holy Monastery.* The Devil therefore disclosed his real name, and said, *I will make you and your superiors sorry, and I'll cause their ruin.* Rising courageously to his feet, Joseph answered, *you won't do anything except what God wants.* But the Demon answered with deed and words, giving him a violent open-handed slap on his back which horribly burned Joseph so that the Custodian, when he learned of it and when he saw the burn mark, had the chamber of the Servant of God blessed as a protection against diabolic abuse.

But nobody visited this rare prodigy of holiness with greater veneration than the Infanta Mary of Savoy, a princess of great piety and great understanding, daughter of Charles Emmanuel, and Catherine of Austria. This great Lady, a devotee of the Third Order of Saint Francis and a devout royal pilgrim, visited all the sanctuaries of Italy and afterwards betook herself to visit that of Saint Francis of Assisi. She wanted to see the copy of the Saint's portrait held by the Blessed Joseph, since Innocent X had not granted her permission to see the original. So she did venerate the image of the Holy Patriarch in the church sacristy, the one that belonged to his most devout son Joseph.

She was left so taken by Joseph's holiness that she stayed for some days in Rivotorto where the Seraphic Order had its beginnings, and some months in Perugia from where she betook herself several times a week to Assisi to confer with the Servant of the Lord about matters of her soul, and she passed whole days in sweet colloquy which never ended without a flash of some miraculous event. The Infanta was deaf, and couldn't hear other voices except through a silver trumpet held next to her ear. But when the Blessed One talked, she could hear him at a distance without the trumpet, and that's how their pious conversations were held. When her finger was badly bruised and was causing her great pain, she wrapped Joseph's girdle around her finger, and immediately she found herself free from the pain.

On one occasion while participating in Joseph's Mass, she saw him rise three palm-widths off the ground as he raised the host. One morning she wanted, with permission and in the presence of the Superior, to have breakfast with the Blessed One in the sacristy of the larger church. Joseph went with the food that he brought from his cell, saying that he was bringing something to eat to a poor pilgrim, but at the third bite he went into ecstasy with outstretched arms, and his eyes fixed on the Most Serene Infanta. Ordered back, he fled to his cell, silently and with bowed head, without anyone being able to hear any of his words except *fiat cor immaculatum, ut non confundar* (let my heart be immaculate and not confounded). That evening a fellow Monk, said to him jokingly, *I'm joyful that this morning you spoke and broke fast with the most Serene Infanta of Savoy.* Joseph answered seriously, *ah, be quiet; we have two Saint Clares, one alive and the other dead. I saw in her face a certain splendor and for that reason I was unable to stay, and I bowed down.*

The Infanta then sent a messenger to Joseph for some reason that I don't know. The unfortunate man had fallen into a sin of the senses and in that state he appeared before the Servant of God who upon seeing him said, *ah, you wretch, what have you done? Go and confess, and then come back.* He went, confessed, and then came back and was received with a welcome that was fit for his penance

The Infanta departed Assisi, but even at a distance she preserved the memory of Joseph's holiness, so that one of her letters is recorded in his beatification file in which she says, *I want to provide you with all things that you might need so that nobody else has to worry about you, so let me know your needs confidentially.* Joseph who trusted in God alone answered, *by the guts of Jesus Christ I beg you to let me stay in my usual state of poverty, which is the biggest treasure that I can have.* Even though he wanted nothing from this holy princess, she wanted something from him. She made him a new undercoat and requested the Father-General to exchange it for the old one that Joseph wore. The task was entrusted to the Custodian who, to overcome Joseph's aversion, required his obedience. Then, not only with alacrity but with fury he took off his habit and when upon putting on the undercoat for obedience's sake said, *I am pleased for you to take my tunic and my undergarment, [and if you want my flesh then take even my skin.* So that clothing passed as a relic to the Most Serene Infanta, and the heroic act of Joseph engendered love in the heart of God.

Some other ill-advised ladies did not enjoy such luck. Artemisia, Marchioness dei Medici, sister of the Duke of Corgna, gathered with some ladies from Perugia to go to Assisi to see the raptures of the Blessed Joseph, having agreed that the other ladies would present themselves ahead of her in Church, so that when she herself joined them invoking the names of *Jesus and Mary*, everyone would see the Servant of God in ecstasy. It went as they had planned, but when the Marchioness appeared, Joseph turned to her in disdain and said, *why do you come here out of curiosity? Don't you know that God makes miracles with this piece of wood? Go away in the name of God.* The Marchioness was left stunned and she closed her deposition thus: *I was left like a wet hen and from this I gathered that he knew the secrets of the heart.*

In the midst of so many visits by such distinguished personages when people were honoring him, and among the greatness of so many gifts by which God favored him, Joseph continued to care for his soul, so when asked by a confidant if vainglorious thoughts ever passed through his mind he was able to answer, *yes, but they come and go and by the grace of God they don't stay.* So it was his custom during visits by the most renowned people to kneel, kiss the ground and say *non nobis Domine non nobis, sed nomini tuo da gloriam* (give glory not to us, Lord, not to us, but to your name) thus attributing to the Lord every instance of glory that is His. So, being full of Christian humility, and understanding that all good comes from the Father of Light which descends from Him to the hearts of men, Joseph did not neglect any means to set himself in virtue, and in that way he became great.

We know that Joseph had a high regard for holy indulgences, not only the ones stemming from the holiness of the Roman Pontiffs which kindly profited the Order of Minor Conventuals, but also of those granted to the pious confraternities. Thus, when the Venerable

Archconfraternity of the most glorious Saint Anthony of Padua was set up in the Basilica of the Twelve Holy Apostles of Rome in 1649 during the happy commemoration by Innocent X of his first birth, Joseph's distinguished name is glorified in the rolls of its illustrious and devout brothers. Also, in the celebrated Company of Saint Stephen of Assisi, one can see this new light of holiness recorded in its annals.

twelve

Taking of the Blessed Joseph from the holy Monastery of Assisi to the Monastery of the Capuchins of Pietra Rubea (Pietrarubbia), and his stay there of about three months.

The Holy Inquisition in Naples had already fully approved Joseph's holiness. So had the Supreme Pontiff, Urban VIII, who with great astonishment admired Joseph's ecstasies. The Pope decided with his enlightened judgment to take this great treasure from the public and hide him in a remote spot, thereby reserving him intact for God, who would want him for Himself. And it would be left to God through his secret and wonderful ways whether to display Joseph to others. Such was the intention of the highest authorities; an intention that was attested frequently in the examination of Joseph's life during the process of his beatification.

By command of the Pope, who at that time was Innocent X, the Tribunal of the Holy Inquisition in Rome required that Father-Master, Brother Vincenzo Maria Pellegrini, Inquisitor of Perugia, transport Joseph immediately and with honor from the holy monastery of the Minor Conventuals of Assisi to the monastery of the Capuchin Fathers of Pietra Rubea (today Pietrarubbia) on the slopes of a rugged mountain. There he was to be handed over to the monastery's Father-Guardian along with instructions that will be outlined shortly.

The instructions were executed quickly, yet the Blessed One did not find them completely unexpected. A few months earlier, the Lord had revealed to him *that he had to stay under a certain mountain, but at that time Joseph didn't know nor could he discern the full significance of the revelation,* although he did understand it when he was quickly taken from Assisi and then saw the site of his new residence.

The Inquisitor notified both the Father- Custodian and Joseph of the most holy command. The Inquisitor, traveling in a carriage to the holy monastery, kindly invited Joseph to enter the carriage with him. The Blessed One entered without even minimum resistance. Instead he had a joyous and laughing expression, enlivened by the gentle manner and soft words of the Inquisitor that he should not fear anything. The Inquisitor added that Joseph should ask for anything he wished, and that he was ready to provide it before beginning the journey.

With similar displays of benevolence, this wise and discreet superior, in accordance with the pontifical commands, conducted Joseph to the city of Castello and lodged him in the Monastery of Saint Domenico, where Joseph was received and treated courteously. We are assured of this by Monsignor Libelli, Archbishop of Avignon, who was a confidant and friend of the Blessed One. The prelate describes as much, for he happened to visit Joseph in Castello, his own home town, where he happened to be. Libelli says, *I closeted myself with him in his room and asked him if he was happy. He replied that any place satisfied him because he knew that God could be found there. We passed on to discuss spiritual matters, and the discussion turned to the ingratitude of men. Joseph said that he was in wonderment that every man did not become moved at the sight of a crucifix, and he began to enumerate the sufferings of the Lord: the agony, the beatings, the thorns, the nails. And while he was talking like this I noticed that his mouth grew tight as if dipped in strong vinegar. At the same time I saw him in a single movement fall to his knees from a chest on which he had been sitting, and he made such a noise with his knees that I thought he might have done himself great harm. I don't know how, but his eyes became thunderstruck, that is with the pupils rolled up under his eyelids and his arms arranged like a cross, just as Saint Francis is depicted when he received the holy stigmata. I too kneeled to thank the Lord, and carefully studying the position of Joseph's body I tried to move one of his arms which I did with difficulty. But it hung from his shoulder, and when I made it dangle, it seemed to shake, and the arch of his back seemed suspended in the air. After a good quarter of an hour he returned to his senses and said in Neapolitan, forgive me but I'm sleepy, and he went back to sit on the chest.*

The Archbishop added that he reproved Joseph, exhorting him to keep from letting these disconcerting movements happen, and the Blessed One answered him that *he with his prayers would have been able to help him receive such a gift from God, for which he had prayed many times but without result.* The prelate went on to ask what God showed him while Joseph was thus removed from his senses. He answered *that many times he could see many things about God, mixed together, without being able to distinguish one from the other; at other times he could witness some specific mystery, as it seemed by his divine will.* And here he begged the Archbishop not to take advantage of him by questioning him *because he was ignorant and was unable to discourse.*

So, the trip through the countryside continued, and there were miracles at every step. Joseph sat on a litter, which by necessity passed over rugged and dilapidated roads. The leader of the voyage was dispirited, and despaired of continuing, but the Blessed One said, *take heart and let the mules go where they want, for he who guides them knows full well how to guide them.* And one could see that the one guiding them was an angel from heaven, for the mules that bore the bars of the litter leapt, surmounted, and went over impossible roads as if they were walking in a spacious meadow and not in places where things that were made of wood had never passed, or where if anyone had ever tried to pass would have fallen pitifully from the highest crags. It amazed those who saw these strange happenings, during which Joseph, always smiling, was saying *oh brave mules, o brave mules,* raising his eyes to heaven thanking God for their success.

After such a distinctive string of ecstasies and miracles, the Blessed One arrived at the Capuchin Fathers of Pietra Rubea but did not wait to be handed over by the Inquisitor to its Father-Guardian, who at that time was Father Giovanni Batista of Monte Grimano, who had come promptly to the gate of the Monastery with all his monks. Instead, Joseph descended from the litter and ran straight away past every other friar, and threw himself on his knees in front of him and said bless you Father-Guardian. He, in turn, surprised at being greeted by someone who did not know him by sight, asked, *and how do you know that I am the Guardian?* Joseph answered, *I know you and I have seen you and the other brothers of your monastery, and your monastery itself.* It is attested in the legal beatification proceedings that *during the trip that he had just made, he had seen everything by divine revelation.*

By the command of the Supreme Tribunal, the orders from the Inquisitor were left in the monastery, fixed on the door of the refectory and on the door to Joseph's cell, that under pain of excommunication, nobody should allow Joseph to speak with anyone except the Capuchin fathers of that monastery, nor write to anyone, howsoever eminent his rank, nor receive letters, nor leave the monastery. In a word he must remain there sequestered from any secular contact.

The Blessed One, silent and mute, not only read these insistent orders but also heard them read out loud, displaying an imperturbable and placid expression along with a satisfied spirit, without asking either then or later the reason for which they were issued, or why the holy monastery of Assisi had him transported away. Such a heroic resignation to divine will showed that he had every faith in God alone, and he used that faith to teach anyone who might be pressed in spirit or anguished in body to be *joyful, my son; put your hope in God and don't doubt.* In fact, God, who either in a dream or more likely in a vision had shown Joseph the cross before putting it on his own shoulders, never let Joseph want for anything. Nor did he diminish the affluence of his gifts, but in fact increased them greatly. As a result of the Inquisitor's haste to obey his high-level orders, Joseph arrived at Pietra Rubea without his eyeglasses and his hat, without asking about them or complaining, having miraculously known everything ahead of time already.

Father Giovanni Maria of Fossombrone, Provincial of the Capuchins, gives us an authentic description of Joseph's incomparable resignation, patience and spiritual fortitude. After describing the hardship with which Joseph was brought to Pietra Rubea, and his incomparable patience regarding his suffering in being taken from the holy monastery of Assisi, he says, *the day after Father Joseph's arrival, when I was the Provincial Superior, I found on the door of the refectory a bunch of very strict orders from the Most Reverend Father Inquisitor concerning Father Joseph, which our monks were to follow strictly, that he should not speak with any other secular or religious person, or ecclesiastic of any rank or condition. I found similar orders fixed to the aforementioned father's cell that was assigned to him by the Father Inquisitor, which was the meanest and darkest one of that monastery. Upon entering the cell to visit him, I found him joyful and happy, like a jewel in paradise. I stayed with him for five days, and always saw in him the same joyfulness, without his asking me if I knew the reason why he was taken from the holy monastery of Assisi and placed with such strictness in our monastery of Pietra Rubea, or what was expected of him.*

In accordance with his apparent joviality, Joseph bore a lightness of heart whereupon he sang songs composed by him more with a divine than a poetic spirit, and he wanted the monks, particularly the older ones, to sing them with him. One of them, which he repeated many times, went like this:

Gesu', Gesu', Gesu'
Vieni, vieni consolami tu
Vieni, vieni, e non tardare,
Senza te non posso stare
Senza te non possoi piu'
Vieni, vieni consolami tu.

(Jesus, Jesus, Jesus,
Come, come, console me.
Come, come and don't be late,
I can't be without you,
I can't go on without you
Come, come, console me.)

During some particular distress, in jubilant rapture, leaping and singing, he would exclaim:

> *Amore, e carita'*
> *E una gran felicita',*
> *Chi ha carita e felice, e non lo sa.*
> *Chi ha pazienza in ogni loco*
> *Non fa poco, non fa poco*

> *(Love and charity*
> *Is a great happiness.*
> *He who is charitable is happy but doesn't t know it.*
> *He who is patient everywhere,*
> *Doesn't do little, doesn't do little.)*

And so great and heroic was his patience that at some points he almost lost all sense of the things of the world. When frequently asked if his victuals were well prepared, he always answered immediately, *they're good, they're good.* Never from his mouth would one hear, *this makes me feel sick, this is good, this I don't like.* To whoever had the job of providing his meal at Pietra Rubea, he said, *I always fast; I am always in Lent; don't take the trouble of bringing me food; if you bring it I'll eat it; if you don't bring it I won't eat.* In fact, he never asked for anything to eat, nor did he ever leave his cell without a specific need, or else in obedience to the superior. But having the normal need to eat, he did it with simple vegetables, or a few nuts, or bitter herbs, and water lightly mixed with wine, gulping it all down rather than eating, as if either detached from his senses or disdainful of providing relief for his body, as if its natural weight afflicted his soul which was desirous only of sweeping through the upper regions of Heaven.

Despite this, he was always flying towards his God with miraculous and continuous raptures. When celebrating Mass, which used to last two hours, he was incessantly ecstatic. The wonder of it all was that when he came back to his senses, he punctiliously followed the correct words and the ceremonies so that it seemed that an angel was giving him each syllable and guided the ritual. On some occasions, by command of the superior, he would go to the orchard of the monastery, and there he would usually go into a rapture, either when considering the divine wisdom behind the creation of some plant, or at the song of some little bird. In his cell, all he did was weep over the passion of Jesus Christ, and, because of it, fly quickly towards Heaven.

One morning while celebrating Mass, an angel told him that he should finish it quickly since the assistant at the Mass who was Brother Michael of Saint Amore, a Capuchin layman, had to go make the rounds to seek alms. Joseph obeyed and finished the sacrifice with great brevity. While removing his holy vestments he asked the layman, *what is it that you have to do?* He answered, *I have to go around to seek alms,* and the Blessed One then added, *the angel has already told me, which is why I hurried to finish the Mass soon. Now go in the name of God.* This monk, who later was to die in a state of great holiness, deposed as follows in the beatification process, *Father Joseph many times would tell me, this morning at Mass I saw a little lamb, by which he meant Jesus in the sacrament.*

With the utterances of the angels, Joseph's ecstasies were accompanied by miracles and prophesies. Giustina of Antimis, tormented for several years by a tumor, was conducted to Pietra Rubea from her town of Macerata, for the sole purpose of participating in a Mass given by the Blessed One, which she did and was healed. In Urbino, Pier Santi, who went blind from an obstinate excretion of fluid, recovered his sight by the touch of Joseph's cap, and exclaimed, *mother of mine I can see, mother I can see,* filling the whole household with wonder and consolation. One evening, the Guardian of the Monastery of Pietra Rubea, lamented to the Servant of God, *that there was no more wax for candles for the very long Mass which Joseph was to celebrate the following morning.* Joseph answered *have faith, son, have faith, don't get annoyed, for the little old man will provide it for him.* By little old man, he was referring to the Capuchin Saint Felix. That morning, upon the opening of the Church, some unknown person had placed on the altar a bunch of candles that were enough for the Blessed One's Masses for as long as he stayed in that monastery.

For as long as Joseph lived there, God provided in abundance for that religious family. When a Capuchin of Monte Baroccio had lost certain clothing, he sought recourse from Joseph, who immediately upon hearing of the incident told him, *go to such and such place and you will find them.* He went, and find them he did. To another Capuchin, who came before him, Joseph said in his ear, *with such and such a person in your cell you spoke badly of your superior. Go confess yourself.* Thus pricked in his conscience, the Capuchin confessed his sin and what had happened. And so, interrupting the discourse of another Capuchin who was speaking to him, Joseph said, *go and open the gate to such and such a monk, who at this moment* (and it was close to two in the morning) *is arriving at this monastery from Urbino.* And just then the stranger knocked, and when the messenger arrived and the gate was opened, each was in wonder as to Joseph's miraculous prediction. Many more such accounts are left to mention, which will be spoken of elsewhere

We must not pass over here without great awe the deepest secrets of God. To curb the gathering of half the world which had betaken itself to venerate our Blessed One in Assisi, Joseph was thus hidden by men in a Capuchin Monastery among inaccessible cliffs and crags so that, buried thus by the threat of excommunication and the interdiction of human contact, that worker of miracles, that prophet, that celebrated saint which he was, not be known. But here particularly God, who had placed in Joseph the thundering of His grace and pleasure, raised him higher than ever for the veneration of others, before the gathering of the people, and the acclamation of the world. To avoid verbosity, we will be content to cite only a couple of testimonies.

Father Giovanni Battista of Saint Agata, the Capuchin Vicar of the Monastery of Pietra Rubea, attests, b*efore I went as Vicar to the monastery of Pietra Rubea, the public would gather there, as many as thousands of people, and the great multitude even uncovered part of the roof of the church, which I have not yet seen repaired completely, but upon my arrival by order of the Superiors I did not permit that Father-Brother Joseph should be seen any more by others except by us monks.*

The previously mentioned Father Giovanni Battista of Monte Grimano deposes as follows, *from the first when Father Joseph lived in our Monastery, so much of the public would gather from surrounding areas and from far away to be at his Masses, that people even climbed the roofs, and on one occasion he was seen by secular people while he was in ecstasy.*

Father Brother Giovanni Maria of Fossombrone, Provincial of the Capuchins, narrates more specifically, *many people, ecclesiastical and secular, and even lay people from distant towns, flocked to our monastery of Pietra Rubea to hear his Masses, which he celebrated publicly in that church of ours, and to gaze at him and admire his ecstasies and his raptures, and to be supported by his prayers in their needs and infirmities. These gatherings were so numerous that inns were built around the monastery, and a shelter was built for the comfort of those who came but who were unable to fit into the church when the said father celebrated Mass, and they removed parts of the roof and made openings in the very walls of the Church.*

Now, to get a fair idea of such a great gathering of people it is enough to say that on the day on which falls the Feast of Saint Augustine, so large was the number of people from far-off towns who mustered in the Church of Pietra Rubea to hear the Blessed One's Mass, that the Superior forbade Joseph to celebrate it that morning. The Devil, who envied the holiness of the Servant of God as much as he could, wanted personally to bring Joseph notice of this ahead of time. Taking on the appearance of a young tramp, he impetuously opened the door of his cell and pointing his finger at him menacingly said these words, *you will not, will not say Mass this morning.* The Blessed One replied imperturbably, *I'll do what God wants* and, unmoved, he indicated his preparations. When the command came from the Guardian, he obeyed, illuminated by the divine, and said, *melior est obedientia quam victimae* (better it is to obey than sacrifice).

thirteen

The new taking of the Blessed Joseph by order of the Holy Inquisition to the Monastery of the Capuchin Fathers of Fossombrone, and his stay there of around three years.

It had been the intention that Joseph be completely hidden in every way from the eyes of the world, to be noticed only by the eyes of God. For that reason, the Holy Inquisition decide to move Joseph from the Capuchin Monastery of Pietra Rubea, where the Lord had revealed in him so much of the splendor of his wonderful gifts, to the Monastery at Fossombrone, of the same Order.

Urgent and secret orders to transport Joseph elsewhere were sent to Monsignor Ascanio Maffei, Archbishop of Urbino, who deputized for that task the Canon Priest Mario Vivian, an ecclesiastic of great integrity and great skill who was the Arch-Priest of that Metropolis. When he arrived at Pietra Rubea he communicated his high commands to the Father-Guardian, and to Joseph who immediately asked *where he had to go.* Upon hearing from the Vicar that he couldn't disclose it at that time, Joseph asked if it was a place where God could be found. When told yes, he said, *well then, let's go joyfully because the crucifix will aid us,* and it helped him so prodigiously with its presence that on that happy trip there were perhaps more marvels than miles, more ecstasies and raptures than there were steps.

Meanwhile, mixed rumors regarding Joseph's departure ran through the towns of that province, and there wasn't anybody who didn't try to find out the road that Joseph would take. But, since God would not bring his servant along those hard roads if men didn't give him reverence, miracles followed Joseph. A mule pulling the archbishop's litter had previously been reluctant and spoiled, but on this trip was obedient and faithful. An unruly horse which had refused to carry any weight, got down on his own and accepted his burden. A downpour that soaked everyone down to his undershirt didn't even lightly sprinkle the Blessed One. Sudden ecstasies would surprise him, and he worked miracles which, over that thirty-mile trip, underscored his holiness and added its luster to his name.

And so they arrived at Fossombrone, a city surrounded by some mountains, on one of which at the top, a mile away, was the Monastery of the Capuchin monks. There Joseph was handed over to the Father-Guardian with the same stern orders as at Pietra Rubea. He stayed for three years with the same acceptance as before, the same holiness of life, and the same resignation, never asking why he had been taken about in the world. He continued his fasts with only Lenten food, with his penitence, with his bare feet covered only with threadbare slippers, and living in poverty with his patched up tunic which he only changed when his co-religionists sent him another one from the monastery in Assisi. In short, in Fossombrone, he was known as *that so holy monk*, as he had been called in Assisi, and continued that way until his death.

For his heroic sanctity, by now known everywhere, the Capuchin monks suffered a great deal from inquiries and petitions, inasmuch as the knowledge filtered throughout that city that Joseph might be in their Monastery, and the monks didn't know how to handle those who begged to see him to commend themselves to his prayers. And for that reason the place was crowded with such a great throng that one could well understand the undoubted writing of the Apostle that *such is the good odor of Christ* that one can't stay hidden for the fragrance that it sends forth.

With such a rich treasure of sanctity lying within, great were the offerings that the people made to that monastery for the upkeep of the Servant of God as well as that of the good monks, who well appreciated the gifts but absolutely rejected them.

While living with the Capuchins, Joseph was asked if he knew *that taking upon one's self the rule of Saint Francis was to be blessed by the Holy Father.* He replied that he knew that well, *but that it was better to carry it out than to take it on,* meaning that it was better to observe the rule than just to know it.

There was in that Monastery one who with juvenile capriciousness made fun of Joseph's holiness, and there was a novice who took little care in observing the monastery's rule. Each one conversed with the Servant of God in his cell. One of them left venerating him, and the other was transformed into a penitent and became a perfect monk.

When Joseph was invited lightheartedly by a monk to stop his rigorous retreat and take part in a procession of the *Corpus Domini* that was then in progress, Joseph gracefully replied, *truly such a desire took hold of me even in Assisi when I was in almost the same straits as I am here in Fossombrone, and I told myself that everyone is going to accompany the Emperor of Heaven, and I, useless and unworthy, am left in my room without being able to revere or see him.* Fixing his mind on that observation, and repeating the same lament, he was raised by God to think of higher matters, and he miraculously saw the whole procession which was proceeding through Fossombrone, and also saw all the oversights and defects that the monks committed who were accompanying it. And he knew with distinct mental clarity that he himself could fall into the same defects. Upon recovering his senses, he threw himself on his knees, vigorously thanking the Lord who, in such unusual ways, kept him far away from doing evil.

Great was his kindness towards the sick, and whenever a person in that monastery found himself that way, Joseph was consumed by compassion. Often he found himself with Brother Antonio, an old lay monk with the gout. With a joyful face Joseph would say to him, *my Brother Antonio, patience, patience; he who everywhere has patience does not accomplish just a little.* The monk learned those words, and whenever he was with the Blessed One he was the first to repeat them, and Joseph would laugh and answer, *oh what a beautiful song, oh what a beautiful song!*

In exercising obedience, Joseph had no equal. He had permission to roam the monastery and he had access to the cells of the monks, but he still didn't leave his own cell without orders from the Superior. When invited to take some air in the garden, or to betake himself to another part of the monastery, he always answered, *is there permission from the Guardian?*

On Easter Day, the Guardian ordered him, as a matter of obedience, to eat meat that morning despite Joseph's custom of always eating Lenten food. Joseph answered immediately, *yes, my son, let's eat meat.* And when the Guardian made as if to send for it, the Blessed One added, with complete resignation and humility, *father of mine, at the moment I feel something—I know not what—that eats at my conscience, so may your fathership know that when I used to eat meat among my monastic fathers, it made me ill, but I want to believe that to eat it now out of obedience, it will not do the same.* The Guardian replied, *if so it is, so be it,* and bothered Joseph no more about it.

One evening, the above mentioned Father-Guardian entered Joseph's cell while a layman was preparing him for rest, and with a joyful voice said, *what is going on here Father Joseph?* Joseph answered *one is burying the dead.* The Guardian, noticing that Joseph had his back and his head resting against the wall and the rest of his body stretched out on planks, added, *it will do you ill to sleep with your head leaning that way against the wall; it is necessary to attach a headpiece there.* Joseph replied, *yes, son, get a headpiece, for it will be better.* And so, he left his personal governance wholly to the superior.

Joseph's obedience is shown emphatically regarding the following matter: The provincial chapter of the Capuchins was to meet in

Fossombrone, so Joseph by order of the Sacred Congregation of the Holy Office was supposed to be taken to the nearby Monastery of the Order in Monte Vecchio, and then be brought back afterwards. Since there was no litter available, the bishop's vicar sent a horse for the Blessed One, who having been informed of the command said, *Let's go joyfully,* without thought of the discomforts of the ride or of the advanced age of a person ruined and exposed by his penances. Two Capuchin fathers were deputized to help him along the steep and damaged roads. But as soon as Joseph got into the saddle he did it so badly that the Guardian realized that he would fall off right away. As soon as they were out of sight, the Guardian, fearful that over some steep crag he might lose that treasure entrusted to him by heaven, sent a messenger after them recalling Joseph to the monastery. Upon arriving, the Guardian said, *Father Joseph, you said that you were an excellent rider, yet you sat on the horse with so little grace that it seemed from moment to moment that you were going to fall.* The Servant of God answered, half joyful and half thoughtful, *listen, my son, I mounted the horse for obedience's sake, but when the horse began to walk I immediately heard a voice which said to me repeatedly, go back for you will break your neck and I answered if it be the will of God he will inspire my superior, whom I hold as to speak for God, to recall me; and having recalled me I think that God has inspired him.* But, the Guardian added, *nevertheless it's necessary to leave, and since we can't find a litter and you don't know how to ride a horse, could you go on foot?* Joseph replied, *yes father, yes father, for obedience will bestow wings on me.* So, with a staff in one hand he joyfully set out walking, without saying anything else but the word *obedience obedience*. After the Chapter had met and Joseph was conducted back to Fossombrone, he told the monks that he had stayed with greatest satisfaction at Monte Vecchio, where Saint Felix had appeared to him and consoled him beyond description, assuring him that in a short while, a similar order from Rome would have him conducted back to Fossombrone, which is what happened.

His return, and his three-year stay there, was a continuing paradise of ecstasies and raptures up to God. Here we will merely mention them, leaving us to speak of them in detail elsewhere. Joseph could not see a devotional picture without, with his usual scream, going into ecstasy and into a rapture that again brought his body up into the air. He could not hear a word about the passion of Jesus Christ, or a word of praise of his most pure Mother without falling into a sweet swoon. And when a Capuchin friar in the garden wanted to recall to him the greatness of Mary, Joseph immediately threw himself against him, both falling to the ground with Joseph screaming with the fullness of God, and the Capuchin screaming with the greatness of fright. Their comrades heard them and ran toward the sudden noise saying *both have gone into ecstasy*, but they saw that the ecstasy belonged solely to Joseph who lay prostrate and motionless, unconscious for an hour, the Capuchin friar having fled in great consternation.

A similar event happened first in the library and then in the dormitory. Upon seeing a Crucifix, it wasn't long before Joseph collapsed on the ground as if dead with his arms and feet distended, eyes and mouth covered with flies. It being difficult to carry him to his cell, the Guardian commanded him in his ear that, for the sake of holy obedience, he return to his senses, and he immediately did. Upon being asked the next day if he had heard the command, he replied *no*, and when asked further why he returned to his senses, he said,, *it was because God, who is the highest lover of obedience, with one word made Joseph's vision disappear, which had occupied his spirit, which, no longer being occupied, brought back full strength and feeling to his body.*

On a Sunday evening, during which the Gospel of *ego sum pastor bonus* (I am the good shepherd) was read, Joseph and the other monks went to the garden after dinner. There Joseph caught sight of one of the monastery's lambs, and expressed a desire to hold it. One of the monks put it in Joseph's arms, and he hugged it tenderly to his bosom and then took it by its feet and put it across his shoulders. Then, excited bit by bit by the spirit of the Lord, he began running through the garden and the devout friars ran after him wanting to see what was happening. They finally saw the lamb and Joseph both in the air, the lamb having been thrown by him up high by superhuman strength and he himself, by the strength of his spirit, had risen over the top of the trees in the garden, kneeling there for over two hours - that is, until midnight.

But the ecstasy on the morning of Pentecost was prodigious beyond others. As Joseph was celebrating Holy Mass and intoning the *Veni Sancte Spiritus* (Come, Holy Spirit) the abundance of grace and the impetus of the spirit that came upon him was so great that he took flight to the altar, more violently than quickly, like a lightning bolt going around the chapel, erupting in such a strange shout in such a truly booming voice that the monastery shook. The monks left the confines of their cells yelling, *earthquake, earthquake,* which suddenly filled the whole Monastery with fear. Running then to seek shelter in Joseph's chapel, they found him unconscious on the ground, full of that same divine spirit, rumbling with the force and fury that had come down from heaven and had filled the heart of the Apostles at the Last Supper.

On another occasion, *at the second Feast of the Easter of Resurrection, as Joseph was celebrating Holy Mass, Jesus Christ appeared to him in the form of a pilgrim. After Mass was over, the pilgrim went down to the dormitory and Joseph followed him saying pilgrim, pilgrim, and the pilgrim vanished into the dormitory's window where the Blessed One always felt a great tenderness of spirit.*

From being always in loving rapture with God, there came to Joseph a kind of godly transformation, so it's not surprising that almost everything he did appeared full of heavenly qualities. But inasmuch as it is for God alone to know every person's conscience and penetrate its secrets, how remarkable that our Blessed One was also able to do it, so that all those in his presence feared that their consciences might be stained or defective or sinful. Wherever Joseph lived, he revealed to everyone the secrets of their hearts. We have referred to many instances before now, and will refer to many more in another Chapter.

During his stay at Fossombrone, a certain Capuchin, Father Michael, was reciting with him the litany of the Blessed Virgin, but was a bit distracted. Joseph said, *stay here* and pulled him by his sleeve, and Father Michael, confused, returned to the prayer. The same father, while celebrating Mass, showed some spiritual distress, I don't know what, but the Blessed One said to him, *oh Father Michael, the Lord told me that you have suffered anguish in the Mass.*

While speaking in his cell with brother Hildebrand who was a Capuchin novice, Joseph said, *my son, you have a kind mother who blesses you every night with the cross.* And it was true, for his mother from the heights of one of the balconies did bless him every night with a cross.

Together, the Capuchin friar Girolamo of Sinigallia and the Servant of the Lord, agreed to commend each other to God. Joseph observed the promise in full, but not Friar Girolamo who, finding himself together with the Blessed One a few months later, asked him courteously, *Father Joseph did you remember to pray to God for me?* Joseph replied, *I prayed for you, but you never remembered to pray to God for me.* Friar Girolamo reddened and replied, *but, your fathership, you're a holy man close at hand to the divine majesty, so you don't need my prayers.* Smiling graciously, the Blessed One answered immediately, *oh, so you want to compare a Capuchin with a lesser conventual monk?* For a Capuchin was supposed to prevail over a lesser Minor Conventual in degree of sanctity for the rigor of his life.

If Joseph ever said of a sick person *he will die*, his death was inevitable. And if he said the opposite and predicted his return to health, surely his health would follow. On Thursday, January 7, 1655, around the fifteenth hour, having come out of his cell to celebrate Holy Mass in his little Chapel, Joseph saw that the priestly vestments had been laid out of the color prescribed by the ecclesiastical rite for the Eighth Day of Epiphany. He said to his servant, *give me the vestments of the dead because at this point the Pope has died in Rome.* And so it was, the prediction being then confirmed by the dismal news that suddenly arrived. But many similar cases followed to which I will refer in another Chapter in greater detail.

fourteen

By order of Alexander VII, the Blessed Joseph is restored to his Minor Monastic Order of Osimo. His trip from Fossombrone to the aforementioned city.

Pope Innocent X, had been firm in his deep belief that Joseph should be a true saint rather than being acclaimed as one, but it rendered those in Joseph's Order inconsolable in seeing Joseph separated from them. But Innocent X's death motivated the Order to beg the new Pontiff, Alexander VII, for the favor of his return, for which the Order had longed and yearned.

When the Pope had been a cardinal, he had been several times the mediator of these petitions, and now he had moved from being a past intercessor to being the arbiter. Conveniently, in May 1656 the General Congregation of the Minor Conventuals took place in Rome, where eight provincials of the Order prostrated themselves at the foot of the pontifical throne to beg for the return of Joseph to their cloisters.

Alexander saw and took note of the tears in the eyes of everyone in the Order and showed himself inclined to satisfy their wish but wanted to hear in which monastery Joseph should be placed. Everyone answered in unison, *the one in Assisi*. But the Pontiff, whose every word seemed weighty and majestic, spoke as an oracle and said, *no, for it is enough to have Saint Francis in that sanctuary so that the good monks don't lack for anything in such a place which has always been a school for religious observance.*

A few days later he let the Order know that *he wanted Joseph placed in S. Francis of Osimo.* At that time that church was governed by the Bishop Antonio Bichi of Siena, son of the blood sister of Alexander VII. So, through the confluence of blood, prudence and wisdom, that prelate could rightly guarantee to the Supreme Pontiff that Joseph would be treated honorably, and that his complete withdrawal from the world would be ensured, which the pontiff desired completely for Joseph's person. The Pope's intention to move Joseph would have been carried out under the supervision of Bishop Bichi, who was then a Cardinal, if another event hadn't impeded it. The commission that was finally sent went from the Holy Office to Giberto Cardinal Borromeo, protector of the Minor Conventuals, at that time Legate of Romagna, who joined with Father-Master Felice Gabrielli of Ascoli, who was General of the Order and later Bishop of Nocera in Campagna Felice, in entrusting the matter to the Secretary of the Order himself, who with an entourage betook himself to Fossombrone and, competently and with care, implemented Joseph's transport.

Joseph knew nothing of these hidden agreements, being in withdrawal and closed up, and his whole spirit being with God. But God, who communicated to His servant the secrets of others, did not at this time hide His own. As it happened, on the very evening before the second hour when the Father-Secretary of the Order arrived at the Monastery of the Capuchins, Joseph had at the first hour, contrary to his custom, opened the window of his cell and leaned out frequently to see the arrival of those who were supposed to conduct him to his brothers. A layman marveled at this novelty and asked the reason. The Blessed One answered calmly, *my son, don't marvel because I now have to depart from this monastery and return to my Order, and the Secretary of the Order who has to take me with him is already drawing near.*

The layman repeated Joseph's mysterious answer, and it immediately filled the monastery. While the monks were all discussing the matter, the Secretary arrived, gave the dispatches to the Father-Guardian, and wanted to depart right away. The arrival brought tears to that monastery, and all the Capuchins hurried to Joseph's cell, some of them sighing, some weeping bitterly, and some even saying that the territory of Osimo would not allow Joseph the same retreat nor be as peaceful as that of Fossombrone because of all the secular people there who always disturb the minds of monks. At these allegations, the Blessed One turned towards the blessed crucifix and said, *Lord, you well know that I neither desired nor specifically wanted Osimo. But wherever you want me to go, tell me how I can serve you there.*

Upon leaving Fossombrone, the Capuchins accompanied him a mile to the foot of the steep hill road, on the plain where the horse paths had been created, and here is where the usual miracles began, which gave fame to all the journeys taken by our Blessed One. With careful affection, the Capuchins put under his habit an absorbent cloth on Joseph's shoulders and another on his chest to absorb his perspiration and leave his tunic dry lest his sweat, accumulated while moving, should do him harm. But when the cloths were removed, they immediately sent forth such a fragrant heavenly odor that it filled the streets, and when they returned, the odor filled the whole monastery as well.

While continuing the journey through the gloom of night, they missed the road of Saint Vittoria delle Fratte, and instead wandered rather than travelled through the forests of the mountain. Joseph, who was escorted by a better guide, revealed the road. *There,* he said, *go in that direction where the moon is rising.* Even those who claimed to know the way obeyed him and they found themselves under the bell tower of the monastery of that place. Upon arriving they asked the Blessed One what place that might be and he replied, *the monastery of his Order, created and set up by Saint Francis himself.* Joseph prostrated himself and kissed that ground that had been sanctified by footprints of his Seraphic Father, and said, *may God be praised that I find myself among my brethren.*

There he was visited by Monsignor Zeccadoro, Bishop of Fossombrone, who prostrated himself to rejoice in his presence and to receive, along with his family, Joseph's blessing, which he got. The prelate gave Joseph a servant who bore the name *Paolino*, who on the following night accompanied Joseph over very difficult roads using one hand to guide Joseph's horse and the other to hold a lighted candle. Despite a strong wind the candle never went out, nor was it consumed during that trip which lasted several hours. It was later kept as a relic, a splendid testimony of the holiness of the Blessed One.

In order to escape from the popular throng and that of the nobility that had gathered after news had spread of Joseph's adventurous voyage, they avoided the cities, towns, and castles, finding it more convenient to rest in the houses and farms of peasants. So it happened that a poor woman vegetable-seller came to him weeping over the destruction of her family because certain worms had ruined and rotted all her melons. The Blessed One took pity on her and blessed her garden saying, *Potentia Patris, Sapientia Filii, Virtus Spiritus Sanctit, benedicat te defendat, Amen* (May the power of the Father, the Wisdom of the Son, and the Goodness of the Holy Spirit Bless you and Keep you, Amen). And the melons grew again and were so beautiful that none had ever seen such beautiful melons as those blessed by the *Holy Friar*, as he was called by the woman who profited by it.

Upon drawing close to the walls of Osimo they stopped at a farm and Joseph went out on a balcony where, for some while, he gazed at the town as if amazed, and saw the cupola and the upper part of the famous Temple of our Lady, and the Holy House of Loreto that was there. Joseph gave a cry and exclaimed, *Oh God, what do I see! How many angels come and go from heaven. Don't you see them? Look again at how many parcels of grace come down from up there, and they go back and bring some more! Tell me, what place is that?* And when he was told that *it was the temple wherein was venerated the Holy House of Nazareth,* Joseph prostrated himself and turned to exclaim, *no wonder then that a great many angels of paradise go down to that place; look at it and see how divine compassion rains down there! Oh happy place, oh blessed place.* Having said that, he fixed his eyes on the Holy House, went into ecstasy, and coming down from the balcony through the air, he flew in quick rapture a distance of six walking sticks to the foot of an almond tree, measuring in that flight a height of twelve palms.

Upon coming to his senses with more joy than usual, he began to sing his usual little spiritual songs, and while walking and singing he called Father Peter of Urbino over to him, and taking him by the right ear said, *sing this song with me.* The song was *Natum Vidimus & Choros Angelorum collaudantes Dominum* (We see him Born and the Choruses of Angels Joining in Praise of the Lord). The blessed one said, s*ing loudly, Friar Peter.* And while singing together it happened by chance that Joseph suddenly spread his arms, letting go of the ear of his fellow singer, and repeated several times *collaudantes, collaudantes* (fellow praisers, fellow praisers) fell unconscious on the ground in a new and astonishing ecstasy. For half an hour neither blows nor shaking would call him back to this world except for the voice of the Secretary of the Order.

With such wonderful activity of spirit, our Blessed One entered Osimo on July 10, 1657 and went into the Monastery of Saint Francis of his Order, where he continually increased in sanctity and where he would die happily.

fifteen

The stay of the Blessed Joseph among his coreligionists of the Minor Monastic Order of Osimo, until his death.

Upon entering his monastery of Saint Francis of Osimo, to the incredible joy of his Order, the Blessed Joseph found everything in readiness to support well his withdrawal in accordance with the orders of the holy superiors. Here he had separate rooms with a chapel, a garden and a companion, so that he could work his wonders without distraction from the gatherings of people, or the annoyance of outside events.

He then proceeded to embark on his saintly life. At sunrise he rose from his cot and went immediately to the oratory to recite the first canonical hour and other offices until his spiritual father entered to hear his confession. After confession, Joseph prepared for Mass, and then went to his designated chapel to celebrate the Mass privately. Dressed in holy vestments, he would kneel before the altar, and with great devotion would recite the litany of the Blessed Virgin. When finished, he would begin the Holy Mass, which he uttered with great spiritual fervor. It lasted around an hour when he was not in ecstasy, but somewhat less when he did go into ecstasy.

When he had finished Mass, he would linger a short while in the chapel and would then return to the oratory to continue the canonical hours and other offices, that is that of the Madonna, that of the Dead, that of the Holy Spirit, and the seven penitential Psalms with

Prayers. In due course he would recite the rosary. He would busy himself with these holy exercises until it was time for dinner, his meal being brought to him after the other monks had dined.

Hurrying out soon from the dining room, he would go back to the oratory to give thanks to God. If some monk wanted to talk with him, Joseph would listen voluntarily and then went to his room to rest. He would then return to the oratory to continue his prayers, ending by reciting the Ave Maria unless prevented by some monk who might come to him out of spiritual need. At the Ave Maria, his companion used to light a lamp, it being the custom to read spiritual books, including Holy Scripture, until almost the third hour of the night.

Around the third hour, a meal would be brought to Joseph. Upon finishing it, he would return to the oratory where sometimes other monks would approach him to discuss matters of the spirit, or to sing songs in praise of God. It would last about an hour and a half, and he would then remain in the oratory by himself until midnight. At that time he would begin the Matins, and when he finished he would rest until daylight. Such was his daily and nightly activity, which he always followed until his final infirmity, unless some indisposition or sickness prevented him.

Similarly stated, his physical life was as follows. He would eat nothing but Lenten food throughout the year. In eating and drinking, his manner was sober and moderate, and if the necessity for life hadn't required it, he would have abstained entirely. In his dress, in place of a shirt he used an undergarment of light wool made in Assisi. In winter he wore a cloak. He slept dressed in the same clothes, half seated half lying down on three planks, with a small pillow covered with cloth under his head, and a worn bearskin under his waist.

There were two rooms where he usually lived, and there he was kept apart from others for the whole time he lived in Osimo. One room was an oratory, and the other was for rest. Only the most esteemed and wise monks were permitted access to his cell at pre-set times to discuss matters of God and to hear them discussed. But they soon discovered other divine gifts with which the Blessed One was enriched, and they were amazed by them, and they kept these great things in their hearts. They would go frequently to him seeking his prayers for those who had requested them, and he used to answer, *I will send them forth, but it's up to God to give grace. God understands all sorts of speech, so have them talk more with God, and they will be heard more than I.*

And if a specific person were named, or a specific need described, he could speak of it very specifically as if he knew everyone - the nobility, the citizens and common people of Osimo. He knew who their relatives were, their professions, and even the places and the streets where their homes were situated, as well as the straits in which they found themselves. And he also spoke of the city as if he had within himself a book of genealogy and could read everybody's situation.

Yet he had never seen the city, or heard it named, because he had been taken there from Fossombrone in greatest secrecy. So anyone who would hear him recount these things truly had reason to open his eyes wide in wonder, more so because Joseph never went out, neither from the monastery nor even from the rooms assigned to him except when ordered. Despite this, his blessed retreat was so pleasing to him that he used to say, *I am inside a city but I seem to be in a forest or rather a paradise.*

On one occasion it happened by accident that his companion did not bring him his usual meal, but Joseph so esteemed the commands of his superiors that he did not complain or leave his cell because of it, and remained fasting for two days. In fact, talking about it later, he used to thank God, having received from Him that which men had always denied him.

But if any of his Brother Monks were sick, then under orders he would go out to him. And in the same way he went out once to see the church, but with its doors closed and with great secrecy to avoid any secular disorder.

The Devil, envious of Joseph's solitary life and even more of his sanctity, often tried to afflict him with his horrible visits. Thus, displaying himself frequently, either in threatening human aspect or as a wild beast, terrible and fierce, he would pull at him with a thousand offences. But Joseph, strong and enduring, recognized in him a divine intent and struggled with man's greatest enemy by means of constant prayer. Suddenly hearing the sound of chains, cries, and shrieks, some of the monks barred the door of his very cell, others ran from the dormitory, and some almost swooned with fright. That morning when the Blessed One was asked the reason for such a strange din, he was unable to deny it but not wanting to tell a lie said in a composed manner, *it was a joke, and he fell silent.* Asked again if in such a solitary retreat he was ever tempted by the Devil, he answered, *he does not tempt me and he leaves me be, for even though he appears before my eyes with horns that are this long* (he would indicate the length of his arm) *I don't fear him nor am I afraid of what he does because I am always with God, withdrawn from the world.*

Although God was pleased to hide the person of such a good servant, it was not pleasing to Him however to see idle the ability to work miracles which he had given Joseph. A horrible sudden storm rose up in the neighborhood, and two whirlwinds opposite each other threatened to ruin the countryside with large hail and wind, and threatened the destruction of the farms. Every part of the sky had darkened, the wind, was blowing terrifyingly, and the devastating storm was beginning to descend. All the monks of the monastery ran frightened to Joseph's cell. Upon seeing them he said, *don't doubt, have faith,* and facing the window with a cross in hand, he commanded the storm to leave, saying, *go with God, go with God.* In an instant the air became calm again, and the hearts of the monks and of the people were gladdened.

A young man of Osimo, tempted by impurity, and perhaps with a propensity for it, girded his loins with a cordon of the Blessed One, which had been given to him secretly by his confessor, and was immediately cured of that plague, living thereafter in perfect chastity. Camilla Simonetti, wife of Agostino Diotiaiuti, a noble woman of Osimo, was for thirty hours in the agony of a difficult childbirth. Commended to Joseph's prayers by a monk of the monastery, Joseph raised his eyes to heaven and said, *go, for in a quarter of an hour she will give birth*. And so it happened.

When the Blessed one prayed for Olimpia Calvi she was cured of a black dental abscess and an evil fever, and although she usually suffered mortal pain in childbirth to the despair of physicians, she happily gave birth to a little girl just as Joseph had predicted. Scipione Costico, upon touching a handkerchief that was wet with Joseph's blood, was healed of an excessive headache and an evil fever. Captain Stephen Blasii was freed of a fatal sickness through Joseph's intercession. His wife Benedetta Cimarella was instantly cured of a bloody flux when she touched an image of the baby Jesus that was brought to her from the rooms of the Servant of God.

Fifty-six miracles done in Joseph's presence, or by him at a distance, are recorded in a separate catalog in the beatification file, besides the great number described so far. As to those not mentioned among so many, we will say that Joseph's life was, by his virtue, a miracle of sanctity itself, so that ongoing miracles were in themselves a continuous miracle.

Adding to the fame of the miracles were Joseph's prophecies that went on until shortly before his death. Father-Master Roncagli of Mondaino, who loved Joseph a great deal, came to his cell, and Joseph suddenly said to him that he knew everything Roncagli had endured on some of his travels, how much he commended himself to Joseph during some of his tribulations, and other such facts as if Roncagli had narrated them himself.

Father-Master Sylvester Evangelisto of Osimo, while in discussion with Joseph in his cell, was called to the confessional. The Blessed One said to him, *go and kill the scorpion*. He duly went and confessed a young man who, after much obfuscation and with encouragement by the confessor, admitted a sin that, for reasons of shame, he hadn't disclosed in an earlier confession, whereupon the confessor saw issuing from the penitent a scorpion that shortly afterwards disappeared. When the Monk recounted the matter to Joseph the same day, Joseph with his hands and with a laugh applauded the verification of his prophecy.

A young innocent female peasant, mortally wounded by a shot from a firearm when she passed between two quarreling young men, was commended to the Blessed One's prayers. Without hesitation he said twice, *she will not die*, and she did not die even though the shot was certainly a mortal one.

Joseph fervently asked Brother Clement, a layman of the Monastery at Osimo, to pray for him on a pilgrimage that Clement was making to Assisi. Although Clement promised to do it, he forgot and didn't keep his word. Upon his return Joseph said to him, *oh how you prayed well for the old man* (meaning Clement himself) *but you never remembered me*. Friar Clement was struck dumb by such a knowledge of his failure.

Monsignor Antonio Bichi departed from Osimo, and it became known through the city that he had gone to visit Saint Nicholas of Tolentino. When told of this, the Blessed One immediately answered, *eh, be quiet for he has gone to Rome to take the red Hat*. And in fact he went to Rome where, on November 10 of the year 1659, he was proclaimed a Cardinal, having been secretly known as such in the Pope's breast since 1657. Joseph made a similar prediction about Father-Master Lorenzo Brancati di Lauria of his Order. When it was said that he was going to be a Cardinal, the Servant of God answered, *have patience, he will become one, but not now*, and he did become one, but only later during the Pontificate of Innocent XI.

From these predictions of Joseph's, one can see that he dealt familiarly with God, face to face, as another Moses on the mountain, as his amazing raptures so greatly confirm. He was tenderly devoted to the Mystery of the Nativity of our Lord, and as a result he delighted in the figure of the Baby Jesus which gave expression to his most inner feelings, and he honored it with the most partial devotion. So it was no wonder that in Osimo, Jesus Christ appeared to him frequently in the guise of a child, and Joseph would place Him in his arms, caressing Him, and talking to Him with the fiery feelings of that heavenly love which gives peace to saintly souls.

Frequently, in the solemnity of Holy Christmas, Joseph would lay out a little crib, or rather a nativity scene, in his oratory in imitation of his Seraphic Holy Father who had originated it. Joseph would then invite the monastery's masters, monks and novices to a celebration. There he was the first to arouse everyone to holy delight, playing a rustic shepherd's flute, and singing his usual little songs with bright fervor during which he would suddenly fall kneeling onto the ground, and would go into ecstasy. Coming back to himself, and no longer in humble confusion he would send everyone away, begging them *to make allowances for his daze and stupefaction*

He once asked to be lent a wax image of the Baby Jesus, and Father-Master Sylvester Evangelista brought it to him. With absolute tenderness, Joseph received it in his hands, hugging it to his breast, and with increasing fervor in his heart he began to squeeze it with such strength that it would have broken into pieces even if it had been made of wood. Warned of this by the above-mentioned monk, he turned to him, *ah little faith, will you also sing with me?* And during the singing of his usual songs he went with that holy figure in hand turning for a long while ecstatically throughout his cell, with the gestures of singing and with motion of body. Then he gave the figure to the Father-Master so he could put it in a little basket on the altar of his oratory, but as soon as Joseph saw the Holy Child in its designated spot, he immediately leapt from a low bench where he was sitting, went into flight three paces towards the altar, and with sudden force pressed his face onto that holy figure which remained intact even though made of wax.

Upon being visited by the Bishop, Cardinal Bichi, and asked about something spiritual, his answer was to rise up quickly from his chair and to kneel on the ground with open arms and eyes in such a deep ecstasy that a fly walked for considerable time over the pupil of his eye, but Joseph was so removed from his senses that he didn't move his eyelid. His raptures were continuous and we can say that he lived more in ecstasy than in this world.

He was found once in the Chapel beneath his rooms so unconscious and heavy that it took the effort of many arms to carry him like a dead man to his cell. He stayed that way as long as the flood of divinity kept his heart submerged. Upon being visited again by the afore-mentioned Cardinal Bichi, the Blessed One talked about the heavenly court, comparing it to a court of earthly princes. He then uttered a loud scream and threw himself impetuously from his chair onto the ground on his knees. He remained there immobile for a quarter of an hour, and this time again when a fly walked on the pupil of an eye that was open towards heaven Joseph made no movement, completely distracted and absorbed in the joy of the celestial court. When Joseph returned to his senses, the Cardinal asked him, *what accident had befallen and what had happened to him.* Joseph answered with a great sigh that *the greatness of heavenly things, and the miserable baseness of human things had been the reason for his stupefaction.*

sixteen

Illness and death of the Blessed Joseph of Copertino.

Our Blessed One carried out his life of most austere penitence up to his sixtieth year, always in distress from serious and considerable illnesses. With a weakened stomach, bloody urine, sudden bloody vomiting, sometimes the result of rich food eaten under orders, a long seven-year abstinence without bread, and ten years without wine, a full Lenten period without nourishment except for a few nuts, barely able to open his mouth, defective as it was with dryness, sleeping badly at night and worse if he tried by day, with his youth passed with penitential austerities already described, Joseph was so reduced in body, so separated from the world, that nothing was lacking for his beautiful soul to turn to heaven except to be called by God.

And called he was by his Lord, with that voice that usually summons his most beloved servants, that is with a revelation as to the time and hour of the happy transit, a grace desired by many but attained by few. Our Blessed One received it, and it was so precise that one can't tell if death met him or if he met death. When he had set foot in his Monastery of Osimo, he turned to heaven and, with serene countenance and folded hands, said, *haec requies mia*, (here is my rest), and upon stepping forward affirmed that *he had to die there* adding, *if I'm not the first from Copertino who dies here, I'll certainly be the second.* And the prophecy came true; for a few months before his own death, another monk from Copertino died there.

Father Sylvester Evangelista arrived there together with Joseph, and the survivor of the two was to assist at the death of the other. The superiors had meanwhile assigned the former to other monasteries, but after two years he returned to Osimo and heard Joseph say to him, *you did well to come to Osimo, for the time draws near to carry out the promise and to commend my soul to God,* as in fact happened five months later.

During the time for recreation Joseph, with joyful expression, said to the monks, *you know, oh fathers, that on that day that I won't be able to receive the little lamb,* by which he meant the Holy Sacrament, *I will then pass to a better life.* It was a prediction confirmed by facts, because during his infirmity he either celebrated Holy Mass every morning or else was a communicant, but only on the last day of his life, for the violence of his pain, was he unable to receive the Sacramental Jesus.

With such beacons from heaven, he thus detached himself from the earth so that he reduced himself voluntarily to such poverty that he had neither food nor clothing, except for the tunic that Cardinal Bichi, Bishop of that City, wanted to replace with a new one. Joseph didn't seem the same, but with joyful countenance and merry words, all fired by the love of God, he bore the manner of a victor who, already in possession of the enemy's spoils, wants nothing more in his heart than the sole delight of his triumph, rejoicing in that immense good which he hoped to gain shortly.

So, on August 10, 1663, Joseph was attacked by fever that was at first intermittent but became continuous. It degenerated into a fatal sickness, forcing Joseph to abandon his poor little cot where, with glad heart under the authority of his superiors, he entrusted his body like a bag of bones to treatment by physicians, but otherwise perfectly resigned to the divine will. There were those who went to him many times when he was in that condition to urge him to ask the Lord for a return to health. But, although Joseph had obtained such grace for many others, he would always answer, *oh then, oh then, look, look.* Such were his feelings, such were his words, full of love for God, and full of charity for his neighbor.

As his sickness progressed, his love grew. No other voices were heard from him but *oh love! oh love!* and in offering it he would put both hands on his breast, as if he wanted to open it to release a fire that consumed him. To those with him he would occasionally say, *pray to God for the Supreme Pontiff, for the Lord Cardinals, for the union of Christian princes, for all the religious Orders, and for their leaders, and especially for our Order of Saint Francis, for the souls in purgatory, for the sick and distressed, and for those who pray for us.*

The intermittent fevers lasted five days, and during that time he never missed celebrating Holy Mass in his oratory, during which he was always marked by the Lord with those ecstasies and those extraordinary communications in which Joseph partook throughout his priesthood. The most marked, however, was experienced in his last Mass which he celebrated on the day of the Assumption of the Virgin Mary, whom he always held as his dear mother. The files of the process of beatification attest that *he had marvelous ecstasies and raptures, and even his body was raised into the air.*

But as his illness became so bad that he couldn't get on his feet any more, Joseph begged for and was given permission to attend Holy Mass every morning as a communicant. Upon being presented the sacred host he would exclaim, *behold the joy, behold the joy,* and, as if he were no longer ill, the color would return to his face and brightness to his eyes which he would then hold shut after receiving the Jesus Sacrament, and he would then pale as if he had fainted or was dead.

Yet, the more his flesh weakened, the stronger became the vigor of his spirit, and the Lord cheered him with the flow of his gifts. So up until his death, his prophesies continued, as well as his insight into people's hearts.

To the surgeon who was attending him he said, *think better of it; remember where you were on that day and at that hour,* and thus aroused in him such a great spiritual need that he went right away to confess himself. To a nun, afflicted by the news that her father had been jailed in Urbino by order of the Legate, Cardinal Bichi, Joseph said, *eh, be quiet; it's not true, for your father is in the good graces of the Cardinal just as the old man* (meaning himself) *is in good spiritual health!* And so it was, as confirmed in a letter which followed.

To the Vicar-General of the Bishop of Osimo, who came to him one evening after overcoming the objections of his mother who didn't want him to leave home, Joseph said, *vicar, go back home because your little old woman is waiting for you.* And when asked how he knew this, he repeated smiling, *go back home because your little old woman is waiting for you.*

Similarly, he foresaw that the priest Don Carlo Facchio had prepared a small basket of plums to send him which had been suggested in order to overcome Joseph's lack of appetite. Joseph sent the surgeon to seek them, saying, *go to the priest at the gate and you'll find the plums.* The surgeon went and couldn't find them because the priest was not at home, nor had he said anything about plums. Joseph made the surgeon go back to search the cellar better, where he found them on a barrel.

So as not to make the account of these predictions overly long, we'll conclude with the words of Father Giovanni Donato, nephew of our Blessed One, spoken to the Archdeacon of the Cathedral of Osimo, Pier Filippo Florenzi, and to the priest just mentioned, when discussing the virtues of Joseph. The words were, k*now that my uncle is aware full well of everything that happens in this city because the Lord God manifests everything to him.*

Meanwhile, it was not possible to do more to keep Joseph alive. One has to hear from the surgeon who opened his vein and also cauterized him, who said, *during his last illness, while cauterizing the right leg by order of and in the presence of the physician, Signor Giacinto Carosi, I noticed as I carried out the operation that while Joseph was sitting with the leg lying on my knee he was in fact separated from his senses, with his arms spread open and his eyes both open and raised towards heaven, and his mouth somewhat open without giving any sound of breathing; and I observed that he was raised almost a palm's height off the chair. I tried to lower the leg but it was not possible. I noticed further that a fly had settled on the center of the pupil of one eye, and the more I slapped it away the more it returned, so that finally I let it be.*

That ecstasy lasted until Father Sylvester Evangelista arrived, who after seeing it, called to Joseph, requiring him per holy obedience to return to himself. Joseph did so immediately with a smile and placing himself down on his seat, told the surgeon to perform the cauterization. But it had already been done, and when Joseph saw his leg bandaged, he said, *I didn't feel a thing.*

The same surgeon also saw Joseph in ecstasy during three bloodlettings that he performed, during which God showed through His miracles His delight in His faithful servant's affection by healing him and sparing him the pain of the cutting and the fire that, by necessity, accompanies such operations.

Twice again the above-mentioned surgeon, during this last illness, saw the Blessed One in ecstasy in his little chapel where he was hearing Mass, and it happened in the following way: b*eing on his knees at the foot of the little Chapel, unable to celebrate Mass because of his infirmity, Father Joseph gave a great shout which terrorized me. Just as the priest was in the act of raising the holy host, I saw Joseph spread out on the ground in middle of the little church but with his face uplifted and his arms equally spread, detached in fact from his senses; after the elevation of the host, I and Brother Bernardino, a layman who served the Mass, raised him from the ground and put him back in his place.* Thus said the surgeon Francesco dei Pierpaoli, who added, *whatever fear that Joseph's ecstasies caused at first, particularly from his shouts, they nonetheless rendered great consolation, contrition and devotion among those who watched him.*

But since the medical operations ended up being useless, the Blessed One was reduced to the extreme of his mortal life. During the course of his illness he said, *the little ass is beginning to climb the mountain,* and as the illness became more pronounced, *the little ass has arrived halfway up.* When it was recognized that he was about to die, between smiling and suffering Joseph said, *the little ass has arrived at the top of the mountain, can't move any more, and is about to leave his skin.*

Joseph wanted communion by Viaticum, and it was done on September 17. As the sacred host was being brought from the Church, and the monks were walking to the rooms of the sick man, he no sooner heard the bell that always rings whenever the Viaticum is being carried, that he was all invigorated by its sound and lit up by divine love. He leapt from the bed and in a marvelous rapture betook himself in flight through his rooms to the little door at the top of the stairs, where he knelt and received the sacrament of divine love. At that moment his countenance was filled with superhuman splendor, to the affection and admiration of the Episcopal Vicar and others present who thought they saw in him a heavenly seraphim.

Having received the bread of the angels, Joseph fell into mortal weakness, and was carried to his poor bed, saying as he went, *cupio dissolvi, & esse cum Christo* (I want to dissolve and be with Christ). Upon being told, *now is the time to fight*, he replied *victory, victory.* To those who reminded him of paradise, he said irritably, *I certainly don't want to go to hell because God isn't praised there.* He asked next for the holy Extreme Unction, and when it was being administered he said with a sonorous voice, overcoming the extreme weakness of his beaten strength, *oh what songs, oh what sounds of paradise, oh what fragrances, oh what odors, oh what sweetness of paradise.* Then he had them read the profession of faith to him. He asked for forgiveness for all his defects, and begged the Monsignor Vicar and his superior to bury his body after his death without solemnity in some hidden spot, so that it would never be known that Brother Joseph of Copertino had been in the world.

Upon learning from the Vicar-General that the Holy Father had sent him a blessing, he greatly marveled that the Vicar of Jesus Christ would bestow such grace on such a worm of the earth and on the most lowly of his Order. *This,* he said, *is not a blessing to be received in bed.* Agonizing as it was, he betook himself with the help of others to his oratory where the litany of the Blessed Virgin was recited devotedly. Then, on his knees and with great piety he received the blessing from the Vicar.

After this was done, he returned to his bed where he always lay dressed in time of illness as he usually did in time of health, with his eyes turned towards heaven, and he quietly readied himself for the great passing. He appeared to be in pain for some reason or other, and the often remembered Father Sylvester Evangelista, his confidant, foreseeing the reason for his saintly agitation, drew near to his ear and said, *Father Joseph, perhaps this is the effect of the love of God.* Joseph replied *oh you understand.* And turning to the crucifix said, *Take this heart, Jesus, burn it and split it.*

Upon the affectionate recitation of the prayers of some saints, and upon hearing mention of the love of God, Joseph begged with labored voice that such words be repeated, and when saying it he pressed his fingers on the left side of his breast, wanting his heart to speak where the tongue was failing. Nevertheless, one could hear the name of Jesus stammered from his lips, as well as these halting words from his stammering tongue, *may God be praised, may God be thanked, may the will of God be done.*

He also fulfilled his promise to Father Sylvester Evangelista that he wanted to find himself at the point of death, saying to him, *yes, I do want to find myself there, mercy, mercy.* He was so happy when a fellow monk who was present recited to him the Hymn *Ave maris stella* in the common language, that Joseph burst forth in his usual short prayer:

Salve Regina
Rosa senza spina
Figlia d'Amore
Madre del Signore
Prega per me,
Che io non muoia peccatore

(Hail oh Queen
A Rose without a thorn
Daughter of Love
Mother of the Lord

*Pray for me
That I not die a sinner.)*

Finally, upon arriving at the evening of the eighteenth day of September of the year 1663, at five and three-quarter hours of the night, not having been able on that day to receive the Sacramental Jesus because of the seriousness of his infirmity, Joseph gave up his soul to his Creator as he had predicted, with a placid smile that cheered all those around him, with a happy and serene countenance, resplendent with a sudden light, at the age of 60 years and three months, in the monastery of the Minor Conventual Order of Saint Francis at Osimo where he had stayed for six years, two month, and eight days.

The Blessed Joseph was tall and well put together, big boned and sinewy, vigorous, able, and well fitted to endure great but not the greatest suffering, which he took upon himself with the most rigorous penitence, with whippings and fasts, the greatest of which were in his youth. His countenance was bright but, because of the elevation of his mind, was mostly serious and majestic.

He had a full beard, thick around his chin, which was blackish in his youth but in advanced age became more sparse and white all over. He had lively eyes, black as his hair, but because of the habit of ecstasies they were always turned gracefully towards heaven. The whole carriage of his body was so attractive that in its activities it evoked the spirit of God, all humility, simplicity, and gentleness.

In his speech he was affable, cheerful, and in his words he imparted a distinct and natural charm to the rough speech of his native town which he always kept in his mouth until his death.

seventeen

His Burial; the flocking of the public to his Sepulcher.

If in life our distinguished Blessed One brought wonder through Europe, no less was the fame of his death that went out to nearby and far-off peoples, accompanied as it was by the concern of Popes, the distress of Cardinals, the gathering of the people, and the glory of miracles.

News of his serious illness having arrived earlier, Cardinal Chigi, under orders from the Supreme Pontiff, wrote Monsignor Antioco Onofri, the Vicar-General of Osimo on September 22 that *if the Father Joseph of Copertino were to be called by God to the other life, the Vicar-General should see to it that his body be put into a casket (even though that was unusual) and that he be buried in a sepulcher that, in the Vicar-General's judgment, might be most appropriate.* But the Vicar and the superiors and fathers of the Monastery of Saint Francis had already foreseen the orders from Rome with praiseworthy efficiency.

Following the death of the Blessed One, after it was made known to the public by proclamation, his body was opened and embalmed with spices and aromatic herbs. In so doing the surgeon not only found the pericardium shriveled but also the ventricles of the heart without blood, being actually arid, and the heart itself dried up not from the natural heat of fever but, attributed by the surgeon who knew from long experience, to the supernatural flame of divine love

Upon washing the body with strong spirits, the sheet that was under it caught fire, one doesn't know how, and as it flared up it seemed to spread hotly over Joseph's face, so the hearts of those around it beat most strongly in fear of seeing it all deformed. But when the fire was extinguished the face appeared again intact and whole, and not one hair on his head or chin was seen to be burned, to the great joy and wonderment of those present.

To avoid turmoil among the people, Joseph's body was not displayed in the Church but in the sacristy instead, with a wooden fence around it. Four Canon-Priests, eight noblemen, and eight monks of that monastery were deputized to oversee it. This protection was very necessary because of the innumerable throng that came from nearby and outlying areas, for whom it was never possible to see Joseph alive but who now came to see him dead. In those six years, two months, and eight days that the Blessed One was in Osimo, his withdrawal from life was so great, as was the obedience of his fellow monks to the pontifical instructions, that nobody knew for certain of his stay in that monastery regardless of the continuing rumors that he lived there, so now those who venerated his holiness desired to see the person.

Ambassador Cesareo, on his way to Rome had passed deliberately through Osimo and had made strong and urgent requests to see Joseph and to speak with him, but he did it in vain. Princes and knights from here and there and from beyond the Alps, made the same trip, but they also did it in vain so that one of them, a member of the Visconti family of Milan, to whom the Guardian denied that Joseph was residing in that Monastery, replied *that is what they said you would say*. Some Frenchmen also went there and said, *where is Father Brother Joseph, who is spoken of in France as another Saint Francis?* But even they were not lucky enough to see him.

That barrier now being broken with his death, and the prohibition being ended, a single cry ran through the city, then through the outlying areas, then throughout all of Italy, and then through the whole of Europe, *that the Holy Priest is dead who used to be in the Monastery of Saint*

Francis in Osimo. But so great was the flow of those who gathered, that the houses, the nearby districts, and outlying lands were depopulated in order that those who hadn't the good fortune to see Father Joseph of Copertino alive could now at least gaze at him dead. The rush of countrymen and outsiders grew like a torrent, so in order to satisfy the devotion of each one, permission was given for everyone to enter the sacristy up to the third hour of the night, allowing the most worthy of them to kiss Joseph's hands and feet.

On the following day, when the funeral rites were ended in the presence of the chapter, the clergy, and all the orders, public devotions were permitted until about the fifth hour of the night. Then the cadaver was laid to rest in a wooden casket in order to inter it the following morning. But that decision was prevented by a new throng of people. What followed was a rare case when the casket was reopened and brought back into the sight of those who would have no peace if it had been taken from them. It was then displayed again in the same place with the same guards until such a time that, either with entreaties or with threats, the people were pushed out of the church. The Holy Body was placed in a casket of cypress, which was placed into another casket of oak, and brought to his Church of Saint Francis, where it was buried in front of the Altar of the Immaculate Conception in a newly-dug sepulcher.

Our worthy Blessed One was thus buried, with a noble and numerous throng of people showing clear signs of reverence, devotion and esteem. And that good God, who renders glorious the sepulchers of his beloved faithful servants, wanted to glorify Joseph's Sepulcher on that same day of his funeral with a clear and splendid miracle.

For five or six years, Vittorio Mattei of Osimo bore on the edge of his right knee a cystic tumor that is commonly called "*natta*" that had recently grown to the enormous size of a large loaf of bread. He was distressed by such an uncomfortable annoyance and also endured hard pain in that knee, particularly when walking or kneeling. Nevertheless he never searched for cures to get rid of it and to free himself. When the pain became a lot fiercer and unbearable in the final stage of the infirmity, and the tumor had become a total impediment to his movements and to the bending of his knee, the afflicted Vittorio called the surgeon to attend him, who upon seeing that the tumor had aged and hardened, stated that it couldn't be operated on without mortal danger, and that it would be better not to touch it in any way.

With indomitable patience, Vittorio continued to endure his tormenting and incurable disorder until moved by the clear knowledge of the holiness of the Blessed Joseph of Copertino, who had flown to heaven but was not yet buried, he entertained the firm hope of being freed by God with the powerful intercession of this his great servant. So, even though in deep pain, Vittorio courageously betook himself to the Church of Saint Francis, going through the devoted crowd of people to visit the sacristy where the cadaver of the Blessed One was displayed. From there he went to Joseph's room and carefully placed himself on his little cot, and finally betook himself to the chapel where Joseph usually celebrated the Holy Mass when he was alive. The bystanders showed Vittorio the imprints of the knees of the Blessed One on the dais in front of the altar where Joseph had long prayed. There, moved and comforted by his living faith, Vittorio forced himself to bend the afflicted knee. He had barely touched those sacred vestiges than all his pain ceased immediately, and the persistent deformity immediately disappeared without leaving any sign of it on the knee, leaving Vittorio healed just as if he had never had such a nasty affliction.

Vittorio's son followed his father, whose knee had been instantly healed, and was himself miraculously healed by our Blessed One in a more delicate part of the body. The son, named Stephen, who was later a Monk of the Minor Conventual Order with the name Anton Maria, was at that time a youngster twelve or thirteen years old. On November 2, 1663, that is to say a month and a half after Joseph's death, while playing with someone the same age who was throwing stones at him from afar, suddenly felt the center of his right eye struck hard by a sharp splinter of stone, and was so hurt that he was left completely blind in that eye. Since the outer membrane, the cornea and the inner membrane were lacerated, and parts of the pupil destroyed, not only did watery fluid pour out mixed with blood, but when he was brought home and placed in bed, the eye dripped that night as seen the following morning in the wet sheets. The physician and the surgeon were called and both knew the loss was irreparable, and all that could be done was to prevent inflammation, and ensure that the eye be as little deformed and sunken as possible. After ten or twelve days of useless treatment for this misfortune, the parents urged their son to commend himself to the Blessed Joseph, whose image was hanging at his bed. The youngster did it with sincere faith, and his mother, Lucia Fortunati, begged him to place on the useless and blind eye a piece of the Blessed One's tunic, hoping that through his intercession, the eye and his sight would recover.

With sincere faith he betook himself with his good mother to the tomb of the heavenly intercessor, and with more fervent prayers, applying again the above portion of the Blessed One's tunic to the eye, he begged sincerely for his recovery. He reverently leaned the damaged part of his body on the tombstone, and while there he immediately experienced in himself a divine beneficent hand. From that cold stone beneath where the mortal remains of the Servant of God rested, a supreme goodness emerged, and in an instant not only was the sunken eye filled with fluid, but the membranes were fixed, the whole eyeball completely re-formed, and suddenly clear and perfect vision returned as it was before the savage blow, leaving only a simple scar to marvel at. Full of joy and gladness, the son and the mother rendered humble thanks to their distinguished benefactor, and upon returning home, their relatives and neighbors rejoiced and joined in venerating the greatness of the miracle, by which the eye was not only bright and clear but regenerated and remade.

As son and mother are so closely related, one cannot omit the mother of the afore-mentioned Stefano Mattei, who was also favored by our Blessed One. This woman, named Lucia Fortunati, as we have said, was on her way to the Festival of Remission at Assisi and lost her bundle of linen and wool cloth. Upon realizing the loss, she went back three miles in search of it but without success. So kneeling with sincere faith she said *that since the Blessed Joseph had made her son recover his vision, she was hoping that he would recover her bundle for her,* and she continued on her journey. As it happened, upon returning she arrived at the windmill of Macerata where she had noticed her loss, and spoke of it in a loud voice with those of her party. There was a poor little peasant ahead of her who told her that he found the bundle, and he gave it back to her. *From that incident,* the woman's deposition concluded, *I was left full of amazement considering that I found the lost clothing after many days on a road that was frequented so much at the time of the festival.* Therefore, remembering the favor of the Blessed One, we add this to the listed favors, as a crown of our immortal debt to him.

In the chapters that will conclude the second part of this book, we will mention many miracles wrought by God through the intercession of the Blessed Joseph at his sepulcher and in many parts of the world, even though we can't mention all of them because it would take too long. Chapter XII, the last chapter of Part II, will list twenty-two splendid instances that are no longer crying out to be known, since we have the great fortune to have beneath our eyes the original authentic depositions which we have portrayed with complete fidelity.

Meanwhile may we give praise and glory to God, who authors and bestows all that is good, and may we praise the Supreme Shepherd of the Universal Church, Benedict XIV, from whose revelation we are assured of the eternal happiness of Joseph among the Blessed of Heaven. So we place under his infallible judgment what we have said so far, and what we are about to say in the second part of this book.

End of Part One

THE LIFE OF THE B. JOSEPH OF COPERTINO

SECOND PART

one

Of his great love towards God.

He who doesn't know God is surely blind, and he is surely without heart who doesn't love Him upon looking at and considering those appreciable things that He created by which He provided to everyone a magnificent testimony of His virtue and His ineffable goodness

But, oh, how much more sublime, how much more lovable does it all appear to one who, on the wings of faith and animated by God's divine charity, rises to contemplate Him. By these two heavenly virtues Joseph was exalted to know the immense greatness of God and to contemplate His lofty worth and infinite beauty. It rendered Joseph so in love with God, and so softened by that superb and tender love, that when we closely examine everything Joseph did, we well understand that he could have neither heart, nor mind, nor spirit, nor strength for anyone else than for God alone.

For that reason, so engrossed was he in the flame of divine love, that he felt himself taken up in a swoon whenever he heard God named, not only in his cell or in the monastery, but also on public roads where, intoxicated by divine charity, he went about shouting, *oh, love! oh love!* and very frequently would repeat *he who feels charity is rich but doesn't know it.* To weaken the flames of these fires that burned in his heart, Joseph used to sing devout little songs. Among these was one to his personal intercessor, Saint Catherine of Siena. Upon arriving at the words:

E dal Celeste Amore
E sue man fu ferite
i piedi, e il cuore

(And from Heavenly Love
His hands were wounded,
and his feet, and his heart).

Joseph would break out in a flood of tears, shaking all over as if he wanted to rip open not only his clothing but his very flesh, and he would say, *open this breast of mine, split my heart,* and turning to the crucifix he would repeat with the Apostle, *cupio dissolvi & esse cum Christo* (I want to dissolve and be with Christ). So, with various gestures, as when one is suddenly and greatly agitated, he would sing, weeping,

Gesu', Gesu' Gesu',
Deh tirami lassu'
Non posso star qua giu'
Deh tirami lassu', dove sei tu
Gesu', Gesu, Gesu.

(Jesus, Jesus, Jesus,
Come, pull me up there,
I can't stay down here;
Come, pull me up there, with you
Jesus, Jesus, Jesus).

Even though the affection of Joseph's heart towards God was continuous and never interrupted, nevertheless great things appeared to him during those mysteries which the church in its solemnity conveys regarding Jesus Christ. It was amazing to see Joseph exult during the days of the Holy Nativity, along with the shepherds and with the angels, inviting everyone near the crib of the Holy Child to sing along with him the simple little song that he had composed:

O felice Capannella
Dove sta la Verginella
E Gesu nella cestella
O felice Capannella.

(Oh happy Little Shelter
Where stays the Little Virgin
And Jesus in the Little Basket
Oh happy Little Shelter).

When Lent came, Joseph's withdrawal was so great that it was understandable that he called it an abandonment. During Holy Week, by virtue of his great love towards God, Joseph used to weep and say to anyone he found in the dormitories, *don't you know, my son, that Jesus was scourged, and crucified, and died.* Likewise at other times, as if present at the passion of his Lord, he would shout, *behold Judas is coming; flee, Jesus.* And he would walk with halting steps, as if following his divine love who had been despised and betrayed, and he would exclaim sighing, a*h, the son of God interrogated by a man! Ah reckless Caiphas! Ah wretched Pilate!* And following his Lord hand in hand to Calvary, he would remain to the end nailed to the same cross by his great love.

During those loving ecstasies, he would console himself with his suffering Jesus, singing some verses with other monks, and his most beloved song was this one:

Son peggio de' Giudei
Mentre te crocifiggo e so chi sei.

(I am worse than the Jews
While I crucify you I know who you are).

On Holy Thursday, when the altar is divested of its covering, he would stay in the shadows for six or seven hours, all frozen as if dead on earth. On one occasion, when the evening of Good Friday came about, he was led to the Church to attend the Holy Sacrament on the occasion of the Burial, and he fell into a great swoon of love so that they had to carry him away lest he be seen by some secular people who were beating the door to come in. But passing through the narrow door of the gate in front of the greater altar, he slipped out of their arms so that it was necessary to drag him with great force along the ground into the chorus. Even though they pressed him on parts of his body, and called him by name more than once, he remained immobile without feeling. Brought into the monastery, and finally back to his senses, he began to weep. Asked why, he answered, d*on't you want me to weep if Jesus Christ is dead?*

Likewise on another evening during Holy week, he was found genuflecting on the ground with his head bent back in a posture that is naturally difficult for the human body, and his eyes were full of tears. Being a very cold season, he was brought up the stairs on someone's back as if he were a cadaver, and was placed on his little cot where he persisted as if dead for six continuous hours, so great was his pain caused by his love for his suffering God. But when Holy Saturday came, he would jump up and with the greatest happiness sing *hallelujah* which lasted two whole hours, and with the same abundance of spirit he used to celebrate the most holy Festivals of the Resurrection, of Pentecost, and of Christmas.

From such a great and keen love towards God, which nobody can attain or express if he loves only himself, it emerged *that even if he were to go to hell, even there he would love his creator, and would always hope for the high compassion of his God.* On other occasions, in talking to his Lord, he would say, *Lord I love you so much that if I thought that when you created me you had destined me for hell, I would still want to carry out all those acts of respect and servitude such as were never performed by the great saints in paradise, and if after having thus served you well, you were to send me wherever you desire, I would still be most content.*

One can see from what follows that Joseph's great charity was perfect, being of such sublime virtue that it excluded any fear. Here is a sense of the Blessed One's heart: *I don't serve God for fear of hell, no, no. I serve him only for Himself. I seek Him. I desire Him, and I want nothing more. If for my sins I were to lose Him, and if it would become necessary to send me to hell, I would like to be in a place in hell separate from others, so as not to hear Him being cursed and blasphemed, and in that separate place, with hell on top of me, I would still want to bless Him and praise Him.*

Endowed with such constant heroism in loving his God, there was for Joseph no other absolute prince than God, nor was there any other greatness than being able to arrive at God's love. For that reason, to Cardinals, to Sovereigns, and to anyone of high status who might betake himself to Joseph, he would say frankly in his speech and with fixed repetition, *you came to this world to serve God and to love God during these few passing days that you are alive, not to be a Cardinal or a Prince, about which nobody will ask you in the next life, but only if and how you loved your creator.*

In the case of someone who, instead of serving God and loving God, offended Him, Joseph would be so distressed that on one occasion he fell to the ground for that reason, and couldn't then get up without loud lamentations and with his disdain for living anymore in this world where one could not only be offensive but where such great goodness could be offended.

For that reason, completely burning with heavenly love, he used to seek to give blood for blood and life for life. When a desire was born in his heart to go on the most arduous missions among the non-believers in Africa and America, words sprang from him which said, *oh how voluntarily I would yet go to carry out the work of a missionary.* But then, turning one eye to heaven and the other to his own low condition, he would add humbly, *but it would be necessary for a learned priest to come with me so that he could preach and teach, and I'd be his companion, helping him and offering continuous prayers to receive martyrdom.*

His desire to shed all his blood for the love of his God often made him say, *for my part, I would choose to be deprived of the consolation of paradise if only to contemplate the great mysteries of God, and to give all my blood and my life for Him.* But then he understood from the Lord that he could be a martyr many times over by suppressing his own will, whereas by steel he would be doing it only once. So Joseph, from then on, replaced the sacrifice of death with his own mortification.

And understanding that in death he would benefit only himself but that alive he would benefit his Lord alone, bit by bit it awakened in him the knowledge of the incredible burning of those who offend God's ineffable clemency. It so deeply wounded his heart, that bitter tears flowed from his eyes and blood came out of his mouth. Equally great were his lamentations and his exclamations at any suspicion that God might be offended.

For that reason, whenever he heard of outbreaks of war among Christian princes he would break out in a sudden cry and would say, *oh God is placed aside in a corner and is made subordinate to a palm-width of land.* Also, upon seeing neglected church buildings, he would shout full of zeal, *if a prince were to come here, oh how it would be adorned, yet the King of Kings resides there. You put off reverence for God for the sake of reverence for a living creature. Oh, love where are you! Oh faith where are you!*

A strong desire rose up within Joseph to fly about the whole world to announce the greatness of God to all men, but he did not have wings of suitable size for such a flight, and he was closed up in his cell. So, instead, he invited senseless creatures one by one to bewail such evil and to love that God whom man dishonors so badly with words and with deeds. Many times again while in the garden, upon considering the teaching of the All-Powerful as seen in the little herbs and flowers, he would sigh and say, *oh love! oh God, unknown yet so visible! God offended, yet so worthy of love!*

To finally understand the quality of Joseph's love towards God, one example is sufficient to show his zeal for the honor of the divine. During a journey that he had to make, he found himself at an inn where he heard a coachman blaspheme God. Joseph rose, fired up with great fervor, but for a short while he kept himself from throwing himself upon the coachman to choke off the horrible blasphemy from his evil mouth. He might have even done it, if he had not a great horror against force and had not fainted to the ground, pierced through the heart by his understanding of the divine offense that had been intended.

What has been said so far is but a spark of that great fire which flared in the Blessed Joseph, and from whose effects one can understand the greatness of his love towards God.

two

Of the continuous praying of the Blessed Joseph.

Our Lord Jesus Christ teaches that it is always good to pray tirelessly, and his Apostle advises us to pray always without interruption. Those who do it with lively faith, firm hope, and burning charity have their minds raised to God and they direct everything to the greater glory of God, even when they act for the needs of the present life. Thus, S. Augustine, in explaining these divine and apostolic utterances said, i*n ipsa fide, spe & charitate continuato desiderio semper oramus* (we always pray in continuous desire for faith itself, and for hope and charity). (Epist. 121 c. 9 to 2).

When speaking of the prayers of our Blessed One, it can be said that they were continuous for faith itself. For even if the ecstasies that engrossed him with God did not always alienate his senses, his mind was always raised to God. Thus he stayed for a very long time in prayer, as averred by witnesses *who many times saw the vestiges and imprints of Joseph's knees on the dais of the altar and on the planks of his oratory*. And hence came Joseph's bursts of tears, and it happened *that sometimes when speaking to him, he didn't understand what was being said.*

Regarding this continuous elevation of Joseph's mind to God, Father-Master Antonio of S. Mauro, Provincial head of the Minor Conventual Order of S. Niccolo of Bari, gives an example. He attests that, having taken Joseph as a companion during his visit, more as an example to the people than for Joseph's services, he wanted to test Joseph's continuing meditation, so he said, *Father Joseph, if you could meet any woman you wish, which woman would that be? And Joseph replied, the Most Blessed Virgin. On another occasion he replied Saint Catherine, and on yet another occasion Saint Claire, depending on what was on his mind. The Father-Master asked Joseph, if he were to meet some old man or a young man, who would he want him to be? Joseph answered that the old man would be Saint Peter, and the young man Saint John. Upon being asked f he were to meet some monk, who would it be? And Joseph answered Saint Anthony, Saint James, etc. That is to say, every natural thing served Joseph as an approach to the supernatural.*

Through such steps, Joseph reached a union with God that was so intimate that Father Girolamo Rodriguez, a Portuguese of the Company of Jesus, a man distinguished in doctrine and in piety, departed Rome to talk with the Blessed One in Assisi. Having done so, he deposed the following oath, *that Brother Joseph was always in complete unity with God, and that his heart was much disposed to union with God, even more than dust which will flare up at any small glimmer of fire.*

Even when praying out loud, Joseph gave specific evidence of this wonderful union. When he recited the Office in the chorus enclosure, he would often weep abundantly with extraordinary sobs so that it became necessary for him to remove himself and go to his cell to give vent to his love through his tears, and when he returned he would begin to weep again. He was seen many times unable for the whole day to recite the canonical hours, and to have to postpone them to the evening, since God wanted him all day for Himself with tears in his eyes and his mind in heaven.

In experiencing these consolations, Joseph so savored prayers that he didn't know how to pass a moment without engaging in them, as was also said in Chapter XV. Knowing how much prayers were necessary for everyone, he instilled them in everyone with great urgency, particularly to anyone who begged for his own prayers. He would say to them, *do it yourselves and I will do it too, and in that way we will obtain the grace we request because God understands all languages, and wants to be prayed to.* To his fellow Monks he would say separately, *say your prayers, and when spiritual drought or distracting thoughts draw you from prayer, recite the Our Father out loud with care, and in this way you'll make an oral as well as a mental prayer.*

There was one person who Joseph knew was perhaps in need of prayer, and Joseph exhorted him with great seriousness to do it, but received the answer *that he was lazy and that in the morning he couldn't get out of bed at a good hour.* Joseph responded half playfully and half zealously, *I'll throw a stone at you and you'll get up.* And on the following morning for a long while the person felt such a strong urge to pray that he jumped out of bed with a lot of devotion, prayed, and went on forever rising at that hour to pray fervently.

To another person who was very slow to betake himself to prayer in the chorus enclosure because it was very far from his rooms, Joseph made his voice heard, saying, *to Matins, to Matins.* Others enjoyed hearing Joseph so much that another person, while at his meal, was moved to say, *praise to God and prayer,* and immediately with his mouth still full left the table in a great hurry saying, *let's go to praise our God in the oratory.* He remained with his fellow monks for a long time in prayer, forgetting his appetite and the requirements of nature. The Blessed One certainly had a strong and correct reason for those assiduous and untiring prayer of his, inasmuch as the sooner he turned to God, the sooner he was fulfilled. His prayer flew to heaven with an escort of the most beautiful qualities.

The order provided for Joseph, charity inflamed his desires, and faith gave undoubted witness of the highest power and infinite goodness of the Lord. And Joseph displayed the need for humility in total submission to the great Father of Mercies. And so it was that he never doubted. For that reason, one reads in the legal processes for his beatification, *that the prayers of Father Joseph were never empty, but whenever* he asked he always received something for the health of bodies and souls. *In fact, the people who entrusted themselves to him expected that at the moment he prayed for them they would receive the grace he requested.*

As confirmation, we will report a fact not touched upon elsewhere, even though it is no less resounding and actually more resounding than we have narrated in our account of his life. Giovanni Alcide Fabiani, wanting to betake himself from his native Assisi to Spello, wanted first to pass by the Blessed One as a gesture of courtesy, and asked Joseph if there was anything he could do for him from that place. Joseph paused for a while before giving an answer, and then said to him, *go by all means, and I'll pray God for you.* Alcide went to Spello to put an end to a lawsuit that he had with John Mannari regarding an inheritance of a thousand scudi that were given to Europa Corona, his first wife. Mannari saw that the case was going badly for him so he decided to take the life of the claimant. He placed himself in a trench with six assassins, and waited for Fabiani to pass on his return trip to Assisi. But throughout the wait along with his violent accomplices, all of whom were ready for the assassination, they saw everyone who passed along that road but were unable to see Alcide even though he did pass by on horseback in the company of three other people. The Lord wanted, through the prayer of the Blessed One, to render Alcide invisible, renewing the miracle done for Himself when the Hebrews took him to the peak of the mountain and wanted to throw him down, for which reason he was rendered invisible, *transiens per medium illorum ibat* (he passed through the midst of them).

This great event was told to Fabiani by one of the assassins, who became sick shortly afterwards and went to him in Assisi to be cured since Alcide was a surgeon. The assassin said to him, *some days ago I wanted to take your life, and now you would give me mine.* He then revealed Mannari's horrible plot in all its details. Fabiani's deposition ends, *that's how I remember the words of Father Joseph, who surely must have prayed to God on my behalf, and I would argue that it is because of his prayers that I was freed from the mentioned dangers, even though when he said those words to me I didn't reflect on them at all.*

Besides the foregoing, there are another fifty-six miracles recorded in Joseph's life, that God wrought continuously over time because of Joseph's prayers which were so pleasing in their quality and fervor, and which were offered with so much faith and humility, that they captured God's heart.

Joseph was the beloved, the dear one of the Most High. As soon as Joseph lifted his mind to Him, God was immediately ready to light it, to illuminate it, and pull it to Himself. At Joseph's first thought of devotion, feeling himself pulled by a power that was more than human, he would utter a cry and would fly with his soul to the embrace of his God. Following behind his soul, his body would fly as well, and sometimes he would also pull someone whose hand he was seizing, as will be told in the following chapter.

three

Of the ecstasies, and the wondrous raptures of the Blessed Joseph.

Ecstasy, as the Saints describe it, is an alienation of the senses in order to absorb the spirit of God. The rapture that happens after ecstasy is the elevation of the body that follows the flight of the soul. Both are effects of divine love. *Est exstasim faciens divinus amor* (divine love causes ecstasy). And thus the Areopagita, referred to by the Angelic Doctor, (2.2. q.175.a 1) says, *Love is the cause of rapture.*

But so many were the ecstasies and raptures of our Blessed One that we have to say that his love towards God was great to the extreme, always manifesting itself by the loud screams that he put forth whenever he was suddenly taken by the vehemence of his ecstasies or the force of his raptures. For that reason, as he himself said to everyone who sought him out, *he who lights gunpowder in the weapons of war feels the burst and the explosion in the surrounding air, and so the heart of the ecstatic sends forth a shout because it is lit by the love of God.* To tell the truth, his life was a continuous rapture of mind and body in God, and even if some of them are not described, others else are touched on in this story only in passing, yet we will here recount others to complete the narrative.

The first of the innumerable ecstasies and raptures that Joseph had throughout the full course of his life was as follows. Shortly after receiving the priesthood, his superiors sent him, wearing a long ecclesiastic coat, to attend a procession at the Feast of Saint Francis in the Church of the Madonna of the Grottela. As the procession began, Joseph reflected on the venerable habit that he was wearing and on the sacred activity that he was leading. When he emerged from the sacristy, he was first surprised by a brief ecstasy. It was followed immediately by a rapture, wherein he took to flight on his knees to the top of the pulpit of the church, which was fifteen hand-breadths high. Here he remained with arms outstretched, and in his heart he heard, *leave every thought of the world and serve me.* Upon recovering and returning to his senses, Joseph went to his mother's and carried out the expropriation of his shirt as described earlier in the story of his life.

The Blessed One wanted to erect three crosses on a tiny Hill on the road from Copertino to the Monastery of the Grottella to represent Calvary and commemorate the passion of Jesus Christ. He betook himself therefore to the shop of an artisan to encourage him in his work on the biggest of the crosses. But upon seeing the cross there and the nails and instruments of Jesus' pain, Joseph gave a very loud cry and rose in ecstasy, totally beside himself and engrossed in his God. The woodworker was so frightened that he dropped his chisel which made a big cut on one of his fingers. Brother Ludovico then roused Joseph who immediately squeezed the blood from the middle part of the artisan's finger, and upon bandaging it said to him, *hurry, get back to work.* And the artisan's finger was so healed that he scorned the useless bandage, threw it off, and as if nothing had happened, then completed the work he had begun.

Gladdened, the Blessed Joseph said, *let's go, let's put the cross on its Calvary.* It was fifty-four palms high and heavy, because of its size as well as its material which was from a nut tree, so when it was brought to its assigned location, ten people were unable to put it in place. So the Blessed One, with devout impatience, removed his cloak and said, *here I am,* and hurled himself, or rather flew through the air *like a bird* for a distance of almost eighty paces and by himself grabbed the cross in his hands and carried it as if it were light as straw; then straightened it and placed it in its hole.

From then on, any time he saw these crosses, he always directed his veneration and the devout feelings of his heart towards them and so yearned for them that on one occasion he gave his usual scream and, transported by ecstasy, he flew through the air for a distance of twelve paces and came to rest on a nail in the wood of the cross in the middle and stayed there for an hour without any support except that of his God. With a similar flight, he returned from where he started. There he found Pompeo Morelli, who had followed Joseph in this extreme activity, and said to him, *did you see, did you hear?* And when Morelli answered that *he did not see anything, nor hear anything,* the Blessed One replied, *I found, I embraced, I kissed the divine child on that Cross, and in remembrance of it I now feel myself on fire and my heart burning.*

Likewise, seeing those crosses when in the company of two priests, they asked which part of Jesus Crucified he might have kissed, and whether to them would be given the chance to see him on one of those crosses. He answered for humility it was the soles of the feet, and also the holy side of the body which is the source of the sacraments. Then he said, *and I, and I, and I* and three times he said *that most holy mouth.* And completely inflamed by divine love, he ran flying to embrace the cross, resting himself on his knees on the lower nail, over ten palms high off the ground

On another occasion, in a procession going from Copertino to the Grottella, Joseph, upon seeing those crosses from far off, exclaimed very loudly *oh, oh, oh* and flew for a noticeable distance through the air, placing himself in ecstasy on one of them, leaving the public full of holy awe to consider how far the omnipotence would display its marvelous greatness when pleased with his faithful servant.

More than sixty similar raptures in the churches and in the land of Copertino are listed, so whoever wanted to see Joseph removed from his senses, and even see his body transported in the air, had but to remind him of the most holy names of Jesus, or Mary, or else initiate a devout conversation with him.

A monk was discoursing with Joseph on the coming of the Holy Spirit when Joseph gave a loud cry and said, o*h if only the Holy Spirit would come in the form of a fire!* When another brother was passing casually in the corridor with an oil lamp in hand, Joseph renewed his shout and rising into the air four paces through the air toward it and then remained ecstatic for a quarter of an hour while contemplating the burning of an actual material fire and the burning of the most divine spirit.

He celebrated Holy Mass more frequently in the air than on the ground. The usual lifting of his body took place like this. Upon getting close to the consecration, Joseph would rise on his toes, actually on the tips of his largest toes, and stay that way until the consummation of the sacrifice. What was the extraordinary was either taking leave of his senses or else flying backward two paces or else becoming unconscious or raising himself two palms into the air or else carrying out such acts that showed that he either was wholly in God or that God was communicating subtly with him.

Although Joseph's ecstasies and raptures were extraordinary and intense, his person was always well composed. His vestments, either priestly or monkish, were well fitted to his body and appeared carefully arrayed, which was itself amazing.

Secondly, in those moments one could do anything one wanted to him, for he sensed nothing because he was left totally deprived of any sensation, his soul being at that time taken up with his union with heaven. His appearance during these ecstasies was always devout, always likeable in its mixture of piety, love, and veneration, which in some people evinced terror, in many others reverence, and in everybody contrition.

Going back now to the ecstasies and the raptures of our Blessed One, without repeating those recorded in his biography, we will refer to some others since it would be too difficult, not to say impossible, to talk of all of them

When the little chapel where Joseph usually celebrated the Holy Mass in Assisi had to be adorned, three painters arrived at his room to plan their depiction of the mystery. They brought Joseph to the little chapel nearby and after considering many ideas, they concluded that it would be a good thing to paint the mystery of the Immaculate Conception of Mary over the door. Joseph heard that decision and, startled by the greatness of such a privilege, said full of joy, *what are you saying? The Conception of the Virgin Mary! The Immaculate Conception! Ahi, ahi. Oh what a great thing! Oh beautiful thing!* And, being at a loss for words, he fell on his knees in ecstasy and rapture. He stayed there for a whole hour in contemplation of the great mystery.

He did the same on the day of that festival; for upon hearing a monk discoursing, he said with great fervor, *this is our protectress, our lady, mistress, mother and helper.* And, giving a loud scream he raised himself from his seat and threw himself in ecstasy with outstretched arms, contemplating the greatness and kind generosity of the mother of God. On another occasion, fixing his gaze on an image that represented the mystery, which was hanging on the wall of his cell, he first began singing devout little songs, and from there was taken in ecstasy and rapture, rising to the top of his room, whence little by little he came back to earth from heaven. Likewise, upon seeing a similar depiction hanging on the wall of a room of a sick man whom he was visiting, he flew on his knees onto a small table under the sacred image, and then with a backward flight he returned to where he had been without upsetting the small table or the fragile glass objects on it of the kind usually found in the rooms of the sick. And returning to himself, he clapped his hands together in response to the admiration of others, and said, *Oh this is my infirmity! Oh this is my infirmity!*

Upon seeing sacred relics, Joseph was transported by these same raptures. He went to the sacristy of the holy monastery where he was invited to venerate the sacred veil of the most holy Madonna. He kneeled in front of the precious relic but upon moving forward to kiss it, he jumped backwards, flew for eight long paces, and then returned in the same flight to kiss it, after which once again as before, he flew back eight paces. Then he took to a new flight onto the table where the reliquary was resting, and there went into ecstasy with arms outstretched so that that his two hands found themselves on the flames of two lighted torches. He stayed there until the bystanders recovered from their surprise and moved the torch-holders away, and saw with new amazement that Joseph's hands were unhurt and devoid of any injury from the fire.

There was also another occasion in the same sacristy where Joseph was shown the shoes of his seraphic father Saint Francis. When he saw them he moved forward to kiss them, he took them in hand, and said, so *these are the slippers of our Father? Ah, ah, ah,* and when the shoes fell from his hands he was taken in rapture to kiss the feet of his saint.

Greater was the rapture that he had when he was called to re-fold the tunic of Saint Francis in the sacristy, where among those deputized to carry out that holy function there were many monks and members of the nobility. The Blessed Joseph, in the act of folding the habit of the holy father, flew backwards more than three paces, and went so high that he flew over the heads of two deputies who were behind him, and then fell on his knees in ecstasy on the pavement behind them. Then, brought back by the command of his superior, he lowered his hood halfway over his face, and returned to his cell with his head bowed.

Joseph usually endured marvelous and surprising raptures when he said his prayers. Thus, while praying before the altar of Saint Francis, his companion monks could no longer see him. Looking about in search of him they again saw where he had flown sixteen palms high onto the ledge of the Chapel.

In like manner on the following night, Holy Thursday, Joseph found himself in church with the other monks of the monastery at prayers before the sepulcher, which was placed over the main altar adorned with clouds and an abundance of lamps which formed a wide and majestic scene. The Blessed One gave eye to the sepulchral urn in which he found his God alive, although depicted as dead, and paying attention neither to the lights, nor the clouds, nor the ornaments, nor to other obstacles, he went in a single flight directly to embrace the sacred urn where his treasure was placed. He passed through various narrow spots and timbers, without upsetting the clouds or overturning the lamps or dislodging the adornments, and stayed there fixed on his knees for a good while, until the superior called him back to his place, which he did obediently in flight without damage either to himself or to the display.

Even more marvelous was Joseph's rapture while praying in the small chorus enclosure that is attached to the altar of the Most Holy Sacrament. All the public in church saw him with his head leaning forward coming bit by bit through the jalousies of the same little chorus, and stopping in the air with his knees bent, his face turned towards the tabernacle. And *his visage was so resplendent that he appeared like a seraphim.* The Father-Custodian, who noticed him, ran to the small chorus, and called to him by voice and hands to obey and come back from the jalousies. Joseph then re-entered by the same route, having used every opening as a doorway when he was carried by rapture to his God.

When reciting the litanies, or even more at some invocation or praise of the Most Holy Virgin, Joseph used to hurl himself into flight to embrace the image of the Mother of God. Once in his leap, he caused a lighted candle which was burning before the portrait to fall on his tunic but not only didn't it burn but his clothing didn't even light up.

His raptures while celebrating the divine sacrifice were continuous, as we have said, but we cannot keep quiet about the following ones. More than once Joseph was seen raising the host while at the same time raising his whole person, carrying himself so high that if his passage had not been impeded by the roof, he would either have been carried and would have carried his consecrated Jesus into the presence of his Eternal Father at the sublime altar of heaven.

Joseph's devout little songs were also prayers in which he united himself closer to his God by gladdening himself with melody. One day while he was singing, a crucifix was placed in his hands. Upon seeing in his hands that beloved object of his joy, his voice emitted a loud scream and, in a great leap he immediately jumped from the cot where he had been sitting to the furthest corner of his cell where he lingered for a quarter of an hour on his knees in ecstasy, pierced as he was by his Lord. Upon recovering from his ecstasy he said, *oh Brother Felix, what have you done?* And he gave back the Crucifix.

We will close this Chapter with another stupendous rapture, since we don't want to refer to all of them so as not to make the account excessively long. The priest Don Anthony Chiarelli, strolling in the garden with our Blessed One, said to him, *Father Joseph, what a beautiful sky God created!* Then Joseph, as if he had been called to heaven, gave a loud scream, jumped from the ground, flew through the air, and went to rest on his knees on the top of an olive tree, *and that branch*, the beatification file says, *waved as if a bird was on it*, and he stayed there almost half an hour. Then coming back to himself said to the priest, *how am I going to come down?* The Priest went to get a ladder, and that is how he came down.

The spectators of these amazing raptures were cardinals, princes, monks and priests, nobility and public, and in fact one of them was the actual Supreme Pontiff, as we wrote elsewhere. They all supported the testimonies in the beatification file, whose authenticity was declared by the authority of the Apostolic See. We may, therefore, admire them and give praise to God who is pleased even more to glorify highly His faithful servant in the eyes of men.

four

Of the tender love of the Blessed Joseph towards the Mother of God.

Anyone who tries to take a serious, reverent and devout look at the most pure Mother of God would find it too difficult not to fall into saintly love. For no matter how much you gaze at her you'll never find anything stern or frightful, only unassuming yet resounding sweetness and gentleness. Saint Bernard said, *Quid ad Mariam accedere trepidet humana fragilitas? Nihil austeum in ea, nihil terribile, tota suavis est* (Why should human frailty fear to approach Mary, for in her there is nothing stern, nothing frightening, and all is gentle.) (Ser. 1 de verb. Apocalyp.)

Our Blessed One gazed at Mary often, and was so strongly taken by her that perhaps none of the saints above him had more tender affection or more ongoing adoration for her, so much so that he seemed born for her. And she seemed to have taken him up from his birth and to have held him under her maternal protection from then on. For that reason, even as an old man Joseph always called her *his mother*, in the way of a child, but called her who had borne him *his nurse*, not recognizing any other true mother than the most holy Virgin. I have already spoken in this biography of Joseph's reverence as a layman. Of his reverence as a monk, and the grace that he received from her, we will speak presently.

Joseph's rise to such a high level of perfection had its beginning in his devotion to the Mother of God. For having been asked how his conversion began and for what reason it got its impetus, he replied, *I was in Copertino in the Monastery of the Grottella, and I gave myself to the devotion of the Most Blessed Virgin which is worshipped in that church.* In that regard he explained *that he was so devoted to the Most Blessed Virgin of the Grottella that both night and day he was almost always praying before her.* Every day his prayers out loud to the Most Blessed Virgin consisted of the Rosary, the Office, the Litanies, seven Our Fathers, seven Ave Marias, and Seven Salve Reginas in memory of her seven sorrows and, also every day, nine Our Fathers and nine Ave Marias in honor of the nine months during which she lived in the womb of Saint Anne, as well as other devout utterances all of which came from his reverent spirit.

Joseph used to say, and would procure to say every time he saw the image of the Virgin Mary, *Refugiam peccatorum, Matre Dei, mementa mei* (Mother of God, refuge of sinners, remember me). As witness of this tender love of his are the little songs he composed in praise of the Mother of God, regarding which the files of the beatification process say, *upon singing them with great fervor he was on frequent occasions taken up in God and there are about one hundred such incidents compiled.* One of these songs was:

Vergine gloriosa
Prudentissima, e bella,
Gi Agioli, che ti miran si pietosa,
rendon ragion del tuo puro amore;
E vedendo la tua faccia si bella,
Non si posson saziar del tuo splendore

(Glorious Virgin
Most wise and beautiful
The Angels who seet you so compassionate
Convey your pure love;
And seeing your face so beautiful
Can't get enough of your splendor.)

Burning as he was with such a chaste love towards the Mother of Holy Love, those flames spread abroad, *so that a great number of people gathered at the Madonna of the Grottella from near and far-off towns. And the Most Holy Virgin dispensed much grace because of the intercession of her devoted servant, since his holiness had been initiated by Mary.* Thus Joseph's fame and renown grew greatly throughout that province.

Inasmuch as Joseph would always undertake to imprint his devotion to Mary in his heart, he also never failed to adorn her. Knowing the good humor of such a dear mother, he used to say with playful piety, *my mother is capricious; if I bring her flowers, she says she doesn't want them; if I bring her other ornaments, she says she doesn't want those either; and when I ask her what does she want, she tells me I want the heart, for I only graze on the heart.* And he gave her his whole heart. So, upon being asked what he wanted in the whole world, he answered, *nothing more than, with permission of my superiors, to stay in the Monastery of the Grottella where the image of the Most Blessed Virgin is located, which I love and revere.*

Inasmuch as he had made Mary the gift of his heart, he undertook that everyone else should also give his own heart to her. When people feigned their devotion to her through external means, he found it useful to penetrate the depths of their souls. To some people of Copertino who came one day to his cell, he said at their first meeting, *what did you come here to do? Maybe to visit My Lady?* When they answered *Yes,* Joseph replied, *and what have you brought?* They went on to say, *the religious service and the rosary.* The Blessed One then asked, *what service, what rosary? For my Lady wants only your heart and your will.* For he knew from other devout people that they had gone there out of curiosity, and to amend for their defect he had them recite the litanies. But when they reached the words *Sancta Maria* (Holy Mary) *he gave a scream and was left in ecstasy with his face towards Heaven, with his arms extended, kneeling like a statue.*

His practice for inculcating in the hearts of the faithful veneration towards God and devotion towards Mary was this: *every time someone* went to his cell he had to kneel and recite with Joseph the litanies of the Most Blessed Virgin. Whenever someone was in need, he would invite those present to recite the litanies, and at the end he would preach about the matter at hand. He would always recite these before Mass, and also in his cell whenever there wasn't a topic at hand for discussion, saying, *let's not waste time; let's recite the Rosary or the litanies.*

Whenever the Most Blessed Virgin is pleased by such reverence, it shows itself distinctly as a generous reward, such as those she bestowed on our Blessed One. She filled his spirit with so much such sweetness that when he uttered her praises or heard others praise her he would be separated from his senses and she would carry him to herself. On one occasion, Joseph came down from his cell to participate in the litanies, and upon going into the Church and hearing the People sing, *Sancta. Maria ora pro nobis* (Holy Mary pray for us), he gave a scream, took to flight, and hurled himself onto the altar, passing high over the heads of that numerous gathering. On another occasion, while celebrating Mass at his altar, a large number of those present saw him in ecstasy raised into the air, and heard him say with tears in his eyes, *praise her with your songs you holy angels, for I am completely consumed and cannot worthily praise her.*

In the beatification process it is deposed that on one occasion he was raised in rapture by the intonation of *Janua Coeli* (Gateway to Heaven) and another time by *Sancta Dei Genirix* (Holy Parent of God), and on yet another occasion by the words *Mater divinae gratiae* (Mother of Divine Grace). Three times she was addressed as *Sancta Maria* (Holy Mary), and on one of these occasions he flew up over the heads of three ranks of monks who were in front of him in church on their knees reciting the litanies.

But these raptures upon hearing the praises of the Most Holy Virgin were so frequent in him that we can say they were continuous; the same with his ecstasies. A Dominican father told of his noble vision of the glorious Patriarch Saint Domenic when the Blessed Virgin discovered two of his monks under his mantle. In Joseph's beatification file it says that when Joseph *heard this he gave a shout and went into ecstasy, and having been in that state for half an hour, the Dominican ordered him to come back to himself, and Joseph, for the sake of holy obedience, immediately came to, and after a short while sought pardon for having thus fallen.*

The same thing occurred to a Capuchin Father who upon telling Joseph of having read regarding the Most Blessed Virgin, *that just as in the creation when the first thing God did was to make light burst forth all beautiful, so he made Mary, all beautiful and full of grace in the first instant of her own conception.* Upon speaking of this, the Blessed Joseph immediately changed coloration, and with his usual shout, was prostrated on the ground with incredible spiritual force, going into ecstasy and staying there almost an hour and a half.

Yet again, when Father Niccolo' da Moresco, a Capuchin preacher, was discoursing on the greatness of the Virgin Mary, Joseph said to him, *you are very devout, and you are discoursing very well about the Most Holy Madonna,* and then he immediately with a scream became immobile and ecstatic. With regard to this, there are thirty-two instances recorded in Joseph's beatification Process, which would be too long to record here.

Neither the ecstasies nor the raptures were the only rewards that Joseph received from his tender love towards the Virgin. It is narrated in the beatification file that on some occasions, the Most Holy Mother spoke to him and provided him with valuable favors as comforts, turning his compassionate heart into a recorder, interpreter and almost a judge in the dispensation of grace.

Francesco Boni was at the Church of the Grottella, unsure as to whether he should ask that Holy Image for a certain grace. Joseph, who even though far away could penetrate inside a person, betook himself very hurriedly from his cell, ran to the Church and facing the door of the sacristy told Boni in a high voice, *seek her out, seek her out, for she will do it for you.* And he sought her out and obtained it.

Regarding a blind woman, Joseph touched her eyes and said, *the Mother of God will heal you, and immediately she regained her sight.* For a dying man he placed some liquid in his mouth - which is not named in the beatification process - and he was immediately cured, and Joseph said to him, *don't say anything about me to anyone, only that you were rendered healthy by the Mother of God.* With the recitation of the litanies, Joseph used to squeeze Demons from bodies that were hurt, and said that he couldn't find any exorcism more potent. So, in difficult childbirth he would seek recourse in Mary with his praises, and miracles happened right away.

In a word, as one can read in the process of beatification, Joseph *was most devoted to the Most Holy Virgin from whom, as he used to say, he recognized every goodness, and to whom he gave his heart from the beginning of his life, and it was to her that he ran with great confidence for his needs.*

Along with his love for the Mother, there was an equal love in him for the divine Son, so his tenderness was equally great for Mary and the Child Jesus. Joseph had a Capuchin monk, who was a painter, depict on a cloth the Mother of God in the act of placing the Baby Jesus on her holy, virginal breast, in a way that the Mother would look at the Son, and the Son would look at the Mother. Enriched by such a treasure, he prayed before it day and night so that he merited, as he himself admitted, *that the divine infant revealed many secret and hidden things, of which Joseph may have been the only trusted recipient.*

It is no wonder then that the Venerable Sister Cecilia of the Nobles of Nocera, a great servant of God, while seized in ecstasy during the Feast of the Portiuncula, known as the Pardon of Assisi, would see the Blessed Joseph being caressed by the Most Holy Mother as a favorite son of her own divine Son, who would die in her hands breathing out his soul with the sweet words in his mouth, *monstra te esse Matrem* (show that you are the Mother.)

five

Of the gift of penetrating the thoughts and secrets of others, bestowed by God on the Blessed One.

According to Jeremiah, God declared himself the searcher of hearts, *Ego Dominus scrutans cor* (I the Lord search the heart) (xxvii.20), knowing that He alone formed that which is in the heart of man. Such penetration is reserved for Him, and as a great favor He sometimes communicates it, albeit with great limitations, to His favorites. He granted this abundantly to our Blessed Joseph, and it rendered anyone who dealt with him uneasy.

Above all, when anyone who was stained with sin happened to come before him, Joseph would smell the odor and say, *go and wash your face, for it is dirty with ink.* Or else, *accommodate the crossbow,* that is, one's conscience. And when anyone answered that *they did not remember any sin,* Joseph would promptly inform them of the time, place, and manner in which the person had committed it. And when they came back after making a confession, Joseph would receive them with a joyful face, saying to them, *oh, now you are well.*

With some people, he wouldn't even wait for them to come before him, but upon hearing their light tapping at his door he would tell them from within, *go first to confess yourself, and then come in.* Such happened to one Giovanni Battista Paolini whose bad tendencies Joseph revealed to him, and also his disobedience to his parents, and the sin in which he found himself.

The same happened on the road upon meeting Francesco Allegretti who had a guilty conscience for I know not what sin. Joseph took him by the head playfully and said to him warmly, *sad man, sad man, go to confess yourself and make yourself good.*

To a young woman who was confessing to him, he told her the whole confession item by item asking her at the end if *she had any other sin to confess,* and when she said *no,* the Blessed One added, *confess yourself of that thought which you allowed the day before yesterday in such and such a place,* and the penitent knew that it was true, and admitted it to the great benefit of her soul.

To a novice of the Order who wanted to make a general confession to him prior to solemnly professing his religious vows, Joseph suggested that he set down his sins on paper. The penitent did so, but upon giving the paper to the Blessed One, he heard Joseph say to him, m*y son you haven't written it well here because it wasn't the way you have written it, but it happened in such and such a way,* and he was equally corrected in every other sin which he thus amended in his confession.

Joseph also knew one's defects at a distance, and addressed them with graceful reprimand. Giovanni Battista Mazzicchi confessed himself one morning and upon going back home got angry with his servants. The next day he ran into Joseph who immediately said, *oh what a bad thing you have done; after communion you lost your kindness and your patience! Don't do such a thing anymore.*

To a tertiary who had come to the Grottella innocently with a young man who in turn was bringing his beloved with him, Joseph said, *go and admonish him so that he'll mend his ways.* The devout tertiary feared an insult from the young man if she were to carry out the task, but the Blessed One responded, *go, for you will find him like a lamb; he is supposed to become a priest here soon; you'll die before he will, and he will say*

Mass and remove you from purgatory. The tertiary obeyed and the young man placidly received correction and became a priest. He outlived his benefactress, so one can infer that both parts of Joseph's prophesy were fulfilled.

One day the same tertiary called on Joseph, being desirous of conferring with him on the affairs of her soul. But she did not dare to speak to him, and he said to her, *of what are you afraid? Tell me the thing freely,* and here he revealed to her what she herself had thought to say but had not done so, perhaps terrified by the fame of his holiness. He often said to her, *yesterday you carried out the discipline, did such-and-such of a mortification, and had such-and-such thoughts. So now for the future do such-and-such and don't do such-and-such.*

Penetration of hidden secrets and miraculous healings brings us to the following event. Andriella Gravili, a Lady from the town of Salice, was brought to Copertino by her parents and with the sign of the cross she was cured by the Blessed One of a sudden distortion of the left eye and of the mouth towards the ear that both afflicted and deformed her. Upon first seeing that girl, Joseph called her by name without ever having known her. He healed her in an instant, and told her to recite an Our Father and an Ave Maria every day. He wanted from her a little cross that she wore in her rosary, and he gave her a medal in return. When she returned to Salice she recited the Our Father and the Ave Maria only once every eight days, and she lost the medal. A year or so later her father married her off. While in the married state, as she was dressing herself one morning, she was so surprised by an intense darkening around her that she fell to the ground and almost died. The efforts of the physicians were useless, so her father again took his daughter, who was almost dead, to the Grottella, and she was assailed by even worse sickness. Upon arriving at the church she was placed on the dais of the altar. When Joseph was summoned, he told her to walk. She walked and felt her head getting light and her sickness disappearing. She was then led then off to the side onto the dais of the altar, and Joseph told her *that she hadn't recited the Our Father and the Ave Maria for him every day, but only once every eight days, that she lost the medal, and that her marriage was going badly because she was so young, and that's why she had hit her head and had torn her hair.* All of this was true, which greatly amazed her since she was the only person who knew all this. Finally, he comforted her and told her to be in good spirits, that her husband would hold her dear as his lady, which in fact was what happened. *So, being very content* (as the lady said in closing her narration), *as were those of my household, we departed with my having regained my health, for which we thank our Lord God.*

To these revelations of one's thoughts and secrets, we will add another to further confirm this gift of Joseph's. Margarita Natali, having been suddenly assailed by sharp pains over her whole body, sent her servant to summon Joseph. But the moment Joseph heard his voice, and without waiting to find out who it might be or what he might want, said to him, *my son, go back home, for the pains have already stopped, and your lady is cured.*

The Canon Father Mazzicchi, went to the Blessed Joseph to commend to him his nephew Baltassare who, as Mazzicchi was notified, had been reduced to extremity because of illness. Upon seeing Mazzicchi, Joseph said, *now in fact your nephew in Rome has gotten better, and you will not lose him this time.*

Ottavio Ottaviani commended to Joseph his son Ruggiero who was ill in Rome. The Blessed one answered, *pray to God for him.* When Joseph heard that the grieving father gave vent to his bitterness to other people, Joseph said, *what did you want me to say?* And he added casually, *did you want me to tell him that his son had already died? That poor old man would have fallen dead in front of me in his grief.* And eight days later they learned of the death of the son.

Don Bernardino Benaducci, oppressed by internal and external temptations, met up by chance with the Blessed One who said to him, *my Don Bernardino, be strong, for you are greatly tempted,* and it was a great comfort to this troubled priest that his trouble was revealed to such a great Servant of God.

Also made free by virtue of Joseph's penetration into the thoughts of profound melancholy and regret of other people, was a fellow monk who was afflicted for having professed himself among the Minor Conventuals instead of the Reformed Fathers. For that reason, one day when the regret was very strong, by good fortune he met with Joseph and heard him say, *what's the matter; why are you so melancholy? Can't you also do that which the Reformed Fathers do? Be joyful in the Order to which you professed yourself.* With these words the monk's regret and melancholy vanished, and he realized that an Order doesn't make its monks holy, but the monks make the Order holy.

Elsewhere we have referred to the marvelous penetration of the secrets of Cardinal Rapaccioli, but here we should not keep silent about yet another. This purpled lord betook himself from Terni, where he was Bishop, to Assisi for the festival of Saint Francis. There, he talked with Joseph who said, *you, Lord Cardinal, when you are alone and shut in your rooms, go sometimes to one painting, or sometimes to another, and to one of them you say prayers to the Most Holy Virgin, and to the other to Father Saint Francis, and to other Saints that you have in your rooms, and then you shout Father Joseph help! Father Joseph help!* And indeed it was, as the Cardinal himself deposed.

A novice was singing psalms in the chorus but his mind flew to the garden. Joseph reprimanded him for not paying sufficient attention during the assigned hour for the Terce, but the novice excused himself by affirming that he had indeed been paying attention. *Yes,* said the Blessed One, *today you want to climb that fig tree in the woods, and oh how many you want to eat,* and one by one he retold all those thoughts which the novice had indulged in while singing in the chorus.

To anyone nearby who might be reciting the office with him, or the litanies, or the Rosary, but was distracted, Joseph would poke him with his elbow or pull him by his clothes saying, *stay here,* or he would tell someone precisely, *you were completely distracted when you said the Our Father.* To another who hadn't recited the office that day, he said, *and where is the office? The Breviary calls after you,* and they all admitted their distraction and their shortcomings.

More beautiful was Joseph's revelation of an innocent thought to Brother Antonio Pecorella, his companion. When Brother Antonio was returning together with the Blessed One from Leguile with a goldfinch, what was running through Brother Antonio's mind was, *to whom will Father Joseph give this Goldfinch? To so and so? O r to so and so?* Suddenly Joseph said, *I don't want to give this little bird to any of those people whom you have thought about. Rather, I want to give it its liberty. Open the cage and let it fly away.* Brother Antonio was stunned and he flushed, showing thereby that he knew that he was walking in the company of a great saint.

During Holy Week, Benedetta Cimarella, a lady of Osimo who was dedicated to Joseph's holiness, had painted some eggs with her own hands with the intention of giving them to charity. At the same hour, the Blessed One summoned a layman of the monastery and said, *go to the house of the little lamb who has prepared painted eggs to give me.* He went and returned with equal awe both for her who made the gift and for him to whom he brought it. Joseph called this noble Lady by the name of *little lamb,* knowing well, perhaps with supernatural light, the delicacy of her conscience, and he described her qualities, her features, and her height, even though he had never seen her nor associated with her in view of the strictness of his retreat in that city.

Furthermore, very celebrated is the testimony about our Blessed One rendered by Father Pier Francesco of Levanto, a Minor Observant, who was also President of the Monastery of the new Church of Assisi. He deposed that the first time he went to Joseph without ever seeing him before, Joseph narrated to him in detail all the things of his life, particularly internal matters regarding his soul known only to God. He also told him many things that would happen to him in the future. Among these were a storm that he would experience at sea, and which he did experience in the year 1650, from which he was miraculously saved with his companions, having been inspired by God to throw into the sea an image of the Most Holy Madonna on parchment that the Blessed Joseph had given him.

Father Pier Francesco also said that a Sicilian father of the Third Order recounted to him that the servant of God, who had never known him before, revealed all that was inside his heart, and that this monk, having a serious affliction on one of his legs, begged the Blessed One to make the sign of the cross over it, and when it was done the leg was made healthy again. Likewise Father Pier Francesco knew from the same Sicilian father of an esteemed woman who was injured and was commended to the prayers of the Blessed Joseph, but Joseph said without seeing her that *it was not true that she was injured but it was her love of the world, as it was later learned.*

The attestation by an accredited monk was followed by that of an accredited Doctor. Don Giulio Cesare Lezzi of Copertino got definite news that his Uncle, Don Jacopo Antonio Lezzi, Vicar-General in the City of Fiano in the Terra di Lavoro had a fatal illness, and that the physicians despaired of it. Don Giulio betook himself with his five sisters and his mother to Joseph at the Grottella to ask him to pray to the Madonna for the afflicted one. The Blessed One recited the litanies of the Most Holy Virgin, while they responded *ora pro nobis* (pray for us). When finished, Joseph got to his feet with a joyful expression and told them, *be joyful, for you have received grace and on such-and-such a day, which he named, you will have news that your (mother's) brother-in-law who is your uncle is well, and in fact has gotten better.* And the news came as he had predicted.

The above-mentioned doctor, who had gone to Loreto and then passed through Assisi along with his company, went to visit Joseph who revealed to him a fake pilgrim who had gone with them, who called himself Joannicchio. Joseph told the doctor, k*now then that he was the Devil who, by recounting various stories of war, tried to distract you from your usual prayers with the intent to hurl you down. And he would have hurled you down if my Madonna had not helped you. Upon hearing this,* Doctor Lezzi deposed, *we were left stupefied and frightened not only because of the danger* we passed through, but also because we heard Father Joseph tell us something that he could not have known naturally.

It has been told elsewhere but it would be suitable now to describe at greater length a terrible diabolical secret taking place in Copertino. While the Blessed One was in his Monastery of the Grottella talking late one evening with his Father-Guardian, he exclaimed horrified, *oh what a stink! It is the stink of hell.* Without further ado Joseph asked permission to betake himself to a certain spot in Copertino. Along with Brother Lodovico he set off there at a brisk pace. Upon arrival they went straight to a certain house and, upon knocking again and again, the door opened and there he found Warlocks, Witches and Enchanters who were handling unguents and oils some of which had been put back in vases and flasks, while others were still boiling in cauldrons. Upon seeing Joseph, the wicked ones were all filled with horror, and Joseph, filled with holy fury, struck those Devilish instruments here and there with a stick which he purposely carried in hand, breaking and smashing them under his feet, and reducing them to minute pieces. He appeared in this effort so terrible in aspect and his eyes so blazing that those evil ones, not wanting his stick on their heads, removed themselves by fleeing precipitously.

Hell wanted to avenge them, so when Joseph and his companion returned in the dark, they were surrounded by a fiery comet that threatened to reduce them to ashes. Brother Lodovico shouted, *my Father Joseph, we are dead!* The Blessed One said, w*hat dead, what dead! Faith, Faith! Hooray for God!* The comet vanished, but it changed into a great serpent also of fire, with its mouth open, and it came towards both of them to swallow them. Firm in his Faith, and fixed upon God, Joseph laughed and prayed that most holy name to which heaven, earth and hell kneel. And the dragon disappeared. So, the Servant of the Lord, victorious, returned safely to his Monastery of the Grottella.

And this is enough regarding our Blessed One's penetration of the thoughts and secrets of others, with which he was so familiar.

six

Of the continuing and admirable gift of Prophesy of the Blessed Joseph.

In order to organize this chapter well, it would be necessary to weave again the whole life of the Blessed Joseph since his life was itself but a continuing prophesy. Since a prophet is a person whose mind is raised to God who shows him things of the future or things far away, then our Blessed One was a wonderful prophet, for his mind was always with God. His predictions were so numerous that every time someone would speak to Joseph, Joseph would speak a prophesy to him. He could distinctly see things that were coming in one's life just as another person would see them in his own life after the fact.

Even as a young man Joseph could see the religious Order in which he would have to embark, his miraculous attainment of the priesthood, his call to the Inquisition in Naples, his transport to Assisi to two monasteries of another Order, his return to his beloved Minor Conventual Brothers, and finally his saintly death in Osimo in circumstances that we have noted in the appropriate place.

If someone predicts events pertaining to other people, it draws more awe to himself than if he predicts his own events. Joseph's further predictions regarding others spread throughout his life which makes us understand his justly-acquired fame as a prophet for everyone, and why every word of his was justifiably taken as an oracle.

The Cleric Giovanni Francesco della Porta of Copertino was very worried because he had no news of his brother who for some time was residing in Bergamo, especially because Giovanni was waiting for a legal authorization from his brother to conclude a matter of serious import in the town. While distressed about this, Giovanni met with the Blessed One. Upon being greeted, Joseph answered, *God be with you, God be with you. What's new? How are you?* The Cleric, in one breath told him the reason for his distress and concluded, *I don't know what has become of my brother, whether he is alive or dead.* The Blessed one replied, *he is not dead, no.* And raising his eyes to heaven, he added with a joyful face, d*on't doubt. No. On Monday a letter will arrive from your brother, and with the authorization.* And so it was.

Joseph also promised good health to Francesco Boni, who was in the last stage of consumption, saying to him, *put your hope in God, for nothing will happen.* One day Francesco got worse and was assumed to be dead, but Joseph exclaimed, *what do you mean dead, what do you mean dead! He* hastened to him and put a basin in front of him saying, *vomit in here.* Francesco obeyed and cast out from his mouth all the sickness in him, and was left healthy. A year or so later in the Monastery of the Grottella he got sick again with a fever. Joseph went to his bedside and said, *get up from that bed; this is not to be your cross; your cross is in your home.* So he sent him home healthy, and the next day his mother fell ill there. Her illness lasted thirteen months, to the great distress and expense of her son who felt the cross heavily just as it was prophesied by the Servant of God.

To a certain person in Copertino who commended to Joseph someone in Galatone who was ill, Joseph immediately answered, *he is dead; pray for him,* and it was just then that he had died.

A crippled woman, along with her mother, was dragged to the Grottella. Before any request was made for good health, Joseph said, *you can't have two paradises either in this world or in the other; be patient because you will suffer a lot; your mother will die and you will be left alone, and you will suffer much.* The mother died a few days later, and the daughter was left in great distress.

Joseph predicted misfortunes for two young men if they did not abstain from secretly frequenting certain far-off houses. One of them disdained to obey him and a few days later was killed.

He foretold suffering and disaster to a monk who wanted to go to Palermo for his own pleasure. The monk, preferring to carry out his own intentions rather than take the advice of the Blessed One, was poisoned in that city. It was only by a miracle that he was he able to get back to his town, but he had lost his voice and remained without it from then on.

Joseph predicted to Clarice Bibiena the end of a great enterprise of hers that was taking place in Rome, and it came true at the hour in the place and in the circumstances that he told her.

When the Blessed One entered the land of Leguile he met Orazio Saluzzi, son of the baron of that place, who was sick and was going for a cure with his household servants. Joseph said to him immediately, *today in good form, and tomorrow in the sepulcher* (rhyming in Italian: *oggi in figura, e domani in sepoltura*). He died that night, and was buried the next day.

Further regarding Joseph's prophetic spirit, he announced the death of two popes, Urban VIII and Innocent X, and many other people who have been mentioned elsewhere. In item 38 of the beatification file, there alone are over twenty cases recorded. In those, he distinctly predicted the deaths of diverse people with such specificity in his words as to the circumstances that it would take too long to refer to each of them, but it would be neglectful not to mention some.

A mother presented two of her sons to Joseph for his blessing before being sent to study for their doctorates in Rome. *What Doctors, what Doctors in Rome, Joseph* answered. *Doctors in Heaven instead!* And in fact instead of a trip to Rome, they made one to eternity.

A monk by the name of Ignatius was always called *Ignatius the Martyr* by the Blessed One. When Ignatius asked why Joseph always called him that, Joseph answered with joyful expression, *you will be a martyr soon.* And soon Ignatius was dead under the feet of a throng during the procession of the Portiuncula, because he had run to the aid of two young clerics, wanting to rescue them from the stampeding crowd, but did so at the cost of his own life in his charitable sacrifice.

And there was a priest who wanted to forego saying Mass in order to go and help his dying father. Joseph said to him, *go and say Mass, for your father won't die until you get back.* The priest celebrated Mass, went back, and Joseph then added, *oh, now he will die.* And then he did die.

A person commended his health to Joseph after the physicians were in despair, and was concerned about the effect of his death on his wife, his father and his mother. Joseph said, *what wife, what father, what mother! God wants you. God wants you. Heaven. Heaven. A beautiful thing is heaven. But have a bit of patience.* The person recovered from his illness to everybody's amazement, but one month later he died unexpectedly.

During a casual meeting one day, Joseph told an ordained monk, *my brother, don't ever rejoice in anyone's death even if he is your mortal enemy.* And saying this he continued on his way. Not a week went by that the monk received news that his worst enemy had died.

What has been said so far regarding such prophecies is enough, so we will pass to other events.

Father-Master Raffaello Palma, custodian of the holy monastery, used to visit the Blessed Joseph frequently, and every time he would enter his cell Joseph would put his hands on his head and say, *oh what a lovely head; oh how well a miter would fit on top of it.* A few years passed, and Palma was made Bishop of Oria, where he died with a distinct reputation for religious fervor.

Monsignor Niccolo Albergati, who was later called Cardinal Ludovisi, visited Joseph in Rome. Joseph, without ever having seen him or knowing who he was, received him at the outset with these exact words, *and how is it that a Cardinal comes to see a little poor person.* When the prelate told him that he wasn't a Cardinal, Joseph answered, *good, good, good*, and after dinner Joseph sent his companion to him who, on Joseph's behalf, told him not to ridicule what Joseph had told him that morning, and that within a few months it would be seen whether Joseph was fooled or not. The cardinal later deposed, *I sent away the monk but the truth is that our chat was in May 1644, and in March 1645 my promotion followed by divine clemency.* Through the discussions that this purpled one had with the Blessed Joseph, he conceived the highest reverence for Joseph's holiness, which he continued to maintain along with great faith in Joseph's prediction.

In the year 1649 Portolungone was under military siege by the Catholic King, the fall of which would be of great importance to the interests of Prince Ludovisio. The King wrote to his agent in Assisi, and had the Cardinal write him as well, telling him to go and commend to our Blessed One a good outcome for this enterprise and to try to learn from Joseph what the outcome would be. The Agent importuned Joseph again and again, and Joseph always avoided the matter by saying, these things God only knows, and that he could do no more than pray about it continuously, as he was doing. But one Sunday morning, the Minister of the Prince was waiting for the Blessed one in the old chapter building after Mass had been celebrated and with the greatest urgency in the world and with the most pressing supplications he begged Joseph again to give an answer. The Blessed One said nothing and ran hurriedly to his room, over the door of which there was, and still is, a painting of the Immaculate Conception. Joseph stopped there and pointing with his finger at the painted Virgin, turned to the agent and said, *listen now, write to your master that at the time of her next festival, on the eighth day he will gain victory.* What followed confirmed the truth of the oracle, for on the day of the Assumption the town's capitulation took place in the main Square. Cardinal Ludovisio wrote of this to a monk whom he knew in the holy monastery, and said in his letter, *we have had the victory of Portolungone, the square having surrendered to Catholic arms, thereby verifying what Father Joseph said much earlier.*

Moving from predictions regarding great and momentous events, we come to individual private matters. The Blessed One told Teodoro de Benedictis that he should leave the profession of notary and become a priest or else misfortunes would befall him. The notary didn't like the advice, so he had to submit to a long incarceration after which he assumed the habit of priest. Joseph then said to him, *didn't I warn you that it's necessary to be obedient, that God wants you as a priest, or else you would have unpleasantness? Oh, now learn to believe me at your cost.* Teodoro, confused, replied, *I have submitted to obedience but where is my patrimony?* And the Blessed One added, *be joyful because when the time comes, God will provide for you.* And when the time came, God provided for him by means of a person who was quite rich, but from whom Teodoro would never have expected anything.

After Doctor Graziano de' Benigni commended himself to Joseph's prayers for a male offspring, the Servant of God said to some monks who found themselves in his cell prior to the childbirth, *the Doctor will have a male child this evening, but I didn't want to say anything lest it be said that I play the prophet.* Not an hour passed before Olinda, wife of the doctor, gave birth to Antonio Rutilio. The doctor later wanted another child, and commended himself so often to Joseph that he said, *that man lacks faith,* and then sent a messenger to him with these instructions, *tell him that he should have faith, that he will have sons, and that he should give one of them my name.* When the later childbirths came, he gave one of them the name Joseph.

A nobleman of Assisi expected a canonship, and implored the help of the Blessed One's prayers. Joseph asked, *the canonship will be conferred? How do you mean conferred?* The petitioner added, *the arrangements in Rome are in place; all the procedures are in place, and the funds have been found and sent so that it can be announced.* Joseph answered, *all the worse for you; you will now have neither the canonship nor the money.* And within two days what he said was verified by the confirmation of another person of whom a few hours before, the Blessed One had said, *he is the one on whom it is conferred.*

When Joseph's companion ran hurriedly to his cell to give him the news that had just arrived in Assisi of the election in Rome of the new General of the Order, Joseph said, *oh go on, go on; I already know that Father Catalano is the General.* And Joseph said to Brother Carlo of Corinaldo, who wanted a favor from the above-mentioned General, *listen, my son, commend yourself to a superior who will come suddenly and soon to Corinaldo, because he will soon, albeit after my death, become the General, and it is he, not the current General, who will do you the favor that you desire.* And it was Father-Master Andrea Pasini of Spello, at that time an Assistant of the Order, and then General in the year 1665, from whom the monk attained that which he longed for.

Certain plans for a noble wedding weren't moving forward because of the exorbitant demands of first of one party and then of the other, and it seemed that it wouldn't be concluded until far in the future. Joseph sent someone to tell the father of the future bride that he rejoiced in the newly-concluded family relationship. The father of the bride appreciated the sentiment but he answered that the simple initiation of the process was a long way off, much less the conclusion. Joseph smiled and answered charmingly, *how so? Don't you know that one, meaning the young man, was born for her? Be quiet, because the wedding is made in heaven and soon it will be made on earth.* The difficulties suddenly vanished, the parties came together, and the contract was concluded.

Joseph then created even more awe with a new foretelling. The mother of the bride feared that some evil spell would befall during the wedding ceremony. Without revealing her fear to anyone, she went to beg the Blessed One to celebrate the Holy Mass the coming morning in order to counter the spell. But Joseph, being ill, answered that she should have her parish priest do it, and her wish would immediately be fulfilled. And he added, *go ahead and do the ceremony, because I announce to you that they will have a male offspring.* The mother, confounded by Joseph's revelation of her inner thoughts, through his assurances regarding the wedding and by his announcement of a male offspring, asked him to be godfather at the baptism. *Figure out something better,* Joseph answered, *because I'm dying and won't be alive at that time,* as came true, and in fact came true with a regard to a whole group of his prophesies.

The Father-Regent of the Trave, and the physician Giacinto Carosi, who was present at the last one of Joseph's illnesses, commended themselves warmly to his prayers. The Blessed One replied, *I'll do it willingly, but we'll see each other soon.* Joseph died, and shortly afterwards the Regent and the Physician went after him to a different life.

A man of youthful spirit, who had already secured a post as a subaltern, and after the flag was made ready, wanted to go to the war that was at that time burning between the Pope and certain Italian Princes. Joseph said to him, *it will not happen to you; it will not happen to you.* And the man never went. When Joseph's fellow monk, Father Bernardino of Osimo, said that he wanted to go to the mission in the Congo, Joseph said *you won't go.* And even though Bernardino was disposed to make the trip, he never went.

We've left for last the most noble of Joseph's prophesies which was the one that brought with it some of the greatest miracles of the grace of God. Dianora di Nardo, a vain woman and a prostitute with her body, passed through Copertino all resplendent and gorgeous, going I don't know where. Upon seeing her entering the Church, Joseph told his bystanders, *behold the Magdalene,* and turning to her said, *and when, when? God wants you. Leave that vain clothing, and love God, Magdalene.* Immediately (oh great prodigy of divine grace! Oh great credit to the Blessed One!), she put aside her vain clothes, detested her past dissoluteness, covered herself with coarse wool, and gave herself to penance. The Servant of God rejoiced at the miraculous conversion that was seen, and had been foretold by him from the deep abyss of divine prescience.

And here, in order not to tire the reader, we end the predictions and prophecies of the Blessed One, which were much more gratifying to those to whom he made them, even though with Joseph's simplicity it seemed more as if he cast them out as a joke rather than proffered them with judgment.

seven

Of his great Charity towards his neighbor.

The very practice of charity is born from the love of God and so is the love toward one's neighbor, just as light and heat are born from fire itself. And so Jesus Christ, great master of holy love, joined together these two precepts and called the second the same as the first, the one not being able to exist without the other.

Since Joseph loved God with the most burning ardor, who would doubt that he would love his neighbor with pure love, recognizing in him the image of his Lord? He loved his neighbor greatly, and when a person's situation called for it, Joseph applied himself entirely to the welfare of the soul, and to the comfort of body as well. And Joseph was indefatigable. He preached by example and with words to support good people and to convert bad ones. To this end he would address his prayers and, when they seemed weak, would accompany his prayers with fasts, starvation, and even with his blood that he shed with blows from ruthless whippings, thereby trying many times to atone for the transgressions of others. As is written in the file of the beatification process, Joseph prayed to his God continuously, *since God, with his excess of infinite goodness, had suffered for so many centuries the past sins of the world, so Joseph was equally pleased to suffer for the present ones.*

He turned thus to his neighbor with that amiability that is inherent in charity. He exhorted anyone who conversed with him to frankness, truthfulness and sweetness, and he himself valued those qualities as well, having a great horror for lies, deception and self-promotion. In his conversations, Joseph was most affable, and he used to say about himself, and also imply to others, *no worries and melancholy, not in my house* (rhyming in Italian, *scrupili e malinconia non gli voglio in casa mia*). That's why if someone with worries went to him in anguish, he would comfort him with appropriate advice, and then take a broom, sweep him from head to foot, and say, *there, I've removed all your worries from you; behave well and don't doubt.*

He spoke deeply about religion, yet also humorously and gracefully, and he insinuated himself so much into people's hearts that he made everyone who went to him for advice or with whom he was able to deal, be he religious or secular, into prey for Jesus Christ. He was the patcher-up of quarrels and the mediator of peace, especially when it was needed within the cloister. And when he knew that someone was cooperating zealously to reconcile angry souls, he would, as the beatification process says, *caress and embrace them, and show them great love.*

His charity was ingenuous which is why in some cases he made use of metaphorical and amusing sayings. Thus, it befell that a personage of influence came to him bringing an odd young gentleman. At first glance, the Blessed One understood him and said laughingly, *who is this dark-looking fellow you have brought here? Can't you see how dark he is?* And then, turning to the young gentleman said, *Go, my son, and wash your face.* The young man washed it with the sacramental confession, and when he returned the next day Joseph said with great joy, *oh, now you are good-looking; wash yourself a lot, because yesterday you were as ugly as a Moor.*

There was a priest who was fiercely fought over by two most powerful enemies, which are temptation and comfort. After he and Joseph had spoken of other matters, Joseph squeezed his hand upon his departure and said to him with tears, *my son, resist temptation with courage.* And, upon naming the temptation, Joseph said, *because God so wants you not to offend him. I'm telingl you, my son! I'm telingl you!* And in saying it with such kindness it animated the priest for the battle in which he ended victorious.

The remedy that he gave to those who were tempted were *frequent sacraments because*, he used to say, *where God is frequently present, the enemy can't frequently be there, and in the long run God always wins.*

To monks, spiritual fathers, and superiors, everything Joseph inculcated was compassion and charity, and he himself was so full of those qualities that many times he could be seen and heard running around the dormitories shouting loudly:

Carita', Carita'.
Ch ha carita
E' ricco, e uno lo sa.
E chi non ha caritya'
Ha una grande infelicita'.
Amore, e Carita'
E' una gran felicita'.
Carita non recercata
Iddio l'ha inspirata.

(Charity, Charity
He who has charity
Is rich, and one knows it.
And he who has no charity
Has great unhappiness.
Love and Charity
Is a great happiness.
Charity without reward
Is inspired by God.).

Wherever a need required it, Joseph was reliable in his charity and, backed by God, he emerged victorious and triumphant in his encounters. The cleric Alfonso Montefuscolo, who in his youth was wooing a devout woman who was in religious retreat, deposed the following about himself. One day he finally found himself near the Grottella with the Blessed One, who gently put his hand on his head and said, *Alfonso, Alfonso, mind your own business; go about your own business. Be a good man, my son, leave the little nuns alone, and don't make me have to say it again.* All that was necessary was that warning to change him and make him into a good person.

There was a woman called Antonia Leccese of Veglie who did not have a good reputation. On one occasion certain devout women brought her on purpose to where the Blessed Joseph was. When he saw her he asked who she was, and when he learned her name and her town, he went pale, began to tremble, and with a shout went into ecstasy with his arms stretched out like Saint Francis. Coming out of his ecstasy, after being called by his companion, he turned to Antonia and said, *go, my daughter, and get that spell that you wrote a few days ago and bring it here now.* She, who was half dead and terrified by the ecstasy that she had just witnessed, ran home and brought back the evil thing. The Blessed One burned it immediately. Thus Joseph corrected her greatly, but with such charity that she altered her follies and then carried out a good life to everyone's edification.

This charity of Joseph's did not exclude his love of justice, which he possessed to a heroic degree. Thus, the process of beatification says, *he greatly rejoiced that the demons and the damned were to be punished for eternity, and he approved of appropriate punishments for delinquents as an example to others and for their own correction, and that fulfilling the elements of justice would do honor and give glory to God, and would preserve peace and tranquility among men.*

He was most observant of his monastic rule, and he would pursue with great zeal any transgression against it. He inspired his superiors to vigilance by telling them, s*ince Saint Francis has conferred upon you the mantle of superiority and you have received it from him, so it is intact, and not torn or unserviceable.* And just as Joseph's zeal for the health of his neighbor was such that laymen did not dare to appear before him when stained by serious sin, likewise the monks composed themselves inwardly, more terrified by the perception of his holiness than enticed by the appearance of his affability and sweetness.

He was led to love his enemies by such charity, which is the mistress of patience, and it taught him to endure and reduce any injuries done to him. In Copertino he was subject to insulting words, and was also struck and wounded, but with his generous forgiveness he won over to Jesus Christ the person who wounded him. In Assisi he was menaced by ever hardening torments and even death, but in the face of his placid appearance, his assailant was seen to fall at his feet genuflecting and begging his forgiveness. Whereupon Joseph, who wanted nothing more than to mend the ways of sinners, answered him, *go, confess your sin and pray to God for him to forgive mine.*

Joseph's charity flew from him on wings of fire, even as far as to love Turks and non-believers. When pitying their unhappiness for having been born outside the bosom of the Holy Church and for then entering the profound depths of divine judgment, Joseph went into ecstasy for a long while. When he returned to his senses, he would finish tearfully by saying, *my sons, pray for good people, pray for sinners, pray for heretics, pray for the Turks, pray for the Non-Believers, and finally pray for everyone, for we are all redeemed by the most precious blood of Jesus Christ. But not everyone is elected to partake deservingly of all that blood in the glory of Paradise.*

This and much more was wrought by the love in our Blessed One for his neighbor in connection with the health of people's souls. Nor did he stint in curing their souls nor the health of their bodies. There was one who attested in the beatification *that Father Joseph was a Saint Francis on earth, humble, simple, and chaste, that from his mouth always came nice words about God, and he was so gentle and full of charity that one never heard irritated words. When summoned, he would come into Copertino at any hour to visit the sick. I always saw him barefoot with bloody feet but when he was inside he would put on slippers.* These visits of his were so loving that he would not only feed the mouths of the sick but he would dress their sores, *to the point that he overcame the repugnance of his senses and ate the used bandages full of corruption which had been on a sick person earlier, in imitation of Saint Catherine of Siena, his particular advocate, who upon visiting a sick woman, courageously imbibed the corruption in order to overcome the fatal nausea of one of her sores.*

There were two effects of this great charity of his: either the curing of a sick person, having healed over a hundred people in his life, or giving greater comfort by easing an illness. He usually told the sick that, *the Lord wanted something big from them by the sickness that he had sent to them, and this couldn't be anything but to change their lives or increase their virtue.* And if among the sick he found someone in anguish about his children and in fear of leaving them orphaned and abandoned, he would say, *be joyful, for God will provide.* He insisted above all else on inducing the sick to resign themselves to the divine will, assuring them that this was the most certain and efficient means for getting their health back from God. That's why he told a woman who was agitated over the very serious illness of her husband, who day-by-day was nearing death, *as long as you don't embrace acceptance to the will of God, the illness of your husband will continue to increase, and that she and her impatience rather than the sickness and its violence, were what were killing her husband.*

He also showed the greatness of his charity during the lamentable famine which afflicted all nearby towns including Assisi. For that reason he not only abandoned himself in prayer that God might be pleased and thereby give food to men, but not having permission to go out to beg, he went about the enclosure of the monastery breathlessly inspiring and consoling everybody. And to the sick monks he would hunt up some fruit and bring it to them, always with some uplifting souvenir so that they would be comforted in spirit.

Most tender were his words of regret for their illness, such that among the monks the word spread *that in Joseph's company, one was more fulfilled when ill than when living in health,* since in infirmity Joseph belonged to all of them but when they were healthy everyone belonged to himself. Not only did Joseph belong to all his sick fellow monks, but even his things, although inanimate, worked miracles of a kind. Father Luca Maccatelli deposes *that he was beset by stomach pains, and one evening when assailed worse than usual, he begged the Blessed One to pray for him.* Joseph replied, *willingly.* Father Luca, *a little later, without Joseph seeing him, picked up Joseph's eyeglasses from his altar, and applied them to his stomach, and the pain immediately disappeared.*

Joseph's charity in the relief of his afflicted neighbors even prompted him to write out with his own hand the blessing given by his Seraphic Father which says: *Benedicat tibi Dominus & custodiat te; ostendiat faciam suam tibi & miseratur tui; convertat vultum ad Te & det tibi pacem. Dominus benedicat Te.* (May the Lord bless you and keep you. May he show his face to you and pity you. May he turn his countenance upon you and give you peace. May the Lord bless you.) That was the benediction formula that Saint Francis wrote with his own hand at the request of his companion, the Venerable Father Leo, the original of which is stored in the Monastery of the Minor Order of Conventuals in Assisi, and brought from there in procession to the Madonna of the Angels. And upon entering there with the crucifix, the great treasure is opened, which is famous as the Indulgence of the Portiuncula, that is, the Remission of Sins of Assisi.

Of this, the reigning Supreme Pontiff Benedict XIV spoke and wrote with much learning and profound doctrine in Section VI of the most learned essay that he composed when he was still a prelate on the occasion of the procession of the Portiuncula, which was opposed but without effect by the Father-Guardian of the Monastery of the Minor Observants of the Angels near Assisi in 1720. That benediction originally worked marvels as testified by Saint Bonaventura in Chapter XI of the tale of Saint Francis, and even when written out by our Blessed One, it produced miracles for those close to him.

The first one to whom it showed its benefit and aid was the Father-Master Michel Angelo Catalano, General of the Order, who fell into the River Forma di Canara, which brings an abundance of water to the mills, and upon falling he commended himself to the aforementioned Blessed One, emerging then without any injuries. When he got back to the Monastery, Joseph met him, all happy and smiling, and said, *eh,*

Father-General, you had a great fright; you fell into the Forma River at around ten o'clock when I was saying Mass, and I commended you to God; didn't you still have any of those benedictions of Saint Francis? The General was stunned at the revelation as to what had happened and at the evidence of the miracle, and answered that he had one of the benedictions and two of his letters in his pocket, and he retired in silence to his room, admiring the greatness of the Lord in the holiness of his servant.

That benediction proved itself even more useful and more miraculous by the Father-Master Cicale, a Minor Conventual, who was betaking himself from Rome to Palermo. When his ship was surprised by a furious storm in that gulf, a shipwreck was inevitable. But the monk was armed with a lively faith and he threw the benediction into the sea saying, *I command you by the goodness of Father Joseph of Copertino that if he is really a Servant of God that the storm cease.* And, the storm ceased the moment the words that had been written by the Blessed One touched the furious foaming waves.

Another of these benedictions immediately cured Vincenzio Santucci in Ascoli of an evil fever the very moment it was hung from his neck, and similarly restored the health and lives of three others in that city. Its effect also proved health-giving to Porzia de' Nuti, freed from death that was imminent as a result of a childbirth that she had just undergone, because contact with that benediction and with a handkerchief stained by the blood of the Blessed one happily relieved her, Joseph having sent word that *she should be joyful because Saint Francis would help her.*

Not only in Italy but as far away as Poland, that benediction, written by Joseph's pen, worked miracles. There it gave back the sight to a blind man, and some of the benedictions upon being fixed to the doors and windows of a store, then drove out malignant spirits which in a strange way overturned the grain, fodder and oil.

All these miraculous facts showed the greatness of the Blessed One's charity towards his neighbor, and how so very helpful is the reverence for the writings of the saints, through whom God finds it worthy to work miracles.

To complete the topic at hand, one could add here Joseph's unique gratitude towards those who did him well. It says in the process of, beatification *that he appeared wonderful in the quality of his gratitude, always reminding himself of his benefactors, and holding them in special memory through continuing prayers, whose purpose was to implore the Lord for a worthy reward for them.*

It is not here that we should remain silent as to what one of his benefactors deposed: *When I sent him on many occasions some small jars of wine to restore the strength that had diminished at the beginning of his illness, he showed the greatest gratitude and he sent me word that he would always pray to the Lord for me and we had to do the same for him. In fact it made me and still makes me experience the effects of his gratitude, because one of the jugs of wine that I drew especially for him but kept in hand for my whole family after his death, lasted four times longer than usual. And when I receive from the Lord God something good with my family, I accept it as coming from his intercession.*

Likewise, he would teach by saying, *ingratitude is a great sin. When one has received a benefit from someone, one should be grateful to the benefactor and also thank the Lord God.*

eight

Of the unsullied purity of the Blessed Joseph

Blessed are those, said the Redeemer, who are clean and pure of heart, for to them will be given to see God. Of such a pure and clean heart, and so chaste of body and so unsullied was Joseph, that his bodily and mental righteousness rendered him an angel incarnate, so that it is no marvel that his spirit was continuously taken with God and his body was often raised up in the air to contemplate up close those things of divine and superhuman beauty.

But who can ever say how many thorns would be necessary to turn this white lily into a hedge to protect him from diabolical attacks. The Angel of Darkness, who takes advantage of the rebellion of one's senses and the intemperance of one's lusts, tested Joseph horribly, just as he tested the great Apostle, of whom Joseph seemed a copy in the depth of his ecstasies and the sublimity of his raptures.

For that reason, God wanted to keep Joseph firm in knowing the great truth, that God alone was the very person who raised him and lowered him and from whom alone he could hope for help and comfort, be it a little before or a little after any disturbing excesses of his mind. So he allowed Joseph to be assailed with such hateful lustful apparitions, with such obscenities and with such disgusting thoughts that to emerge victorious later was a miracle of endurance and grace. On many occasions Joseph begged God, as did the Apostle, with his heart on his lips, to free him from such infernal plagues which so frequently upset him with damnable apparitions, and he heard himself likewise being answered, *sufficit tibi gratia mea* (my grace is sufficient for you).

Here it behooves us to narrate things worthy of compassion rather than merely tell a story, so that man, however just and holy, learns in what mass of mud he lies as long as he lives in this mortal flesh. Encounters with evil women would besiege Joseph, sometimes in person, sometimes through letters, sometimes on the pretext of seeking advice, sometimes openly with great demands. Demons appearing like women broke his solitude and his evening sleep, and frequently with evil representations of the most obscene things to torment his most pure spirit. He always prevailed over these hard assaults, either by avoiding them, or by throwing the infamous letters into the fire, or by calling for help in the highest and most powerful name of the Virgin Mary.

But Joseph's long-sought peace did not return to his soul, even after his victories, since the enemy did not desist in often portraying to his thoughts those hated, nocturnal phantoms, although they agitated him only a little since he was diligent and prompt in squashing them, even if he might have had pleasure in absolutely consenting to them

But even though this saintly man was restless through his uncertainties, he understood in the end that it was divine help that had preserved him. For that reason he couldn't keep himself from repeating, *ah, my God, I know that everything you do is good, and that I did not sin during those temptations thanks to your grace, but I wouldn't want either to feel them or try them.*

He knew, on the other hand, that often the fear of the enemy wreaks more damage than the enemy himself, so that it behooves a person to disappoint his efforts. So, many times he would rise up from his praying or from his seat, and jumping around his cell would sing

> *Gesu', Gesu', Gesu'*
> *Vieni vieni consolami tu*
> *Vieni, e abbrucia questo cuore*
> *Con il tuo divino amore*
> *Vieni, vien, non tardare,*
> *Che piu' non posso stare*
> *Senza di Te Gesu'.*
> *Vieni, vieni consolami tu.*
>
> *(Jesus, Jesus, Jesus*
> *Come, come and comfort me,*
> *Come and burn this heart*
> *With your divine Love.*
> *Come, come, don't delay*
> *For I myself can be no more*
> *Without You Jesus.*
> *Come, come, and comfort me).*

In this way he commended himself to Jesus, as we have said at greater length in the chapter on his prayers. Thus, when he tore himself with pitiless penitence, it directed his thoughts elsewhere, turning his attention as to why he humiliated himself in the presence of the most high, which was to acquire the valuable gift of purity which is a gift from heaven. And until his death he received the gift and he persevered throughout his most horrible internal and external temptations, it being attested in the process of beatification *that he possessed the virtue of chastity to such an eminent degree that his confessors have asserted many times that it was true that they never knew in him even a shadow of dishonesty, but always found him most pure in mind and body, to the point that his mind seemed angelic rather than human.*

All the depositions conclude in the same way, reporting his unsullied virginity all the way to his death. Joseph cultivated this rare virtue with great scrupulousness and care. With the same care he would inculcate it in others, and thus would frequently say *that a pure soul is like a clear crystal vase, clean, crystalline, filled with fresh water, which everyone likes during times of drought, and can be for them something of great value, but if you put a single drop of oil in it, all that water goes bad and becomes unpleasing.* And he would add, *it is a dangerous thing to deal with women, who bring only harm to anyone who wants to be of God; one should flee from them, flee away from them, and only for obedience sake should one deal with them.* And many times he would thank the Lord for having, during the visit of the Consort of the Admiral of Castile, alienated him from his senses and putting him in rapture, as we said elsewhere.

As much as Joseph loved purity, he hated the opposing vice, and he smelled the stink of anyone stained with such guilty iniquity. One day he was seen disturbed and restless, and when asked, *what was the matter,* he answered *that he had just spoken with a woman filthy with sensuality, and that she had left such a stink in his nostrils that he couldn't remove it.* For that reason one shouldn't wonder that he frequently repeated to everyone that *impure people stink in the divine presence and in the presence of angels and men, whereas chaste people have "Christi bonus odor et odorem notitiae suae manifestant in omni loco"* (the fragrance of Christ, and of their reputations are evident everywhere).

By virtue of his unsullied purity, Joseph was rewarded by God with the prized gift of fragrance sensed by everyone, which was so pleasing, so continuous in his body, in his clothing, in his cell, and finally in everything he touched. It stupefied anyone who smelled the fragrance, and will stupefy in the future anyone who hears this certain and authentic narration: *Father Joseph of Copertino* (so deposes Father Francis Maria de' Angelis, a monk of the Minor Order) *sent out and exuded from his body and his clothing a most sweet odor, which was unlike any natural or artificial odor I have ever smelled. And the same fragrance spread from him throughout his whole room, and on his implements, and was even diffused outside his room. It was recognized as his, and he left his fragrance wherever he passed by, which I smelled throughout the whole time that I was active in that holy monastery, and which I have meant to say publicly, and which lasted until his death as a sign of his purity and chastity.*

The same was deposed by Father Peter Francis Levanto, Minor Observant and President of the Monastery of the New Church of Assisi, who said: *I know that the room where Father Joseph lived in this holy monastery, like the clothing he wore, yielded an odor and fragrance of Heaven, it not being possible for it to be anything natural, and I couldn't determine its nature. . .When I used to return to the monastery after having gone to Father Joseph's room, the fathers would ask me what I was wearing on my body, and I would tell them truthfully that I was not wearing anything with a fragrance, but the fragrance came from my having gone to the room of Father Joseph, and at times it stayed on me for fifteen days.*

Don Girolamo degli Angelucci added, *as corroboration of Joseph's chastity, God had bestowed a great and most sweet fragrance upon him, that covered his body, his clothing, and everything he touched. . .and anybody could easily find his cell because the fragrance spread even beyond it. . ...I could not tell you what strong natural odor it resembled, but I and others have always valued it as a gift of God.*

The same is deposed by Doctor Baldassare Massichi, and the Father-Regent Barnanei, and the Gonfalonier of Assisi, Graziano Benigni. And, Father Brother Giovanni Maria Cappuccino of Fossombrone attests that *the fragrance that emanated from the body of Father Giuseppe was so abundant and pleasing that it cheered all those who entered his cell, and was spread even outside, a sign to those who might not have known where Father Joseph was that he could be found by the sweetness of the fragrance. That fragrance spread to all the cells where he might be visiting for a short while, in the clothing he wore which, even though I had them washed many times with lye and soap, never lost their sweet odor. So it was on the priestly vestments used by him, which not only retained the fragrance but communicated it to the chests where they were kept, and then to other vestments, and the same happened with the things that he touched.* So everyone concluded that any such odor *was the odor of paradise, the fragrance of paradise.*

To these noble testimonies we add the deposition of the surgeon, Francis Pier Paoli, who testifies, *it is most certainly true that, as a sign of Father Joseph's most clear purity and chastity, the Lord God, endowed him with a most strong fragrance which always breathed out from his body, and I know it because all the time I attended him, as I said many times before, and handling him and moving him in his final infirmity, I could always smell that fragrance, which one knew full well to be supernatural, there not being any natural odor similar to it, and I even smelled it after his death when I was handling his cadaver which exuded the same odor, and even when his body was open when he had been shot.*

Two most eminent ecclesiastics now close this chapter, and the high quality of these people renders even more authentic the truth of the narrative. Julius Cardinal Spinola, who was an admirer of the stupendous raptures of the Blessed One, also participated personally in smelling the so-miraculous fragrance. *When I entered that small cell I said to him that I felt myself soothed by a most smooth fragrance, a most sweet odor, that I couldn't say what I could compare it to among those of nature or those composed artificially, but it is certain that although all other odorous things annoy me, I felt extraordinary pleasure from that which came from that cell, which even seemed to confer bodily health on me.*

One finally hears Joseph's old acquaintance, that is Cardinal di Lauria, a person well known to the world, distinguished for his piety and excelling in doctrine. In his words, *the notable gift of Joseph's purity has been evident to all those who have either dealt with him or had anything touched by him, for it yielded a most sweet odor, and the things handled by him kept the odor for a long time. In fact, in the dormitories through which he would pass, he left such a discernible odor that in order to find out where Brother Joseph had gone it was only necessary to follow the path of the odor. It is certain, as the teachers of the spiritual life tell us, that a person's odor is the sign of his true purity and the cleanliness of his heart.*

nine

Of his most deep humility.

Humility is one of the most beautiful virtues that can adorn a Christian soul, making one resemble the Son of God made Man, who proposed himself as an example for humble behavior and for the exercise of humility. *Discite a me, quia mitis sum et humilis corde* (Learn from me, for I am meek and humble of heart). The grace of the Lord is promised and bestowed on the humble, and the Holy Spirit rests in their hearts. Therefore it is by the humility of the Blessed Joseph's that we measure the greatness of his sanctity.

Joseph's whole life was a continuous exercise of the deepest humility. He considered himself a disgrace to the world and to be almost the most iniquitous among sinners. He fixed his mind continuously on the great truth that God is the King of Kings and the Lord of the Those Who Rule, and he diminished himself so much in his own view that when he compared himself to even the smallest and most contemptible, he judged himself vile, abject, and worthy only of ill treatment. Not only did he experience the contempt of others, which he endured with ever-lasting patience, but he also felt abhorrence and overflowing of humility when faced with the infinite praise and applause that was bestowed on him. So, one can well say of him, as per Saint Bernard, that this kind of humility is rare and excellent, *rara virtus humilitas honorata* (in those who receive honor, humility is a rare virtue).

Whenever he succeeded well in a notable undertaking, or when the Lord found it worthy to act through him, Joseph would immediately prostrate himself on the ground, kissing it and saying with tears, *non nobis Domine, non nobis, sed nomine tuo da gloriam* (not us, Lord, not us, but to your name give glory). And he would often reply to others very clearly that *if anything about him was good, it all came from God, and that God usually wrought great things in great sinners.*

When asked if, in so many events that befell him, any thoughts of vainglory had ever passed through his mind, he answered, *yes, they come and go but they never linger.* Joseph would give but a quick and serious glance at his own nothingness and then look on that most excellent God and his mind would rise to the highest, which is the source of all that is good.

He tried, furthermore, to imprint on the hearts of everyone those highest and eternal truths that he tirelessly cultivated in himself, especially in the hearts of the novices of his Order. To them he used to say, *some of you will become preachers, but don't become proud. For the preacher is like a trumpet which doesn't play by itself if God doesn't give him breath for it. So when you are about to preach, say these precise words to the Lord,*

> *Tu lo spirito sei, ed io la tromba,*
> *E senza il foato tuo nulla rimbomba.*

> *(You are the spirit and I am the trombone*
> *And without your breath nothing sounds home.)*

In his ecstatic absorption in God, Joseph was at times heard to say, *the Land of Adam can't produce other than spiny growths and thorns.* And, in the act of receiving absolution in the holy confession, so deeply would he humiliate his own person and beat his breast that the confessor would be left more embarrassed and more contrite than the penitent.

Not with his neighbor or his fellow monks, not with some friend or a brother, did Joseph ever use arrogant or repugnant words. When a superior entered his room he would kneel immediately as if it were the Seraphic Father Francis himself who had come in, and Joseph would declare himself unworthy to see him. Joseph was much in the state of spiritual retreat so he did not go out of his cell except to serve his neighbor, or to carry out some very basic tasks for the monastery. That's why he was seen lifting water from the well for the kitchen, washing vessels and dishes, sweeping the dormitories and the stairs, lighting lamps in church, and carrying material for the workshop. In a word, he was being a base servant.

Whenever anyone asked anybody else about him, Joseph wanted them to answer *that he was like a dead man; that the other monks were happy since they attended the church and the chorus, but that he himself was useless and not good for anything.*

As if that wasn't enough, he called himself by the names of the most vile stable animals, knowing that a sinner among beasts becomes the most unfeeling, and he would say that *he was a great sinner, and he would sign his letters "The greatest sinner who lives in the world, Brother Joseph of Copertino, poor little wretch."*

Nor was this quality in him ostentatious or hypocritical, but the product of his great humility which reached its greatest intensity when dealing with the Devil himself. On one occasion, tempted by woman who was possessed, Joseph dragged the Devil and the offending woman to a window that opened to a public street, and forced her to yell loudly, *Brother Joseph of Copertino is the most evil and infamous sinner on earth.* It was a disgrace for which God then compensated by putting truthful praise on the tongue of a child who called Joseph a *great Saint*, to the confusion of the infernal enemy, as we said specifically elsewhere.

The testimonies as to his humility are famous. Cardinal Lauria attests that the humility of this Blessed One was marvelous, *because he never wanted to be a superior, nor did he seek anything from his superiors other than they would let him be alone within four walls. When he was commanded to see some great personage, Joseph would beat his breast in humility and sometimes wept in pain on account of these visits.*

To conceal his raptures he would call them *his dazes and his defects.* He would often say that whenever he heard some lesson or else some other spiritual exposition he would feel an internal arousal and hoping to prevent himself from becoming a wondrous spectacle with ecstasies and raptures, would often say, *enough, enough, stop, stop; no more.*

Father Bernabe deposed on other occasions that *Joseph's humility before God and before men was unique, holding himself very vile and admitting that he was ignorant. In dealing with others, he recognized himself as inferior. So even when those monks who were not priests left his presence and would throw themselves on their knees to beg his blessing, he wanted to receive a blessing from them first, and then he would give them his blessing with these words, Potentia Patris, Sapientia Filii, et Virtus Spiritus Sancti liberet te ab omni malo* (May the Power of the Father, the wisdom of the Son, and the Goodness of the Holy Spirit free you of all evil). Such was also the way of our Blessed One with all the priests and monks. When many of them went to be blessed by him, he either blessed them kindly or else immediately knelt requesting to be blessed by them.

Frequently, then, there were differences among them in saintly humility, but that of Joseph was always triumphant. For when he, having been blessed used to bless others, his blessing was received as of greater worth than the benedictions of others. Even when passing through Terni on the way to Rome, Joseph found the Provincial Superior in that monastery and asked for his blessing, but instead he saw at his own feet the Superior genuflecting to him, each one asking the other to bless him. Finally the Blessed One won, and was himself blessed with these words, *Benedictio Domini Super caput Justi* (The blessing of the Lord on the head of the Just). Before dying in Osimo, the Fathers of the Monastery requested to be blessed by him, but he wanted their blessing first, and then he blessed them with his crucifix while two monks supported his weakened and falling arms.

What more? The Devil himself, pretending to be a monk on his way to Rome for the Holy Year, asked for Joseph's benediction. Joseph looked around and could not understand how he, the monk, had gotten into that little room of his, and asked him if he had permission from his superior. The Devil gave no answer but persisted in requesting the blessing, and when the Blessed One responded again by asking if he had permission, the false monk disappeared. The Servant of God confided this incident to a person learned in doctrine who repeated it to others. But later the Blessed One heard with great displeasure that it was being told to others and said, *I don't want to tell anything anymore to anyone; I will confirm to myself well enough that such an event was very true and in the way that I said it.*

When talking to Joseph of his ecstasies or when praising him, Joseph felt it as a torment only a little less than hell. It says in the beatification process that he *abhorred applause like the plague, as well as praises of himself, and whenever he heard them it greatly saddened him, and it pierced his soul if anyone held anything good about him. On the contrary, he rejoiced over injuries and scorn against his person.* In order not to be an object of admiration and praise, he often prayed to the Lord to deprive him of the heavenly consolation of ecstasy and raptures, and not to have them.

When they happened to him during Mass, which was frequent, immediately after Mass was over he would put aside the holy vestments and run with swift steps to his room. And when God pulled Joseph to Himself, making him into a prodigious spectacle, Joseph's face after coming back from his ecstasy would redden modestly and, sliding his hood over his forehead, he would betake himself confused to his room. Or else he would ask those around him *to make allowances for his bad manners, sometimes alleging weariness, sometimes illness, and always that he was dazed and weakened in his natural makeup.*

It was said that a blind man from Poland recovered his sight upon being touched by one of those blessings of Saint Francis written in Joseph's hand. When Joseph knew of it, he immediately kneeled and thanked the Lord for bestowing such grace at a distance so that he could escape in that way from the praises of those nearby.

He would conceal the fragrance that emanated from his Body and from his clothing and from his cell by attributing it to the fine tobacco of that time, and when he understood that such an odor propagated itself, he began to take fragrant tobacco: *But in truth*, the beatification process says, *many people discerned that it was due to another cause, and they were able to take away the fragrant tobacco and give him some that had no odor, yet his body, his clothes, and everything he touched still exuded the same sweet fragrance.*

Joseph's great humility was further noted in the beatification process where one reads, *Father Joseph, because of his great humility, endeavored to hide from his confessors and his superiors the gifts and the grace that he received from the Lord God, and he tried many times, admitting them only when required by obedience.*

And regarding Joseph's hiding of his gifts, this was shown by the knight Gaglieno Vigilante, who was deprived of sight and who resorted to Joseph to get it back. But Joseph, immediately upon hearing that the knight wanted from him the grace of being able to see, said calmly, *go away*, but then embarrassed and humble he said *go away quickly because I with my sins might make you even more blind and not give you your sight*. Turning then to a priest who was with him, he said, *oh woe is me that I am capable of working miracles! I who am such a great sinner.*

But he didn't answer in that same manner to his confessor who, upon entering his room unexpectedly, found Joseph in an almost ecstatic state discussing spiritual matters with other monks with great fervor. The confessor, in order to test Joseph's soul and reprove him, said, *what are you saying, you hypocrite?* Joseph turned to him and answered both humbly and sadly, *yes my son, you speak the truth, you speak the truth,* and he covered his face with his hands and went silent. But he wasn't silent when he knew that he was to be visited either by Prelates or Princes or Cardinals or Sovereigns, but being surprised by such gatherings he used to say, *I for my part, don't know why these people come to me, who am ignorant and a poor sinner.*

Joseph was so much in love with the beautiful virtue of humility, and had absolutely no interest in himself, that lordship over a thousand worlds wouldn't have made him change his mind. He knew - and this is one of the most beautiful of his worthy sayings - *that the humble spirit is like a small tree of rich oranges; it produces fruits that are much larger and much more beautiful than those produced by large orange trees. In that way, when a humble soul acts, its acts are much more meritorious and a lot more pleasing to God than those of a soul that is not humble.* Therefore, the more the Lord raised him high with favors, the more Joseph probed into the thoughts of his own nothingness.

ten

Of the heroic poverty and blind Obedience of this markedly Blessed person.

Inasmuch as Jesus Christ was the teacher of every virtue, including poverty and obedience, He lived in such poverty in conformity with that first virtue that He didn't even have a place to rest His divine head. And the other virtue of obedience drew Him from heaven to the earth, hammering Him onto the hard wood of a cross. Joseph was an imitator of Christ in both virtues, and the first one of poverty shone in him to such a heroic degree that one could more easily describe what he didn't have than what he did have. He was so un-provided with anything, that he was therefore detached from everything and averse to having anything.

It wasn't enough for him to have nothing of his own and be dependent entirely on his superiors, but he wanted to experience the discomfort that poverty brings with it, which is precisely the perfection in which such a virtue consists. His clothes were simple cover for the nudity of the body except for his tunic which was mostly beggarly and worn out. He never wore anything else but a coarse and crude habit, which was more of a hair shirt than clothing, a pair of underpants of very coarse cloth, and a pair of slippers which he used when he had to appear in public. He had nothing else to protect himself from inclement temperatures, even from the rigors of the harshest winters. He had one single kerchief of grey wool which, during his last illness, was by necessity switched for two made of white cloth, coarse and crude, since he refused those made of linen as being unsuitable for his poverty.

In sum, as the process of beatification says, *Father Joseph during his whole time in the Order never had anything of his own, and only used the bare and necessary clothing given to him by his superiors, even though it might have been furnished by benefactors for the love of God; he was particularly pleased with the clothes he wore at the end of his life because they were provided for him by the most eminent Lord Cardinal Bichi, Bishop of this City. Joseph always lived in perfect poverty, not recognizing anything as his own.*

As for his diet, of which we have spoken elsewhere, it consisted of herbs and vegetables. His beverage was water, but when pushed by necessity he would take a few sips of wine. His bed was composed of three planks, with a worn out bearskin and a straw pillow for his head. In his last illness, when he was ordered to be placed on a woolen mattress with linen sheets, he was able to lie there only a few hours. To console him, it was necessary to put him again on his beloved planks where he found more peace in the abundance of internal consolation that it gave him.

The only other furniture in his cell were a chair, two straw seats, a small table, and some sacred images on paper stuck to the wall that were lent to him by the priest D. Bernardino Benaducci, his devoted confidant. As for Joseph's personal kit, he was asked when he arrived at a Monastery if he had his stuff with him. He answered yes, and it was a small spoon of wood and a small knife to slice bread.

More content with his great poverty than a man with abundant treasure, Joseph would refuse anything offered to him except for fresh flowers which he would immediately give up as an ornament for his altar. Upon seeing him so poor, some rich people sought means to bring him to their homes with the idea of helping him with a bit of money. But upon going there, he refused and was unwilling to receive it, so they skillfully and surreptitiously placed in his cowl a small silver coin worth two G*iulii,* called *Tari* in those parts. As soon as the Blessed One had the unwelcome money on himself, he broke out in a copious sweat as if he were carrying a great weight on his neck. Feeling as if he were about to die, he raised his voice, screaming breathlessly, *I can't endure it any more.* The money was taken away with the same skill as it had been placed, without his seeing it at all. And right away, as if relieved of an unbearable burden, he breathed and reverted to the state he was in before.

Elsewhere we have underscored such refusals, so it wouldn't do to repeat them here. In that heroic poverty of his he always in fact used to say to everyone *that he had nothing, but that God provided him with everything.* In that, he was like his Seraphic Father, Saint Francis, who often turned towards Heaven and said, *Deus meus et omnia* (my God and my all).

Such were the heights to which Joseph's poverty reached, but poverty wasn't the best part of sacrificing himself to the Lord. It is an arduous thing to divest one's self of what one has, but it is much more arduous is to divest oneself of what one is. Such a triumph is reserved in the virtue of holy obedience, for which placing one's will in the hands of others is greater than any other sacrifice that we ourselves can make to the Most High.

Let us then look quickly at the obedience of our Blessed One. He was very opposed to dealing with women and with secular people, to eating meat, to leaving his cell even to come down to walk in the garden in summertime. But he would do any of these things at a simple signal from his superior, whom he held in as much esteem as if he had been Father Saint Francis himself. On an occasion when a new superior arrived at the monastery where Joseph was staying, and when the superior visited him (since Joseph lived in retreat), Joseph immediately threw himself at his feet calling him, *his father, his director, and master,* and expounded to him his way of life regarding his food, his clothing, his practices, his speech, his prayers, and every other of his spiritual exercises up to that time, and which would continue in the future if the superior were pleased. He thus showed himself a faithful servant of his beloved master, with even more resignation than a sick man desirous of being cured would show to a worthy physician.

In fact he even obeyed his lay companion, and every other layman of the monastery as well, so that without their consent he wouldn't even open or close the window of his room. Once his superior required that Joseph not move from his place, and Joseph didn't move even a foot from the top of a tile where he was standing

Joseph abhorred eating meat, but when some cooked meat was brought to his room and he was told with sharp words, with the approval of the superior, *eat some of this meat you big hypocrite,* he immediately ate it with joy, even though it was a big thing for him to swallow it and then regurgitate it, since his stomach didn't want it. The same thing happened in his final illness, in which to strengthen him he was commanded to eat a tasty dish. He said gaily, *so, you want me to pay the price, hey?* And he immediately ate it and immediately vomited it.

And this was not the least of his obedience. He was opposed to giving anything of his to those who devoutly pleaded for them, holding himself, as said, to be a great sinner, but all that was needed was that his superior order it, that he would quickly undress saying, *for the sake of obedience I am content not only that you remove my tunic and my habit, but my hide as well, if you want it.*

So strongly did he love this virtue of obedience that he called it a carriage that bears the soul comfortably and with pleasure to heaven, and that's why one must let himself be conducted just as a blind man lets himself be guided by his dog. In fact, wherever he was called for obedience's sake, he betook himself there with great happiness, and he always ended up triumphant since he acted out of obedience.

He was sent by his superior to free a woman possessed by evil spirits. The Devil, upon seeing him, slapped him so heavily with the hand of the victim that the sound terrified all those nearby. Joseph wasn't at all bewildered by the blow, and he slid out of his pocket the order written by the hand of the Father-Guardian and tossed it onto the person who was invaded, saying, *you, oh you take it now.* That was the powerful exorcism that put the Devil in flight, leaving the fortunate woman free, thus confirming Joseph's deed.

Such were his exorcisms. After uttering the litanies of the Most Blessed Virgin, he would address the Demons, saying to them, *I didn't come here to chase you away from that body, but I'm doing it only for obedience's sake since I was commanded by my superior. If you want to leave, then leave. If you don't want to leave, then do what you want. For me it is enough to have been obedient. In this way Joseph freed many people.* And so it says in the file of the beatification process.

He knew well the power of obedience, having been obedient as many times as it pleased God, and that's why at such times he would exclaim, *oh holy obedience to which God himself brings compliance.* That's why during his wonderful ecstasies and most sublime raptures, the only thing that was necessary to make Joseph come back to his senses was the quality of obedience, when neither sharp pricking, nor stabbings, nor fire itself had the power to do it. Truly, as he confessed, he couldn't hear the orders of his superiors during his absorption in God, but he could tell that *the name of obedience to the Lord sealed the curtain,* that is, it put an end to his communication, *and left the soul free to do its duty.* From this was born his beautiful saying, *better to die than not obey.*

And by the following similar utterance he inculcated in all the monks the need for obedience: *obedience is a knife that kills the will of a man, sacrificing it to God, and it was the same knife that sacrificed Christ, Our Lord, who "factus est obediens usque ad mortem"* (was obedient unto death). It was no wonder that Joseph, in giving an example of obedience, described it as, *to be ready for the sake of obedience to throw oneself into a burning furnace with the firm hope of coming out of the flames unhurt.*

eleven

Miracles wrought by the Blessed Joseph.

One of the main reasons why God works miracles is to display the sanctity of the person through whom it is worthy to work them, wanting thereby to make him an example of virtue to others. *Operatur Deus miracula ad demonstrationem sanctitatis alicujus, quam deus hominibus vult proponere in exemplum virtutis* (God works some miracles to demonstrate the sanctity of whom he wants to hold up to men as an example of virtue.) (St. Thom. 2,2, q.178. art. 2.0)

God demonstrated Joseph's holiness during his lifetime, with all those raptures and stupendous miracles to which we have referred, and He also wanted to demonstrate Joseph's sanctity after death with miracles that we will mention briefly, so that his heroic virtue might become a holy impulse for imitation.

The first to extol the miracles of our Blessed One was the Supreme Pontiff Alexander VII who, to restore Joseph's earthly remains to his Order, wanted the Capuchins of Fossombrone to place them in the Monastery of Saint Francis of Osimo. Before, when that supreme Monarch of the Church had been Nuncio in Poland, he was forced to endure the hard pain of kidney stones from which he emerged happily although not fully cured completely from the discomfort of such a fierce illness. In the eighth year of his pontificate he was surprised by such a stubborn retention of urine that no matter what techniques were attempted or what remedies were employed, it continued for four days and it was impossible to overcome the painful and life-threatening course of the disease. During his spasms, the afflicted Pontiff remembered the holy life of Father Joseph of Copertino, who had died a little earlier in Osimo, and his illustrious miracles which were talked about fully throughout Italy. The Pope, in his extreme need, invoked Joseph with full faith, and devoutly dressed himself in one of Joseph's habits. Suddenly the pains stopped and he spontaneously voided a great quantity of urine. Thus, by obvious miracle, he was preserved for another five years from a harsh death which had threatened to carry him away from his world-wide care of Christ's flock.

Father Antonio dei Giustiniani, assailed by an evil fever in the Monastery of Osimo, was in desperate health. On the fourteenth day of being bedridden he received final communion by Viaticum, lost his ability to speak, was unconscious, unmoving, and it seemed that he had already become a corpse. While in that state, the lay nurse, knowing of Father Antonio's veneration of the Blessed One, went to Joseph's sepulcher, where Father Antonio usually went every day to recite an Our Father and an Ave Maria, and she said in a loud voice, *Father Antonio, commend yourself to Father Joseph.* Upon saying this, the sound was immediately heard by Father Antonio who answered, *I commend myself to him.* He opened his eyes reinvigorated, found himself healthy, sat up in bed, and charmingly set about laughing. And seeing on the little table by his bed a vase of holy oil, he asked what novelty was that? Upon being told that everything had been prepared to give him extreme unction, he said, *ah I am healthy.* Although he wanted to rise to give due thanks to the Blessed One who was his liberator, he was held back by the alertness and prudence of those present. He dined that night with a marvelous appetite, slept well, and the following morning went down to the church to thank his liberator. On the following night, which was Christmas, he participated in the Matins, and sang the lesson in the chorus to the wonderment of everyone.

Father Francis Anthony Vernaleone, M.C., sick with fever, with an inflammation of both salivary glands, and a discharge of blood which had lasted 25 days, was reduced to the extreme to the despair of the Physicians. In such grave danger, a shirt that had belonged to the Blessed One was placed over him on his bed. Immediately, Joseph made himself seen to the sick man, and said to him, *be joyful because you are cured of both the fever and discharge.* And so it was.

But Father Francis Anthony was still in discomfort because of his salivary glands, and was suffering much in his illness. He resorted again to his benefactor, who appeared to him again at midnight saying, *what's the matter that you should call me?* The sick man answered, *ah my Father Joseph, cure me again of these salivary glands and finish the grace bestowed on me.* The Blessed One then added, *I will heal one of them, but not the other, but in the other you will have improved health. You will rise next Saturday from the bed.* What he said is what indeed followed. The other gland was healed by surgery, which succeeded miraculously. The patient felt no pain whatsoever from the tool of the surgeon, thus fulfilling the third part of the powerful aid given by the Servant of God.

While Captain Blasi was travelling by carriage from Corinaldo to Jesi with his wife and a son who was a priest, the air was beset by a fierce storm at the second hour of the night. As flood-like rain descended, one of the horses slipped and fell into a deep precipice nearby, pulling the carriage to its brink. Terrified by the darkness and the pouring rain, and of the horror of the precipice, all the travelers jumped out of the carriage. Biagia, the Captain's consort, who wore on her breast a small crucifix given to her by the Blessed One, raised it with trembling hand and kneeling in the mud said, *oh my Father Joseph, help me and my family in the darkness of this night and in the horror of this imminent danger.* Joseph hastened immediately to their great need. The carriage emerged from the precipice pulled by one horse. The exact words in the beatification file were, *suddenly there appeared in the air a moon that seemed in its fifteenth day even though it wasn't the time for such a full moon.* By its splendor, all were conducted safely to Jesi, and then the miraculous moon disappeared near the end of the trip. Biagia, who had implored the aid of the Blessed One, was privileged even more than the others, because even though she had kneeled in the mud in her daze, she found herself not only clean, but not even wet.

Here, before we go on to mention other miracles, we note that the miracles of the Blessed One had for the most part an instantaneous quality. For this reason, from the unique healings that Joseph wrought, we may exclude the forces of nature, which might have also taken place in due course with the same result but not instantly as one reads in Joseph's miracles.

The Nobleman Graziano Benigni of Assisi was oppressed by a serious illness, and was more dead than alive. He invoked the Blessed One and, being touched by his rosary, suddenly got better and was cured. Giovanni Martelli of Assisi, who was languishing and moving towards death because of a fierce stomach ache, commended himself to Joseph and, as the beatification file reads, *the pain immediately stopped.*

Cornelio Saccalosi immediately found himself free of an evil fever at the mere invocation of Joseph's name and at the touch of Joseph's cap. The children of Countess Ludovica Patrizi of Perugi received similar grace, as did Flamminio Guarnieri who was Canon of Osimo, Donna Maria Leopardi and Donna Maria Angelica Pranzoni who were, nuns of S. Benvenuto of Osimo, Giovanni Battista dei Plodis and his Servant Antonia, Faustina Ambrosia, Francesca Maria Arcangeli, Eugenio Maccatelli, D. Andrea dei Bonfigli, the Priest Guidobaldo Viviani, all of Osimo, and many more whose healings are recorded in Joseph's process of Beatification with these words, *statim, illico, ininslanti, eadem die, prodigiose* (immediately, right then, on the same day, prodigiously) at the sole contact with his rosary, tunic, rope belt, and cap, in fact even upon the taste of a pear, part of which Joseph out of obedience had brought near his lips during his last illness.

Now we will narrate those miracles that were worked by our Blessed One to heal certain definite portions of the human body, whenever he was sought by anyone who was needful of attaining from the Most High a remedy tailored to a specific illness.

Beginning then with those giving birth, Angelica di Costanza, an inhabitant of Perugia, after having miscarried, was surprised by fierce pains for some days. She was sent to the physicians, but was barely alive. So great was the harshness of her spasms that she raised her shrieks to heaven to beg for the cool relief of death. Hastily given communion by Viaticum, the procedures to be carried out after her death had already been prepared, and it was expected that she would expire at any moment. In that extremity, Anastasia di Bastiano, a pious and compassionate woman, took out of a small container some bits of bread from Joseph's table and with them a piece of cloth stained with his blood. She put the bits of bread into a spoonful of broth and had the dying woman gulp it down, and she placed the stained cloth on the dying woman's body, all the while imploring the aid of the Blessed One. Immediately the woman, as if she had never suffered illness, delivered yet a new fetus that was dead but soaking wet. Indeed she was left free of any illness, to the highest wonderment of those around her who in one moment saw her moribund, and then healthy.

Also this topic of good health was shown in the Blessed One's aid to Porzia Sabetta of Copertino. Upon having to go through childbirth, this unhappy woman was sent to a midwife and to the physicians who, after one day and night of vain effort and her incessant sharp pains, intimated her inevitable death since, due to her weakening strength, she would have to be cut at the opening. The husband despaired of human aid so he resorted with lively faith to the divine by imploring Joseph's support. He placed on the body of his weakening consort a letter written in the hand of the Servant of God, and no sooner had it touched her than this patient immediately brought the fetus into the light as if by command, contrary to the expectation of the physicians and of the midwife, thereby filling the mother with joy, the father with happiness, and everyone who was present with holy wonder.

Another person very unfortunate in her births was Anna Caterina Buttari of Osimo, who miscarried nine times because of the weakness of her kidneys. Having come to her tenth pregnancy, she commended herself with fervent faith to the Blessed One, making a promise to God that if her pregnancy were brought to a happy conclusion, she would dress her son in the habit of the Minor Conventual Order to the honor and glory of Joseph. Such was her promise and so was the outcome of her devout desires. She had nine months of happy pregnancy, which she had never experienced before, and with happiness she gave birth to a little boy who was born in perfect health and lived.

But how many more were the Blessed One's prodigies of this kind. Upon contact with Joseph's rope-belt, Countess Anna Maria Montesperelli, Cassandra Girenti, Girolama Mariotti, and Elisabetta Saccalossi of Perugia, along with many others when in serious danger at childbirth, immediately and happily gave birth. If we were to name all of them, the story would never end. A celebrated writer of Joseph's biography, which we have outlined through our own devotion, closes the present subject like this, *we under oath attest in the presence of the Church of God that while writing these things, the time arrived for the childbirth of our daughter in law, and the pain of the mother was increasing as were the danger to the fetus and the fear of our domestics. The patient devoutly invoked the name of Father Joseph of Copertino, and so the birth ended happily so that one can't tell what came first, the imploring or the grace.*

That aid to mothers for which our Blessed One prayed did not ignore innocent children whose health was invoked with faith. A lactating child of Giovanni Canori, Dean of Cardinal Chigi, became ill in Rome and lay on the mother's bosom and was seen with eyes closed, a pale face, and every sign of death. A monk of the Order applied to his breast a piece of the habit of the Servant of God. Upon contact, the child suddenly opened his eyes, attached himself to the breast and with a sweet laugh showed that he knew his mother. Nor did the miracle end here. It was just as if he knew the benefactor and instrument of the health that he so miraculously recovered, for he never permitted himself to be swaddled unless, with his little hands, he had placed the piece of Joseph's habit between his flesh and the wrappings. If occasionally it was misplaced, he refused to lie still but would search for it here and there with his eyes, and upon seeing it would indicate it to the servants, and when receiving it would place it on his breast. It was something that awakened tenderness and devotion in those around him and filled them with grateful veneration towards the Blessed One.

Virginia, a girl of thirteen, daughter of Bartolommeo Tanaglia, a gentleman of Fossombrone, was assailed by an evil fever and couldn't see or hear anymore. Her parents wept over her as if already dead. While she was in this mortal state, Father Joseph Maria, a Capuchin monk, blessed her with a rosary that had belonged to the Blessed Joseph of Copertino. The Monk, who was on a trip to Urbino, departed right after the benediction, but the girl immediately returned to perfect health as if awakened from a profound sleep, not only without fever or a shadow of sickness, but hale, hearty and rosy. When the monk soon returned, he observed the girl, and understanding the miracle, turned with his eyes and hands to heaven and said, *God is wonderful in His Servants, and Father Joseph of Copertino is a wonderful Servant of God who performs amazing works in this world.*

In Copertino, a little boy two months old was oppressed by a horrible unknown disease and was lying spread out and motionless in his crib, putrefying and becoming black, with a stink that was intolerable to the servants. The nurse, Laura Falconieri, inspired by God, wrapped him in a kerchief of the Blessed One, and instantly the rotting little boy regained his color, his flesh bloomed again, and he gave himself happily to sucking the breast, as it says in the beatification process, *and now he is alive,* to the amazement of everyone who saw the miracle.

Pietro Luigi Blasio, a young boy of three or four years, while playing with other boys his age in the courtyard of his house, was suddenly surprised by a fierce pain in his eyes, which he immediately closed, and when doing so emitted very loud cries and shrieks, saying that a wall had fallen onto his eyes. His mother, upon hearing the sound, tried to force his eyelids open, but in vain because once they were opened, they immediately closed again. Upon being visited by physicians and surgeons, they all knew that the nerves were loosened, so the eyes would be drained bit by bit and he would lose his sight. A monk of the Order, who was a nephew of the Blessed One, arrived at that house and was moved by the weeping of the afflicted mother. He said, *let us commend ourselves to our Venerable Father Joseph of Copertino,* and meanwhile slid out from his pocket a little purse of offerings that had belonged to the Blessed One, applying them to the eyes of the patient. *At that same instant Pier Luigi opened his eyes without the aforementioned malady returning, and never again was touched by any illness regarding his vision, being able to see to this day, which is nineteen years after the incident.* So it says in the process of beatification.

The Blessed One was not only generous in his favors to children with regard to illnesses of the eyes, but to people of any age. Sister Vittoria Bruni, a nun of Saint Clare in Copertino, afflicted by a very serious discharge from both eyes, invoked his name and promptly was in good health. A blind man who had lost his sight in such a manner that the very pupils were in fact withered, recovered instantly at the invocation of the Blessed One and the pupils swelled again as the humors once again returned to their visual function.

Margarita Donati of Osimo was born with and always lived with unhealthy eyes, and for months at a time was almost blind and lay in bed tortured by the sharp pain of discharges. One morning she betook herself to the sepulcher of the Blessed One, and leaning her head and her eyes on the ground exclaimed, *here I am, here I am; either health or death; I implore your prayers that you grant to my faith one of your miracles soon.* In that way she declared her need, and that is what followed. When she got up from the ground she could see perfectly, whereas in the past, like the Blind Evangelist, she saw people *sicut arbores ambulantes* (like walking trees). The pains ceased, the blindness ceased, and now being able to see, she returned Home.

Francesca Caldieri in Osimo was oppressed by a similar sickness, and was cured in an instant when she devoutly brought near to her eyes a slipper of the Blessed One. Angela Ratti, stricken by a stick in the pupil of her left eye that became all swollen and lachrymating was immediately free of the swelling, of the pain, and of the tears as soon as the ailing part was touched by a wrapping that contained some hairs of Joseph.

Much the same happened to Anna Cecchi, a lady of Fermo. Pierced unfortunately by a thorn in her eye when cleaning her little garden, she first tried courageously to remove the thorn herself; then upon being touched by a relic of the Servant of God, the eye returned to its natural state, healed as if it never been hurt. The wife of Francesco Morosini received similar grace in the year 1702 in Rome.

So, we've said enough regarding these healings. We will now refer to favors worked by our Blessed One on other parts of the human body.

Cornelia Mattei of Osimo, with a crippled back, a midget in height, always unemotional and mentally obtuse, was brought to Joseph's sepulcher in Osimo. The beatification file says, *she was left free of any illness, and became so beautiful that she no longer appeared what she was before.*

Supported by others, Caterina Blasi was also brought there. She had been sick for two months with fever that had exhausted her strength. Upon visiting the sepulcher, her fever left her and she found herself so vigorous and healthy that she was immediately able to visit other churches and return home on her own feet. Also her servant, Maddalena, upon visiting the sepulcher of the Blessed One, was freed of a discharge of blood that had brought her to the last breath of her life. Again, having been seated at Joseph's sepulcher to implore grace, Antonio Castellani was freed of sharp pains of sciatica which had been tormenting him for two months, thereby filling his wife, son and bystanders with tenderness.

Captain Stefano Blasi was tormented by a fierce and constant pain in his knee such that upon bending he felt as if he were dying from spasms. He dragged himself to the sepulcher of the Blessed One and upon reaching it he kneeled fearlessly, touching the stone ever so gently. He later said, *it seemed as if he were kneeling on soft cotton.* He prayed, and rose up free and healed, and the cruel and painful malady never recurred.

Marsilia Bonafede, and Sister Leoparda Maffucci who was a nun of Saint Niccolo d'Osimo, reported the same grace, having been healed in an instant, the first from a very painful discharge in one knee by a bit of the Blessed One's habit, and the other of a large growth on the left knee, *as big as the head of a lamb*, as the process of beatification says, which suddenly disappeared upon contact with a bit of cloth stained with Joseph's blood.

And finally, Luigi Blasio, whose whole knee had become a sore, brought a slipper of the saint up close to the offending part, first smelling a very sweet odor which he called the fragrance of Heaven, and then finding himself perfectly healed without even an indication of a scar.

Joseph's wondrous intercession triumphed also with the healing of hands, head, shoulders, and throat. Diana Scastiglioni, a seamstress of Osimo, was in spasms for three months from a continuous pain in her right hand, for which reason she couldn't earn a living for herself or her family. Commending herself warmly to the Blessed One, she applied a piece of his tunic to the ailing part, was freed instantly, and was immediately able to take up her work again. The same woman grew a wart four years later near her eye, which bothered her with continuous pain. She bravely scratched it off with her own hand, but such an abundance of blood came out that she was left lifeless, immobile and almost dead. The same piece of Joseph's tunic was placed on the wound and she felt the pain cease immediately. The beatification process says, *the blood was stanched, and the following morning she appeared without any marking on the spot.*

With a touch of the Blessed One's rosary, Giuseppe Risenna of Copertino was cured of incessant, mortal, piercing headaches which were so fierce that they confined him to his home for a full year unable even to sit up in bed. But after one touch he immediately left his house for his work in the fields, cheerful and healthy. A daughter of Laura Falconieri was oppressed by the same sort of pain which was evident from the screams she let forth, but upon resting her head on a letter written in the hand of the Blessed one, was cured in an instant.

A comb of the Blessed One applied to the painful spot cured Antonio of Osimo. A little piece of cloth stained with his blood freed in an instant Andrea Bonfigli of a discharge of blood from his nose, and a kerchief of the Blessed One healed Rosanna Amboni from a very dangerous scab.

With a bit of the Blessed One's blood, Giovanni Battista Pascolini of Assisi was cured of a broken shoulder. Anastasia Risidori of Osimo was, upon contact with the Blessed One's slipper, freed of a fatal pleural infection. One of the Blessed One's rope belts cured the sciatica of Sister Ippolita Galli, a Nun of Saint Niccolo d' Osimo. A piece of a relic of the Blessed one healed Catterina Rossa of monstrous dropsy, and Donna Vittoria Corona Pini of epilepsy, and a nephew of Andrea Massi of a ruptured intestine, and Costanza was freed of asthma, and Donna Vittoria Casponi, a nun of the new Monastery of Osimo, of a nervous disorder.

Antonia Evangelista of Pesaro was cured of a mangled leg, of paralysis of a hand, and of a speech defect. Francesco Cialdei of Urbino was cured of a frightening and precipitous fall down the stairs, so that he was mangled all over and partially broken and came close to a most painful death.

In addition to the foregoing instantaneous cures, as extracted from the beatification files, which glorify the Blessed Joseph and provide manifest proof of the effectiveness of his intercession with God, we describe two more of great satisfaction to anyone who cites them. The Father-Master Francesco Maria Bellani of the Minor Conventuals of the Monatery of Saint Francis of Modena, and Brother Francesco Pavarelli, a professed layman of the same Order, instantly upon invoking the Blessed One happily discharged kidney stones the size of beans without ever having similar pain again, even though they had been oppressed in the past with great torment, as they attest in their authenticated depositions on August 1, 1721.

Following the impulse of piety found in Catholic Christianity, the Blessed One's devotees will want to have some relic of him, so as to have a sure token of his great patronage. But wherever there are some who do not possess a relic, they may nevertheless comfort themselves because that Kind Lord who renders the shadow of his saints living on earth prodigious and beneficial, renders equally wondrous the pictures of those later reigning with him in Heaven.

The pictures of the Blessed Joseph of Copertino abound in grace and miracles, as we will recount below and more fully in the next Chapter. Nor is it too difficult to acquire such pictures, in order to have frequently before one's eyes the image of a person who is so prompt to bless those who, when venerating them, commend themselves with living heart to his effective patronage.

For eight years, Don Francesco Gordini, Canon of Lecce, through his devotion, kept a picture of our Blessed One over his bed. It so happened then, when summer was nigh and the canopy of the bed was removed, the image was also removed without his noticing it. Upon lying in bed that evening, Don Francesco was suddenly surprised by an unusually strong fever which kept him agitated for many hours until morning. Then he searched with his eyes for the image, and not seeing it he called his servants asked, *which one of them then had removed that picture?* Upon learning of the oversight, he went personally to get the picture, and said, *oh Father Joseph, this night my servants made you take air outside of my room, and that's why the heat of fever came upon me.* After the picture was put back in its place, Don Francesco rested in bed, and slid peacefully into sleep, free immediately of any shadow of a fever which in its natural course would have been prolonged several hours into that day, and which never came back. The same Canon, who was a secular layman, added that his daughters by legitimate marriage were freed of a serious illness upon being sent a portrait of the Blessed One. For this reason they became devout, and each of them saw and experienced the portrait's benefits in the painful parts of their bodies, whose pain was relieved by invoking his name.

Domenica Gattucci of Monte Lupone was bedridden for many months due to incurable pains which were thereby prolonging her death rather than her life. Upon bestowing a devout kiss on the picture of the Blessed Joseph, she fell asleep and the very next morning she got up from the bed by herself, healthy and free, and she went to church to give thanks to God and to the intercession of the Blessed One.

Antonia Carella Ciccolini, a noblewoman of Castel Fidardo, was surprised by a very sharp headache that left her beside herself. Then she was taken by an evil fever which left her unable to make her holy confession, so that the only thing that was expected was her death. But, Brother Girolamo, a lay monk of the Minor Conventual Order, arrived at her home and brought with him a picture of the Blessed Joseph. He presented it to the dying woman, telling her in a loud voice, *commend yourself, my daughter, to Father Joseph.* She heard the name of the Blessed One and commended herself to him with living faith and, according to the process of beatification, she said, *I fell asleep immediately and then upon awakening I found myself in full capacity and consciousness, and in such a state that I was fully able to be confessed, and was left improved in such a way that, to the great amazement of the physicians, I was free from any danger, and at the end of four days I was made immune from the fever.*

D. Carlo Marcello Diotaiuti, Canon of Osimo, oppressed without hope of human remedy by an insupportable heart condition which in fact was taking his breath away, turned towards a picture of the Blessed One, *and immediately,* according to the process of beatification, *he felt freed by divine hand from the anguish of death,* and he went to the sepulcher to give devout thanks to his illustrious benefactor.

twelve

Other miracles of God wrought through the intercession of the Blessed Joseph

In the year 1724, Paolino Moretti of Monte Leone in Umbria became ill with a continuous fever, headache, lack of appetite, and great weakness and pain throughout his body and in his nerves, which on June 5 was diagnosed as epilepsy. All human remedies were attempted in vain, even applying a hot iron to the back of the head, which the sick man didn't even feel. On the sixth of the same month, the attending physician put him in the hands of the priests. While Paolino was in this deplorable state, Father M. Felice Fedeli of the Minor Conventuals visited him and, knowing that the sick man hadn't received viatical communion, said, *Paolino, the Venerable Father Joseph of Copertino of my Order is so wonderful and is held so worthy unto the Lord, that you should seek his grace; have faith and ask him for enough time to take the sacrament, and then let the Most High do with you what he wishes; now I'm going to get the relic, and in the meantime commend yourself from your heart and don't doubt, for grace is yours.* The sick man, who until then could hear nothing, deposes that he heard that utterance, and with the utterance of the name of the Blessed Joseph, which had been unknown to him until that moment, it seemed to him that his pains became dormant. In fact, his violent contortions ceased and you could no longer hear his sighs and moans, so there was now some hope for his health.

When the monk returned, the sick man recognized him and was comforted with these words, *here is the relic of your Venerable Father Joseph. Commend yourself to God so that through the merit of this his servant, he will grant you time to take the sacraments.* Paolino was aroused and grace was done which required living faith. Three *Our Fathers* were recited, as well as *Ave Marias* and *Glorias* in honor of the Most Holy Trinity. Then the relic was placed on the head of the dying man. He attests that he immediately began to smell *a certain fragrance, a very sweet odor that he had never smelled in his entire life,* and that the smell cheered him and filled him with faith in the Servant of God, Father Joseph. He opened his eyes, recognized everyone, and turning to the monk said, *Oh faithful father, what an odor, what an odor.* He then confessed himself and took communion through Viaticum, to his indescribable consolation and that of everyone in his home.

When the physician came, he found the sick man in good spirits with little fever and no pain, and he attributed the sudden improvement to the intercession of the Blessed One. Paolino, having obtained the grace of the sacraments, resigned himself completely to God and had no thought of perfect health for his body. So a great fever came back violently on the eighth of the month, and after ten days of illness he was reduced to the extreme. The aforementioned monk, who was aiding the seriously ill man, again took up the relic of the Blessed One, placed it on the sick man's head, and urged him to ask for bodily health, suggesting that he promise the intercessor that he would go to visit his sepulcher in Osimo, and meanwhile the following morning the monk would celebrate Mass for him. Thus aroused, the sick man commended himself to the Blessed One and committed himself to visiting Joseph's sepulcher. That following morning the Mass was celebrated, which was heard on Paolino's behalf by three girls who first confessed themselves and then took communion for him. At the same time that the Mass was being celebrated, the sick man had in hand the relic of the Blessed One, and was commending himself to Joseph with great fervor, whereupon it seemed to him that he was freed from any sickness.

When the Mass was over and Father Fedeli returned, he found Paolo no longer sick, saying, *I am cured, I am healthy so now I want to get up*, and he would have done so if it had not been prevented by the prudence of the monk. They went and called for the physician who came right away, and he was stunned and beside himself with amazement to find the previously dying man now without fever, without pains, with an excellent pulse, and vital and vigorous. Upon learning what had happened, he rendered along with everyone else in the town most humble thanks to the Lord, exclaiming to everyone, *this is a prodigy! Or else Father Joseph of Copertino is indeed a great physician*. The healed man observed that when his great sickness ended, his smelling of the pleasant and very sweet odor which had marvelously comforted him throughout that harsh illness also ceased.

This was not the end of the miracle. Paolino, though he was twice brought back to life from death, instead of going to Osimo to thank his intercessor, on October 6, 1724 he went to Rome to be there for the holy year that was coming. But he became seriously ill there, and was forced to come back to his town. Arriving back there, he was ill from the beginning of December until May 10, 1725 with some kind of very bothersome dropsy. Earthly remedies were useless, so turning to those in heaven he betook himself to Cascia to implore the aid of the Blessed Rita, whose body is venerated in that spot. It was God's will that there, in the Monastery of the Minor Conventuals of Saint Francis, he would find the previously-mentioned Father Fedeli, who seeing him in such a sorry state asked him about his situation and finally said, *Paolino, have you complied with your promise to go to Osimo?* And upon hearing Paolino answer him red-faced that he *had not*, Father Fedeli reproved him for lack of gratitude, so that Paolino took heart and promised to do it immediately, which in fact he did.

So on the day of the Nativity of our Lady Mary, the perpetual Virgin, he set out on foot towards the City of Osimo with difficulty and discomfort, arriving there on September 15 of the said year. He betook himself straight away to the Church of Saint Francis where the Body of the Blessed Joseph of Copertino lay. After performing his devotions, as soon as he kneeled he began to smell from the top of the sepulcher the same very sweet odor that he had smelled during his first illness, and from which he had conceived hope for perfect health. In that place, while hearing Mass, he felt a certain heat from the direction of the celebrant's communion; a heat that began at the soles of Paolino's feet and snaked its way throughout his body with an unexplainable sweetness. He thought he heard a voice from inside himself that told him, *here is your grace, you are already healed.* When the Mass was over, he found himself healthy, vigorous and strong so that he now could undertake any effort. He thanked God and his illustrious benefactor, and returned happy and prosperous to his town where, until 1736 when he made this sworn statement, he enjoyed perfect health through the merits of the Blessed Joseph of Copertino.

Bartolomeo Palmucci, a nobleman of Macerata, was struck in the left eye by a red-hot iron on March 10, 1725. In extreme pain, and lachrymating copiously, he immediately sent for the surgeon to find a remedy. The professor carefully examined the eye and affirmed that the pupil was damaged and did not appear to be dark at all. In fact, since the eye got very white, he feared that the optic nerve might have been touched, so besides being left without sight in the left eye, even the right eye might be left defective as a consequence. Meanwhile in order to mitigate the pain, the surgeon prescribed bandages to relieve it, and these were to be replaced from time to time.

Lady Teresa, the consort of the sick man, was born in Osimo and was most devoted to the Blessed Joseph of Copertino. For that reason, she resorted to Joseph with great fervor. On the same evening as the accident she took a picture of Joseph and placed it over the eye of her husband, and with living faith prayed to the Blessed One to intercede for him with God for a cure.

Because the bandages were replaced, and because it was getting late into the night, the patient got some sleep, but his lachrymating got worse and so did his pain. He woke up, the remedies were renewed, and the eye bandaged again. Thus he slept calmly the rest of the night, and upon waking at the first rays of dawn and finding himself without the bandage, he opened his eye without any pain. He closed his right eye and confirmed that he could see perfectly with his left eye, and for that reason didn't want to undertake any more remedies.

When the surgeon came in the morning, he found Bartolomeo without his bandage. He examined Bartolomeo's eye and to his great amazement saw it free and healthy without the slightest sign of lesion, with no defect, and just as strong in sight as it was before the fatal burn. Bartolomeo remained that way until December 24 of the year 1734 when he made this authentic deposition giving undoubted testimony of having received grace.

For over twelve years, Lady Maria Mausones di Lima, Countess of Castello in the Sardinian City of Cagliari, was afflicted with strange and irregular trembling, sometimes on one part of the body, sometimes in another part, principally in the head but sometimes over the whole body. The best physicians in Madrid and other well-known cities of Spain were neither able to find a remedy or even give a name to the affliction. For that reason there was a suspicion that she was possessed, but no matter how many exorcisms were done, they all were in vain, and it was never possible to tell for sure whether a malignant spirit had invaded her. Finally the judgment was that her infirmity was a natural affliction of the nerves, as were the convulsions. In addition to her great discomfort, for which there was no remedy, another affliction was added when a mark appeared in her eye which got bigger and bigger and impeded her sight, and neither art nor medicine was useful even against this.

God, who wanted the healing of this woman to glorify his servant Blessed Joseph of Copertino, had it that one day when she was going to the Novena of the glorious patriarch Saint Domenico in the Church of his Order, she would meet with someone who was carrying a small portrait of our Blessed One. She was pleased by this effigy and asked which saint it might be. Upon knowing his name, she began to study his life. Upon reading about it and of his resounding miracles, she entertained great hope of having found her liberator. Accordingly she applied to herself a picture of the Servant of God, thinking that she would soon be cured, but it didn't happen that way. Her tremors, which she hadn't felt for three or four months began again, and the discomfort in her vision got worse. Still, she persevered in her faith in the Blessed One, and judged her renewed distress to be a matter of pure chance.

At night, she placed on her pillow the holy image of the Blessed One, hoping in that way to be made healthy, but she did not rest because she was agitated by the usual tremors and by an internal unease that left her melancholy and almost undone. She began, therefore, to become suspicious, especially because when she had that picture in hand, or upon looking at it, she became agitated by the usual tremors, which repeated itself so many times that eventually it led her to believe that her infirmity was caused by an evil spirit and was not, in effect, a natural affliction.

We now come to the exorcisms, but although these were performed when she held her head on the casket wherein reposed the Body of the Blessed Salvatore d'Orta, there was no sign of her being possessed. But upon being shown the picture of the Blessed Joseph, or it being applying to her secretly, the usual tremors made themselves seen and felt. Yet another test was made when the lady was playing at a game, and the picture was secretly applied to her. She immediately felt herself surprised by a pain which, she attested, was greater than any other she had ever felt. Even this was judged a matter of chance. But this was clarified very quickly when, upon being presented the picture, the spirit inside her which had been hidden for so many years manifested itself with words and actions that left all the bystanders full of fear and fright, and they declared it to be a miracle caused by the holy image.

The spirit having been manifested, the exorcist came back the next day with the aforementioned picture, and the afflicted woman was filled with horror upon seeing it, and the same thing continued to happen when the picture was passed before her. And when she saw a painting representing the Blessed Joseph of Copertino, she began to shout, *not that, not that,* and she moved against the wall and grabbed onto people so she wouldn't have to pass before it. Indeed, the repugnance felt by the evil spirit was so great that it threw the afflicted woman to the ground, who being full of faith called upon it in the name of the Servant of God to let her venerate her saint (which is what she called Joseph). The Demon obeyed and left her alone to prostrate herself before the sacred effigy, venerating it and declaring her serious need.

Finally, on July 19, 1727, she betook herself to the Church of Saint Mauro to continue the exorcisms. While the exorcist was enjoining the demon to depart and set free the possessed woman, two monks of the Pious Schools, Father Alonso di Sant'Anna, having been the Provincial of Sardinia, and Father Bernardo di San Giacomo, applied to her body the picture of the Blessed Joseph of Copertino. In that instant the infernal spirit left the body, to the greatest joy of the lady, to the immense jubilation of her most noble household, and to the great wonderment of those who found themselves present at the event.

Besides the acts of gratitude which this fortunate lady obligated herself in order to promote the veneration of her liberator, she wanted the grace that she had received to be made public by printing authentic confirmation so that the whole world might know how effective with God is the intercession of the Blessed Joseph of Copertino.

During the month of June 1731, Anna Teresa Bundari of Copertino, in her forty-seventh year, was troubled under her left breast by a bothersome growth, which was viewed as serious, abnormal, and malignant. It became more and more uncontrolled and obstinate, and didn't yield in any way to medical operations, afflicting the poor patient with sharp pain and incredible discomfort. Near the end of August she was surprised by an un-ignorable fever every day, during which the tumor would get slightly smaller, but when the fever ended would go back to its previous size which was already like a hen's egg. When the fevers ended, the tumor remained as before, with its usual pungent odor. In December, the same fever repeated itself with even gloomier happenings, that is with swooning, palpitations of the heart, and rotten emissions from the breast which increased when pressed, and caused the sick woman insufferable pain. Thus, the attending professor judged it malignant and incurable, and she was therefore exhorted to protect herself with Holy Communion by Viaticum, which she did with full spiritual resignation.

Consoled by those of her household and by others, and urged to commend herself to the Blessed Joseph of Copertino, she summoned the Father-Regent Ruberti, a monk of the Minor Conventual Order, and full of faith in God and in the hope of intercession by her glorious fellow citizen Joseph, she begged Father Ruberti to bring a relic of the Blessed One. The monk came immediately at the second hour of the night bringing with him a piece of the habit of the Servant of God. He had the sick woman and members of her household recite three *Pater Nosters, Ave Marias, and Gloria Patris, etc.* to the Most Holy Trinity, thereby arousing her devotion, and he made a sign over her with the relic. He then left her and returned to the monastery.

Even though despaired of by the physicians, the woman had a lively faith in the recovery of her health through intercession of the Blessed One, and she fell asleep. Around midnight she thought she saw in her room a venerable monk of the Minor Conventual Order, but with hood over his head so she could not see his face. Even so she thought that it was Father Joseph, and she said, *my father Joseph, help me; I pray that you free me of such awful symptoms of fever and of such an evil tumor.* She repeated this prayer and when she tried to take the monk by his habit he disappeared in front of her and she awoke. At that point she sensed no pain whatsoever, felt free of the fever and of all other symptoms, and when she touched the place where the tumor had been she couldn't find it.

Great was the joy in her home, particularly of her sisters who, having been called by her, saw to their amazement that the stubborn, malignant tumor had disappeared. Its departure demonstrated the grace she had received, but it still made itself felt for two or three days by a bit of feverish heat in the neck and foot. After then she was free and clear, without need of any remedies or experiencing unfortunate crises. She was able to go to the Church of the Grottella to declare the miracle publicly and to give thanks to God and to the Blessed Joseph, her illustrious benefactor and fellow citizen.

When Michel Domenico Donato, son of Doctor Giuseppe Casaro and Eufemia Caldrami, was thirteen months old he became seriously ill with pains and convulsive spasmodic movements which also showed themselves in his restlessness and continued crying. In eight days of illness, lying motionless on a bed, eyes shut tight, pale, and so emaciated that he appeared like a cadaver, he was reduced to agony. The loving Parents and Aunts wept inconsolably as if he were dead. An appropriate interment was prepared for when death would occur. His condition lasted from Vespers until the second hour of the night on July 20, 1734, and his last breath was expected at any moment.

The parents and aunts withdrew, leaving a household servant named Irene to watch over the dying child, as well as an upright Canon Priest of the Church. They blessed the agonized child with relics and then saw a picture of the Blessed Joseph hanging near the bedside. They took it and with living faith applied it to the mouth of the breathing child saying to him loudly, *Donatine* (Latin), *Donatino* (Italian), *kiss Father Joseph of the Grottella.* Upon saying those words, the child opened his eyes as if awakened from profound lethargy, began to kiss the sacred image, and in a clear voice said, m*amma, nenna, mamma, nenna.*

At first stunned and then full of jubilation, the Canon called for those in the house and they came running, the father being among the first. They no longer saw the dying son that they had left earlier, but a beautiful child, alert and as healthy as he was before his evil infirmity. His father, at his peak of joy and spiritual happiness, took the picture and said to his son, *Donatino, kiss the image of our Venerable Father Joseph through whose merits you are healthy and safe.* And the child kissed it over and over again, and gave a sign that he wanted to get up and run into the arms of his nurse who was present and took him up and happily put him on her breast, and he sucked as he used to do when in health.

In order to render thanks for such a marked evidence of grace, everyone in that household along with the healed little son betook themselves to the Church of the Grottella at the monastery of the Blessed One, to the altar of the Most Blessed Virgin, offering first their devout souls, and then offering the child's clothes and wrappings, which had already been prepared for Donatino's funeral. Upon their return, Donatino, happy and gay, looked frequently at his feet saying, *the slippers, the slippers,* the significance of which his parents didn't understand. But after he repeated it over and over again they finally grasped that they hadn't left the little shoes of their child at the church. So, to confirm the certainty of the miracle even further, they sent even those in order to complete their offering.

In the town of Monte Filotrano in the Marca, Giuseppe Leali, a 26 year-old mason was surprised on July 8, 1735, by colicky and oral pain, which made him seriously ill as they had before. He called for the physician, also as he had before, to have him remedy the sharp pains which wouldn't let him have his rest. The physician set about as usual to cure the illness as his art prescribed but since nothing worked, he finally resorted to opiates which also ended up being worthless.

Several days of his illness had passed when, by order of the Father-Master Sebastiano Beni of the Minor Conventual Order, another monk of the Order went to visit him, bringing with him a priest's hat that had belonged to the Blessed Joseph of Copertino with which to bless Leali. Finding him very agitated due to his pains, *which,* he asserted, *were crushing his guts,* he urged Leali to be patient, and comforted him so that he would confide in the intercession of the Blessed One, whereupon he recited a *Pater Noster* and an *Ave Maria,* made the sign of the cross over him, touching the painful parts of his body with the hat, and inspiring him again to have faith in God and in his servant. Then the Father-Master left forthwith. As soon as the monk had left the house, the sick man felt himself cured and thus free of any discomfort so that he rose from his bed, ate, and found some peace that he had missed for many days.

The following morning the physician went as usual to visit him, and was greatly stupefied to find him perfectly healthy, contrary to every expectation. But his stupefaction changed into thanks to God, for he understood that God's great Blessed Servant, Joseph of Copertino, had healed Leali, and had done so in such a way so that on that very day Leali could return to his work as a mason and labor without any weakness in his efforts. More amazing is that even though his pains had been infrequent, and they had come about more frequently on fast days due to the food, yet after receiving such beautiful grace he no longer had any discomfort even though he fed on lean food on the days that the Church prescribes. To show his gratitude, Leali betook himself twice to Osimo to visit the sepulcher of his pious Liberator in that city, and back in his own country he proclaimed publicly the miracle of his recovery.

Adding to the many resounding miracles of our Blessed One that we have mentioned up to now, we cannot be silent about the one experienced by Sister Teresa Margherita di San Giuseppe, a professed Carmelite nun of the Convent of San Niccolo in Lecce. This noble Nun was, over the course of eight years, oppressed by such a great and tormenting accumulation of pains that even in their first assault, which was through a fierce and hysterical epilepsy on May 8, 1727, she was expected to depart from life. Once free of that assault, she began to be subject in December of the same year to attacks of raging headaches which, bit by bit, became very obstinate and excruciating, and they not only made her delirious but also forced her to beat her head against the wall. Nor could she stay in bed because of her excessive agitation, so she threw herself continuously on the ground. In addition, as a result of the hard blows, a flood of sharp pieces of rough stone affixed themselves tightly to her forehead, and blood poured down as she tried to inflict outside pain on herself to find some relief from the ruthlessness of her inside pain.

For this unhappy woman every remedy was in vain, so much so that the physicians, almost desperate after a thousand efforts, finally resorted to cutting into her cranium with a small scalpel to discover the cause of such rabid pain. They saw in fact, growing on the meninx, a hard and calloused tubercle the size of a large pea, and they dissolved it with medication. But the headache didn't stop despite it. As if it weren't proper for it to worsen alone, it brought forth with it spasmodic pains in the stomach which were killing her, as well as vicious convulsions in her chest which prevented her from breathing, as well as epileptic attacks, and a cough that was so violent that whatever she swallowed she regurgitated, causing the small veins in her throat to rupture very often with such force that she was seen to spit blood.

From such a pile of monstrous afflictions, the nerves of her spine and back were harmed so that the poor patient could no longer stay on her feet, nor walk, and was forced to go on hands and knees on the ground like an animal anytime she wanted to move from one side to another of her cell. Finally she became malnourished, full of ulcerations in her mouth and throat, with many hard tumors on the lower part of her stomach. She had a habitual fever, and her legs and feet swelled frightfully. In a word, she had become a receptacle of illnesses, unable to sleep or rest, and breathing with great difficulty. She became nauseous when taking any food, and was tormented all over with unbearable pains in her nerves and in her muscles, and with other terrible symptoms.

The physicians recognized that there was nothing to be done regarding such an infirmity with so many great manifestations, and they despaired of healing and curing her. This opinion was confirmed by an extremely acute inflammation and fever that overtook her in September 1735, which assailed her with such great fury that she was soon reduced to the extreme. She was provided with the sacraments, and she commended her soul. She lost the use of her senses, and a fatal cold sweat impaired all her members. She fell into a deep lethargy and her passing was un-remediable and imminent.

Then a paper image of the Blessed Joseph of Copertino was brought to the convent, and given to Father Anastasio di San Giuseppe, a Carmelite monk who was a regular confessor of the mentioned Convent. Between the second and third hour of the night of

September 16, he placed it with lively faith on the dying woman, and fervently commended her to Joseph so that she might be deemed worthy to obtain health from the bestower of all that is good. The good monk begged the heavenly intercessor to give him some sign that God would grant his prayer, and he did receive it, because at the eighth hour of the same night, the suffering woman opened her eyes and offered some words. At that time another monk of the same Order, who had taken the place of the confessor who had left, was able again to grant her sacramental absolution and had her renew the vows of her Order, to which the dying woman, having improved, answered by saying that she remembered them fully. Once this was done, she fell again into her previous lethargy.

The Confessor returned on the morning of the 17th at the crack of dawn, and heard that the sign he had asked for had been forthcoming. He betook himself with great faith to celebrate the Holy Mass with all the fervor of his devout heart, and prayed to the Blessed One to intercede with God for the life and perfect health of the dying woman. He had not yet gotten to the consecration when suddenly the dying woman sat up in the bed and felt herself completely healthy. The sharp fever had gone away, as had the pains, the convulsions, the headache, and every evil symptom, leaving her in fact free. She immediately got out of bed, and dressed herself once again in a fresh clean blouse and her nun's clothes. Sitting down in a small chair, she learned from another nun that the Blessed Joseph of Copertino had been her liberator. She took the image of him that was there, and kissed it many times with great feeling of piety and tenderness, and was heard invoking his name while doing it, *her strength reinvigorated and her senses at the ready*, as she deposed. Being restored to perfect health, she then undertook and carried out the usual offices of her religious community along with other duties, rendering thanks to God and to his holy intercessor, who took her from death and restored her to life.

Ferdinando Giuseppe Venturi, Duke of Minervino, finding himself in the City of Lecce in November 1737 in the home of Signor Niccola Montefuscoli, his uncle, was taken on the 27th of that month by a slight pain on the underside of his right jaw, but did not pay attention to it at that time. But on the following day the pain became very sharp and forced him to think of remedies. None succeeded, and the pain became unbearable, so the physician of that city was summoned to cure him. When he came and examined the painful part, he saw no sign of any infirmity. Nevertheless, he ordered a certain liquid to prevent spasms, but it didn't work.

When Don Niccola saw this, he told his nephew, *inasmuch as human remedies are useless, we must resort to heavenly ones,* and assured him that he could trust firmly in the intercession of the Servant of God, Father Joseph of the Grottella, and that if one of his relics, which he possessed, were applied to the painful part, he would be healed at once. The ailing man answered that he had faith, and begged him for the relic. Don Niccola went right away to his quarters to search for it, while the Duke prayed from his heart to the Blessed One that, *by the great love that Joseph had brought to the Most Holy Virgin, whom his living mother used to call upon, he might be pleased to free him of such an intolerable pain.*

He then undertook as best he could to recite the rosary with one of his chamber attendants and with one of his servants. At the third part of the recitation, Don Niccola came with the relic. The patient felt himself taken by an internal joy and a cold shudder. In a soft wail he cried, *oh Venerable Father, if you love your mother, by the love that you bear for her make this spasm cease.* Upon saying this, the relic of the Blessed One, consisting of a small portion of his undergarment, was brought close and touched to the painful part, and he was at the same moment instantly healed of his fierce spasm. He finished his rosary with unspeakable happiness, and then he fell into a very sound asleep. When he awakened in perfect health, he rendered most humble thanks to his holy intercessor, the Blessed Joseph of Copertino, and then testified to the effectiveness of his protection, and always testified to it thereafter.

Not being over seven to eight years old, Filippo Sebastiano Felice, son of Signor Antonio Molineri, a physician of Torino, and of Ottavia Faggiani, was at childish play when a bean, called an "eye bean," got into his right ear and stayed there for two straight years without his ever telling his parents for fear of punishment. In that time he experienced lachrymation in his eye, pain in the ear, swelling of the jaw, and deafness. Finally the father learned of the matter through his older son, to whom his little brother had recounted the incident. The father immediately summoned one of the most worthy practicing surgeons to extract it. But as much as the surgeon tried, and with great torment to the patient, he finally had to abandon the effort, admitting, as he later deposed under oath, *that it was completely impossible to pull out the bean naturally*, and therefore advised the father to place his son in the hands of God, and not count any further on his life.

Things went ahead in this way for some months without a cure until on February 17, 1742, while the young lad was hearing Mass, he was taken by an attack of dizziness. He fell to the ground from his bench and was taken home by his fellow students. There he was placed in bed and came back to his senses thanks to some restoratives that his mother, Signora Vittoria (sic), gave him, whereupon he begged to be sent to a surgeon to cure him, asserting that he would suffer otherwise.

Therefore his father summoned another good professor who, in order to be able to operate safely, had the patient tied with two wrappings and held down by three men so that he wouldn't move. But even though he tried with his instruments at four different times on four separate days to cure him, the operation didn't succeed since the bean was so deep in the ear that he had to desist. But the pain that was suffered, and the violence done to the ear caused a high fever in the lad which offered him no respite for eight days and nights, and required that he be bled which caused the fever to go away, but the pain and the deafness persisted.

At the peak of such a desperate illness, it was the will of divine providence that a devout person should suggest to the Doctor Molineri that he commend his afflicted son to the Blessed Joseph of Copertino and hope for a remedy through Joseph's intercession. The loving father accepted the advice and he hung at the bed a picture of the Blessed

One, instilling in the soul of his son that with lively faith he should thus commend himself, and suggesting to him in the meanwhile that God would immediately heal him through the intercession of his great servant and that for Joseph's glory would produce and manifest His grace.

It was on March 5 and one and three-quarters of an hour after noontime that the father retired after keeping before his son's eyes the picture of the Blessed Joseph, and sighing and begging from his heart for his cure. And, behold, the sick lad, now full of joy, started to shout and called that they should come and get the bean which, by itself, had emerged from his ear without the least pain, with neither a discharge of blood nor any slowness of movement.

The mother came running and seeing the damaging vegetable at the outer opening of the ear, she took it with great ease with a pair of scissors, and the son who was now perfectly healthy, along with his parents rendered their most humble thanks to God and to the Blessed Joseph of Copertino, recognizing that such a miraculous and instantaneous healing came from him. So, for the glory of the Servant of God, all of them - father, mother, older son, and the healed younger son, and the two surgeons - deposed the fact in authentic formats, always blessing God through His wondrous saints.

Doctor Francesco Valentini, first Physician of the City of Assisi, deposed on January 9, 1744 under oath, that in previous years he has often visited Sister Maria Imperatrice Romana, a Nun of Saint Quirico of that City, and had medicated her for an incurable illness that consisted of a semi-paralysis of the two muscles that open and close the mouth. But they still remained for some months so uncontrolled and devoid of movement that she couldn't open her mouth to nourish herself, and it became necessary to introduce fluids through one side of her mouth where she was lacking a tooth. Otherwise, the nun was healthy of mind and suffered no other discomfort. The attending physician, aware of this after visiting her for several months, left her with the prognosis that she could not be cured, and later a foreign professor also confirmed the same prognosis.

In her great need, the nun suddenly called on and named the Blessed Joseph of Copertino, commending herself with a lively heart. Right away she opened her mouth, returned to health as before, free of the fierce discomfort, and shouting "miracle." *So the Nun said (as the before-named Physician indicates in his deposition) and so do I attest that I found her without that illness since I was immediately summoned to admire the instantaneous miracle wrought by God through the intercession of his great servant, the Blessed Joseph of Copertino.*

Pompeo, a child about one year old of Signore Antonio Ottaviani of Camerino and Signora Felice Giacometti di Macerata, was reduced to the extreme by smallpox which reached its peak on the seventh day, with almost continuous discharges from his body and a very burning fever. His illness was even more desperate because at such a tender age the physician was not able to aid him with remedies, and judged him to be at his end. The child, thus being consumed, lasted in this way from August through all of September of the year 1744, and the clothing and candles had already been prepared to send him to his grave. Meanwhile Signore Paolo Bianzani returned from Macerata on the evening of October 2, and brought the sick child's mother a reliquary in which was a thread from the pocket of the Blessed Joseph of Copertino, for which she had urgently asked Signore Giovanni Giacometti, her Father. Upon receiving it, with lively faith she made the sign of the cross with it over her child who, already unable to move, was immediately seen to the amazement of everyone to remove the covers in the crib where he was lying and playfully raise both his legs in the air, and at that moment began to improve. The child woke up the following morning and began to sing and play, to the wonderment of those present, and was in fact free of the above-mentioned sickness. On the third day he wanted to get up from his crib, enjoying perfect health from that time onward.

But the miracle didn't end here. For an excrescence of flesh was left on the child, a polyp the size of a pea, which affected the sight of his left eye. His mother, who desired full grace from the Blessed One, made the sign of the cross with lively faith over the eye of her child and to her great happiness and wonderment saw the hostile excrescence disappear in an instant, and the eye return to its natural function. For that reason, she and the boy's father rendered their devout thanks to God, recognizing that the child's life and health came from the intercession of the Blessed Joseph. And for the greater glory of the holy intercessor, they confirmed jointly with the attending physician and other eye witnesses that which we have recounted now.

Doctor Jacobo Bussi, one of the two main physicians of Ancona, betook himself to Osimo in 1746 in the last days of September to venerate the Blessed Joseph of Copertino, who had died and was entombed in the Church of the Minor Monastic fathers of that City. After Doctor Bussi performed his devotions, he obtained from the Father-Guardian of the Monastery of Saint Francis a small piece of the outer casket which contained the body of the mentioned Servant of God. Then he departed for Loreto, but before arriving at Castel Fidardo he had to get out of the small carriage in order to avoid danger, since it was a rainy day and the ground was soggy. But the place was very narrow, and in getting out he received an abrasion or a scrape on the shin of his right leg which he did not pay attention to at the time. After returning to Ancona, for three days he busied himself visiting his sick patients even though he was feeling pain. On the night of October 4 he was overtaken by a grave fever and swelling, by intense pain, and by an inflammation of the skin on the leg. The discomfort increased and by October 4, the Festival of the Patriarch Saint Francis, the leg was swollen to almost twice its normal size, purple in color, almost livid, and with extremely sharp pain. Since no remedy worked, he feared it would degenerate into gangrene.

In his affliction, he resorted to the intercession of the Blessed Joseph of Copertino, and begged his father confessor, a monk of the same Order, to place on the painful part of his body some shavings from the casket, already mentioned, in which Joseph's body had been. Around the 24th hour of that day the monk did so after reciting some prayers, while the ill man commended himself with lively faith to the

Servant of the Lord that he might intercede with the good health he was sighing for.

He continued to suffer until the 5th hour of the night, and then fell asleep. He slept until seven, and then upon waking he felt no more pain. He felt his leg and saw it was no longer swollen. He felt his pulse and understood that his fever had stopped. Thus comforted, he went back to sleep peacefully. On the following morning before daybreak he had a lamp brought to him, uncovered his leg, and found it in a perfectly natural state. The swelling had vanished, the inflammation and lividness were gone, and it had regained its original natural coloration.

He rejoiced at such a perfect and instant cure, and rendered due thanks to God and to the holy intercessor, whom he chose to be one of his advocates. He published the miracle, spreading the account of what happened. As proof of his gratitude he promised that at new year's he would visit the sacred resting place of the Blessed One, and would bring a silver offering depicting a leg so that if the holy Mother Church ever decreed permission for Joseph's worship, it might hang next to his holy image.

Giovanni Battista, son of Doctor Domenico Zacchieri of the Terra di Dozza in the Diocese of Imola, from the age of nine or ten was in medical discomfort because of an intestinal rupture, and could never find a remedy. In fact it was judged incurable by those who attended him in Forli and by those who examined him in Faenza and in other places. He suffered during changes in the weather, when eating vegetables and fruit, and during his trips, and the painful swelling increased. He protected himself with wrappings as well as he could, but he clearly knew that a miracle was necessary to cure him.

Through his own good efforts, he became devoted to the Blessed Joseph of Copertino upon hearing of Joseph's virtues from a monk of his same Order. He tried to obtain a miracle, since he had Joseph's picture and his biography. Upon reading the biography and holding the picture affectionately, he became fervent in his faith and devotion, and adopted the custom of reciting evening and morning a *Pater Noster, an Ave Maria, and a Gloria*, praying to the Blessed One to free him from the rupture that tormented him.

Meanwhile on August 6, 1747, before his thirtieth year, having to go from Savignano to Rimini and experiencing great pain in the sick portion of his body, he recited the usual *Pater Noster, Ave Maria* and *Gloria*, imploring the patronage of Joseph for his healing. He promised that he would never cease his devotion to him, that he wanted to establish that devotion in his family and promote it in others, that he would have many Masses celebrated, and vigils and fasts for his glory. With this there was born in him a lively faith in God, and a firm hope for the intercession of the Blessed One, and it passed through his mind to touch the sick part of his body with Joseph's portrait. In fact he did so, and immediately felt a very great abatement of the discomfort in that part, and in the stomach. Feeling himself, he found the swelling had vanished and the pain was gone.

Seeing himself become healthy in an instant, he gave affectionate thanks to divine clemency and to his intercessor to whom he insisted over the passage of time that he was eternally grateful. He never again in the future experienced the same pain or the same swelling, or any discharge from his intestines, even though he unfastened his bindings and he undertook many tests to see if he had really been cured. In fact, still not satisfied, he had himself examined by a surgeon who assured him that in the mentioned part of his body there was no defect whatsoever. So, on December 20 1747, he made the miracle known publicly so that the glories of the Blessed Joseph of Copertino would be made known even more.

The Priest Don Giuseppe Brunetti of Osimo was confined to bed from January 19 to January 23, 1750, by a very serious headache and a discharge from his left eye, unable to find rest day or night. On the evening of the 23rd, the pain got worse to the point that he couldn't endure it any more. He began with fervent prayer to implore the support of the Blessed Joseph of Copertino so that the Lord would give him a cure. Meanwhile he fell asleep and during his brief sleep it seemed to him that he was commended to the Blessed One, and to have before his eyes his picture, and he was speaking as follows, *my Father Joseph, grant this grace; intercede for me with the Lord God for my health.* Praying thus with great fervor, it seemed to him that Joseph answered him in a loud voice and reproved him, *how can you want grace and commend yourself to me while having me under your bed? Remove me from that spot if you want grace, because I want to be seen and I want to be venerated.*

The priest was awakened in a great sweat by this reproof, and he began to weep. He called those of his household who were in the adjoining room and told them, *quickly take away from under this bed Father Joseph who has reproved me for keeping him so badly.* They slid from under the bed a small chest, opened it, and extracted a hollow bust, or rather a plaster mask stamped with the countenance of the Blessed One after his death. The priest Don Gregorio Luchetti gave it to be kissed by the sick man, touching it to his head, and behold it was cured of any pain. The Priest Brunetti immediately rose from his bed healthy and free of any illness to the wonderment and comfort of those present, among whom were two priests. One was the blood brother of the no-longer sick man, and the other the Secretary of the aforementioned city, both of whom, together with the two physicians of that place, testified for the glory and praise of God to the miraculous healing wrought through the intercession of the Blessed Joseph of Copertino.

So as not to tire the reader excessively, we will restrain ourselves as much as possible regarding other grace and miracles of God wrought through the intercession of the Blessed Joseph of Copertino, and will mention them in the order in which, bit by bit, they came to us in their authentic format.

Beginning therefore in the city of Osimo where Joseph left his mortal remains, we will say that on September 25, 1733, Signora Anna Menichelli, wife of Signor Domenici Paolucci, would have died while giving birth had it not been for her husband who was devoted to the

Blessed One and had taken a bit of cloth stained with Joseph's blood and given it to the afflicted mother to swallow in a spoon. He then left home to summon a physician and a surgeon to help her.

But before they arrived, the Blessed Joseph had become aware of the woman, and she gave birth to a little boy who came out feet first. It was on the feet that the prompt and prudent midwife actually baptized him before he was fully born. The child died but the Mother was left free of grave danger. Both parents, throughout this great distress, had the spiritual comfort of knowing that their child arrived at the grace of baptism. The grace was made public by the above-mentioned Signor Domenico, who did not cease to give praise to God and to his intercessor, the Blessed Joseph.

On November 20, 1737, in Portogruaro in the Bishopric Concordia, Signora Angela Zotti, wife of Signor Giovanni Battista Piovesana, suffered such sharp pain during childbirth that it was impossible for her to give birth. The little body of the child exited the womb but the head could not, and the suffering lasted two hours so that the matter was desperate for both the mother and for the offspring. During this anguish of childbirth, the mother remembered the Blessed Joseph of Copertino, and having gotten from a monk of the same Order a fragment of the slipper of the Servant of God, it was applied with lively faith and she immediately gave birth to a boy, alive and healthy, even though it was after a pregnancy of only eight months.

Having exited from danger in an instant, to the wonderment and remarkable happiness of the mother's own mother, of the midwife, of another woman, and of the husband, they all together reported this prodigious event for the glory of God, and they blessed and thanked the blessed intercessor who is so beneficent to those who invoke him and resort to his support.

Our Blessed One showed himself to be even more amazing with Signora Rosa Montini, consort of Signor Tommaso Ciapponi, Secretary of the land of Monte dell Osimo. In her first childbirth, which took place on July 29, 1723, she exhausted all her strength and was unable to give birth to the fetus whose head had already appeared, so both the mother and child were in danger of dying. In that very painful situation, her husband gave her a glass of water to drink which contained a small cutting of the habit of the Blessed Giuseppe di Copertino, and happily she gave birth immediately. But the consolation was brief, for as a result of the mother's convulsions and twisting, the baby was suffocating, not breathing, with stilled heart, cold in the extremities and with a weak coloration. He was brought near the fire to warm him and held there for half an hour without sign of life. He was placed in a small straw basket and the women turned back to care for the Mother, who realizing her misfortune, was crying her heart out.

But the husband, although also greatly saddened, told his wife and the other women that all should commend themselves to the Blessed Joseph and, since it was Joseph who caused him to be born, pray that he give him to them alive, and saying he would bestow Joseph's name on him in baptism if he were resuscitated. So they set about praying, imploring with great fervor the support of the servant of God. And in the act of prayer they heard a voice, or rather they heard breathing, so they ran to the child and found him alive and healthy, as he is to this day. They gave him the name Joseph in baptism in accordance with their promise. And because of the greatness of the miracle and its publicity the child acquired in his land the name of "the resuscitated dead."

In the second year of the current eighteenth century, Maria Francesco Cingolani, a baker of Monte Lupone in the Diocese of Loreto, in order to solemnize the transfer of the Holy House as is usually done throughout the Province of the Marca, fired off a small cannon which, upon recoiling, struck him in the shin. The surgeon on duty was summoned to cure him, and after operating on him, he left for his other duties. Maria Francesco was very devoted to the Blessed Joseph of Copertino so that night, finding himself in great pain from the fracture, it was granted to him to hear a voice that said, *get up Maria Francesco, you are healed. I am Joseph of Copertino.* At the same time that he heard that voice, he also heard his leg send forth a certain sound, like crushed bones that were coming together again. In fact, on the following morning upon rising from bed, he found himself free of the fracture, and perfectly healed. In rendering thanks to God and to his blessed intercessor, be betook himself to Osimo to visit his sacred tomb where, with tenderness and tears, he declared the benefit that he had received, and in gratitude he hung there a testimony of the most humble offerings of his devout spirit.

In the same land of Monte Lupone in the year 1692, the nobleman Signor Giacomo Basvecchi was, by means of contact with the cap of the Blessed Joseph of Copertino, cured of an abscess on his head which had lasted for forty days with sharp pains that had reduced him to the extreme. In his serious and fatal infirmity he had promised that if restored to health he would go to Osimo to visit the sepulcher of the Blessed One. In fact, he went there with his consort, along with a monk of the Blessed One's Order, and with two servants. But upon crossing the River Potenza, the horse put his feet in a hole and fell, along with Signore Giacomo who was astride it. He found himself off his saddle, so he invoked the Blessed One, and walked in the water across the whole width of the river to the opposite bank. Having arrived there, the others in his entourage caught up to him thinking him completely weakened and asked him if he wanted to change his clothes. He answered, *look at how much I'm obliged to the Blessed Joseph, for I haven't been touched even by a drop of water.* And so it was, for he wasn't wet on any part of his body or his clothes. Great was the wonderment of everybody, and even greater were the thanks that he gave to the Most High and to his Blessed One, and everyone noted the double benefit that Joseph's intercession had brought.

During the month of August of the year 1751, Medical Doctor Marina Jacopo Presotini, in his town of Recanati was afflicted by a not small heating of the kidneys, accompanied by a sharp and piercing pain on the left side until he urinated blood. He himself, as a professor, knew the seriousness of his illness, which by all indications was getting more dangerous and fatal, so he gave himself to trying to cure it as prescribed by his art. But he saw over some weeks of care that it was to no avail; the sickness was becoming more obstinate, and the blood was issuing more copiously.

Setting aside human remedies, he resorted with great faith to seeking the aid of the Blessed Joseph of Copertino, hoping for health through Joseph's intercession with God. Nor was he disappointed, because when Joseph's picture was applied with lively faith to the painful part, he found himself not much later perfectly healed. So, grateful to his illustrious benefactor, he closed his authentic deposition with *Gratiam itaque mihi licet Servo indigno a Deo ter Optimo Maximo impertitam pro tanti Patroni meritis (nimirum Josefi a Copertino) confitendam esse conteflor, I quoram fidem hic me proprio caractere subscripsi hac die 4 Decembri 1751* (It is thus appropriate that I, an unworthy servant, give thanks to God, the Best and All High, for the many merits of my protector, namely Joseph of Copertino, for which in good faith I have signed this with my own hand this day, December 4, 1751).

Around September 1751, Giacomo Filippo, three and a half years old, son of Giuseppe Maria Vignati and his wife Maddalena, natives of Osimo, was assailed by a distressing illness of the throat with fever, pains, and restlessness that left him no peace. He almost lost his speech and his hearing, and the nerves in his neck were so weakened that he couldn't hold up his head. In that labored state he was seen by the surgeon Andrea Valenti who declared him gone *unless some Saint were to perform a miracle on him.* Nevertheless, he ordered an unction which was applied eight or ten times without effect. Instead, the child's whole body lost its vigor except for his arms which he could still move.

He lasted in this state, barely breathing, until January 6 of the current year 1752, on which day his father, with great faith, brought him to the rooms of the Blessed Joseph of Copertino, and settled d him on Joseph's chair. After emphatic and fervent prayer, he took him up again and one could see that the child was beginning to hold up his head. The father brought the boy home and consigned him to his wife, but upon departing to carry out his tasks, he heard his son say in a clear voice, *where is Dad going?* So he returned to the child and told him to recite the *Pater noster* to Father Joseph who would cure him.

And, in fact, on the morning of January 7, Signora Giulia Magnani, who was passing by, saw the child whom his mother had placed on a bench, playing with his legs, and she called the mother saying, *your son is cured.* The mother ordered the child to get up and walk to her, and he got up immediately and walked, having re-acquired his entire health which he had lost. It was such that the father, coming back home after four days, found him as he had been before, perfectly healthy. The father rendered thanks to the Lord and to the Blessed Joseph, his intercessor, glorifying him by a public declaration of the grace received, as did those who were witnesses of it.

Alessio Starnari of Monte Filotrano, residing in Perugia, and his wife Teresa brought one of their daughters who was thirteen years old to Osimo in April of this year 1752, along with the maternal aunt Maria Cecconi, for the purpose of seeking the intercession of the Blessed Joseph of Copertino for the girl's health. For seven years she suffered a certain indisposition, thought by them to be a fracture, for which they kept her tied down, but having been examined by a qualified Surgeon, among the best in the city, it was judged to be an inguinal hernia.

On the 25th of the said month, they all arrived together at the sacristy of the Minor Conventual Fathers of Saint Francis in Osimo and, genuflecting before the picture of the Blessed One, they prayed with great fervor for the healing of their respective daughter and niece. Having departed on the morning of the 26th for Loreto, the aunt wanted to see her niece and check her illness, but upon untying her, she found her free of it. Returning then to Perugia, they had the surgeon examine the daughter on three different occasions, and he assured that she was free of the above-mentioned indisposition. Grateful to their illustrious benefactor, the Blessed Joseph of

Copertino, from whom they had obtained grace, they extolled the divine compassion and made an authentic public testimony of it.

Let the story of the life, virtues and miracles of our wondrous Blessed Joseph of Copertino end here. It is not because there are no more great and surprising things to tell about him, but because we judge that those that we have already recounted are adequate to form a distinctive idea of his outstanding sanctity, and are of value to excite the piety of the faithful to devotion to this great servant of that eternal and immortal Lord, for whose praise and glory alone we have undertaken our effort, and whose divine help has brought us to the end of it.

THE END

WE THE REFORMERS

Of the University of Padua.

Having seen the Review and Approval of P.F. Paolo Tommaso Manuelli, Inquisitor General of the Holy Office of Venice, that there is nothing whatsoever against the Holy Catholic Faith in the Book entitled *Life of the Blessed Joseph of Copertino*, and likewise by the attestation of Our Secretary, there is nothing against the Princes or against good behavior, grant License to *Giovanni Battista Recurti, a Printer of Venice*, that it might be printed, observing the procedures for Printed material, and presenting the usual Copies to the Public Libraries of Venice and Padua.

Given on 5 April 1753
(Gio. Emo Proc. Rif.
(Barbon Morosini Kav. Proc. Rif.
(Alvire Mocenigo 4. Kav. Proc. Rif.

Recorded in Book and Sheet 5. to Num. 28;

Giovanni Girolamo Zuccato, Secretary

On this day 7 April 1753.

Recorded in the Mag. Eccell. of the Exec.. against Blasphemy.

Alvise Legrenzi Secretary

Made in the USA
San Bernardino, CA
15 August 2017